MAR 2 4 1983

S0-AJK-257

# A HANDBOOK FOR
# THE DISABLED

# A HANDBOOK FOR
# THE DISABLED

## IDEAS AND INVENTIONS
## FOR EASIER LIVING

*Suzanne Lunt*

*Charles Scribner's Sons · New York*

Copyright © 1982 Suzanne Lunt

**Library of Congress Cataloging in Publication Data**

Lunt, Suzanne, 1936-
  A handbook for the disabled.

  Bibliography: p.
  Includes index.
  1. Self-help devices for the disabled—Handbooks,
manuals, etc.   2. Home economics—Handbooks, manuals,
etc.   I. Title.
HV1568.L86   1982        640'.240816        82-5919
ISBN 0-684-17498-7                          AACR2

1 3 5 7 9 11 13 15 17 19  F/C  20 18 16 14 12 10 8 6 4 2

Printed in the United States of America.

*To Laura and Joe Denton*
*with love and gratitude*

# ACKNOWLEDGMENTS

A great many people have contributed encouragement, time, help, and invaluable information to the preparation of this book. Special thanks go to Catherine Liapes, my helpful, patient editor at Scribners. I would also like to thank the following:

Ralph Bent; Jane Blois, the British Red Cross Society; Ardelle Cleverdon, McGraw-Hill Book Company; Pat Colomban, Blakiston Division, McGraw-Hill Book Company; Milly De Riggi, Friends for Immediate and Sympathetic Help; Barbara A. Dryburgh, Donahue Sales, Talon Division of Textron, Inc.; Millicent Fenwick, congressional representative from New Jersey; Evelyn Fisher, Sister Kenny Institute; Margaret Frank, Winfield Co., Inc.; Harriet Fulleylove, Doubleday Publishing Co.; Betty Garee, *Accent on Living* magazine, Cheever Publishing Co.; Ernest Giannone, North Shore Surgical Supply Co.; Robert I. Goldsmith, Research Corporation; Jarlath Graham, Crain Communications; Arthur D. Heyer, Extensions for Independence; Elizabeth House, National Theatre of the Deaf; Peter Isoz, Permobil Division of Saab-Scania of America, Inc.; Jennifer Jones; Mary-lou Jorgensen, King's Point Fund, United States Merchant Marine Academy Foundation; Dr. Herman L. Kamenetz, Veteran's Administration; Dr. Steven Kanor; Rosalyn Kaplan, National Easter Seal Society for Crippled Children and Adults; Judith L. Klinger, O.T.R.,

M.A., Institute of Rehabilitation Medicine; William C. Kofoed, Invacare Corporation; Julius D. Lombardi, Northeast Association Post Stroke Clubs, Inc.; Jack Macauley, R. J. Reynolds Tobacco Company; Marie McLaughlin, Nassau County Visiting Nurse Association; Leila Mattson and Arlene Nevens of the Great Neck, L.I., Library; Sue Owens; Emmett Pittenger, Abbey Medical; Elsa Prigozy, Great Neck Library; Risha Rosner, Great Neck Library; Edward A. Rust, Rehabilitation World; Larry Schneider; Lois O. Schwab, the University of Nebraska, Lincoln; Carole Stoddard, Dell Publishing Co., Inc.; Karen B. Sussman, American Foundation for the Blind, Inc.; JoAnn Thompson, Arlington House Publishers; and Elaine Trinkoff and Sue Wheiland of the Great Neck, L.I., Library.

# CONTENTS

# Introduction

When illness or injury lays you low or when you feel tired, activities you once took for granted start to loom large. Everything seems to take more effort than it did before. You find yourself thinking, "Why hasn't somebody invented something to make this easier?"

Somebody has. There are devices on the market to help you dress, drive, travel, type, bowl, bathe, cook, carry, read, run a business—do anything more easily than you thought possible.

While some simple devices can be made at home in a few minutes from things you have already, others are expensive. But before dismissing a helpful item because of its cost, remember: you may be able to rent it or Medicare may pay up to 80 percent of its purchase price. Medicare is willing to consider this under the category of "durable medical equipment prescribed by a doctor." What is "durable medical equipment"? Medicare defines it as anything able to withstand repeated use; intended primarily for a medical purpose; and not generally useful in the absence of an illness or injury.

I have tried to recommend only the most reputable manufacturers and suppliers and have included only those new inventions that, to the best of my knowledge, have been found reliable.

The purpose of this book is to present the inventions currently on the market, not to recommend specific devices or judge their relative merits.

Written by a layperson for the general reader, the book's aim is to tell you what is available rather than to persuade you to buy anything.

*The responsibility for evaluating and recommending each device rests with your doctor.* There may be ideas and devices that are *not* recommended for you because you need the exercise of doing it the hard way— or for some other reason. What works for one person may not work for you. *Consult a professional before trying anything in this book that could affect your health.* And remember—*any*thing can.

Prices change so rapidly that those given here are guidelines to approximate valuations at the time the book was published. They do not reflect probable future increases.

At the end of this book, you will find "Sources of Equipment and Information." This section gives the names and addresses of the manufacturers and suppliers from whom you can order. Other sources of information appear at the end of many of the chapters and the Bibliography lists a variety of helpful publications. Use these sources to keep yourself up-to-date on the latest equipment and ideas available.

# PART ONE

## MAKING LIFE EASIER

# 1

# How to Do
# a Lot Less around the House

Housework is a job. Anyone who doubts this should be locked in a four-bedroom house for a week in the rain with at least three children and one out-of-order washing machine. Then, when the repairman fails to appear, the wash piles up, the dog throws up, the car won't start, and the children whine and fight, call whoever is in charge of the house who thought housework was nothing at all and ask whether the person has had a change of mind.

## To streamline your chores
Try doing chores in different sequences until you find the routine that saves the most steps. Try doing major jobs, such as cooking, at a different time of day, when the house may be cooler or you may be less tired, or perhaps under less pressure. Try doing them in a new location. Your ironing, for example, might be easier if done near the washer-dryer area. (You can eliminate it entirely if you buy only no-iron fabrics.) Evaluate your own methods of doing each job the way an efficiency expert would. You may pinpoint unnecessary steps or even realize that some tasks can be left undone, practically forever, with no one (except you) any the wiser. The best thing for streamlining is to elicit more family cooperation. Or if you live alone, offer to babysit or do some other job for a neighbor in return for help with your most difficult household chores.

*To save steps*

Put supplies into an apron with lots of pockets (see page 190) or place them in a plastic dishpan on castors and kick it from room to room (see page 5). A castored cart (see page 27) is also indispensable. You can use it to wheel supplies and folded laundry from room to room, transport food and utensils to and from the table, dress a child, prepare food, sew, do art work, do office work and hobbies, even as a dining table.

*To get up and down more easily*

Install grab bars in places where you must stand to work, such as the kitchen.[1] Leave your wheelchair or a comfortable chair or stool (see page 8) near the grab bar to remind you to sit down to rest—or sit to work— as often as possible.

*To save hundreds of hours of housework per year*

Some of these suggestions are initially expensive, but all are worth their weight in gold as labor-savers.

No-wax flooring

Wall-to-wall carpeting rather than dust-collecting rug-and-bare-floor combinations

Stained rather than painted doors, shelves, and woodwork

Varnished or other no-wax furniture surfaces

Scrubbable paint and wallpaper

Fabric window shades instead of draperies

Naugahyde or vinyl upholstery instead of fabric slipcovers

Built-in vacuum system (Sears)

Self-cleaning oven

Clothes dryer

Lightweight "electric broom" rather than a heavy vacuum

Carpet sweeper for once-over-lightly jobs

# CLEANING

*Equipment*

A number of devices will make cleaning easier.

LONG-HANDLED DUSTPAN AND BROOM:    (About $12, G. E. Miller)

SELF-WRINGING MOP:    Can be operated with one hand if you wedge the 47" handle under your arm; easy-to-pull, remote-control lever 20" above floor guarantees that your hands will never touch mop or water. (About $13, refills about $5, Fashion-Able)

FOOT MOP: A terry "mitten" for your foot. Insert foot and shuffle to mop up spills without bending. Almost 11″ wide, washable. (About $6, Fashion-Able)

SPONGE MOP KIT: A 15-quart scrub pail with wringer attachment that snaps onto rim of pail to wring out replaceable-sponge mop. (About $15 for pail and mop, replacement head about $4, Help Yourself Aids)

CASTORED DISHPAN: Lightweight plastic pan with handles mounted on ball-bearing castors. Excellent as a mop pail or for kicking objects from room to room. (About $20, Help Yourself Aids)

WINDOW WASHER: Has foam pad on one end, rubber squeegee on other end. Use it to wash outsides of double-hung windows. Has adjustable 24″–36″ arm. (About $5, Miles Kimball)

CORDLESS ELECTRIC SCRUBBER: Rechargeable, lightweight, 8″ hand-held device with two motor-driven interchangeable scrub brushes for cleaning tiles, vinyl car tops, silver, oven racks, pans, woodwork. Comes with power pack for recharging and one-year warranty. Made by Dazey. (About $57, Joan Cook)

LONG-HANDLED SCRUB SPONGE: Round or rectangular sponge with 18″ handle. (About $6, Help Yourself Aids)

ANGLED SCRUB SPONGE: Measures 20″, with an angled take-apart metal handle that makes it easy to clean hard-to-get-at places. (About $6, Help Yourself Aids)

SUPER-LONG TUB SCRUBBER: Straight-handled 24″ unit comes with attached long-wearing sponge head plus two extra sponges. (About $9, The Ferry House)

## Tips for tough jobs

TO REMOVE BALLPOINT PEN STAINS: Clean with cold or boiling milk.

WHEN YOUR PET PIDDLES ON THE CARPET: Blot with towel, then make suds, scrub carpet using suds, blot again, and pour plain soda water onto spot. Blot slightly and let dry. This removes both smell and stain.

TO CLEAN MILDEW ON TILES AND GROUT: Scrub with a fiberglass scouring pad (available at hardware and variety stores).

I've used these techniques for years. For hundreds of additional ideas to make laundry and cleaning easier, get a copy of *Mary Ellen's Best of Helpful Hints* by Pearl Higginbotham and Mary Ellen Pinkham (see Bibliography).

# LAUNDRY

The best hint about laundry is to do as little of it as possible. Buy easy-care fabrics and teach each child to do his or her own. If you feel guilty about this, remember that it develops a child's responsibility to do chores—and as soon as they leave the nest, they'll have to do them anyway. So there's no time like the present: teach them now!

### To avoid doing laundry by hand

Whenever you are forced to the wall and think you have to do some laundry by hand, take heart. You can avoid it by putting delicate items into the machine in a *Wash Case*, made of white nylon mesh, 16″ x 19″ with zipper. (About $5, Fashion-Able)

If you still insist on washing things by hand, try agitating them with a rubber plunger, which utilizes arm muscles instead of fingers.[2] To wring out laundry with one hand, drape each item over the faucet and "strip" or twist the water out.

### To turn faucets on and off

Use a hammer or reacher or:

ADJUSTABLE TAP TURNER:   With easy-grasp handle and a set of screws that can be adjusted to fit width of straight-handled faucet. (About $4, The Independence Factory)

STAR HANDLE FAUCET TURNER:   Easy-grasp handle has a U-shaped end that turns star-shaped faucet handles. (About $4, The Independence Factory)

### Washers and dryers

You should have a front-loading dryer with a door that opens from the side rather than from top to bottom. This makes it easier to use from a wheelchair. Top-to-bottom doors won't stay open unless opened all the way, and then it's difficult to reach back into the drum. Unfortunately, at this writing, there is not a washer on the market with the side-opening feature.

WESTINGHOUSE LT SERIES FRONT-LOADING WASHERS:   Door opens from top to bottom. One model, a little shorter than most machines, slides under a counter for possible kitchen use, saves steps to the laundry room. (About $300, consult your Westinghouse dealer.)

GE MODEL 510 DRYER:   Front-loading door opens left to right; shallower drum than most machines (although will hold a full load); drum-mounted lint screen just inside door. (Contact your GE dealer.)

SEARS PORTABLE DRYER:   Has above features plus castors so it can be moved (if you can slide 100 pounds without difficulty). (About $190, Sears)

Another Sears model has "Wrinkle Guard": machine continues tumbling without heat for up to 30 minutes after end of drying cycle. (In white, about $220; in wheat, coffee, avocado, or almond, about $250; Sears)

## To *identify laundry*

SOCK LOCKS:   Package of 24 grippers to hold socks in pairs during laundering. (About $2, American Foundation for the Blind)

HI-MARKS:   Applies directly from a tube to make bright orange, raised marks inside collars for easy identification. (About $4, American Foundation for the Blind)

## *Ironing*

Since it's so much less tiring to sit while ironing than to stand, consider having someone cut the legs of your ironing board. Or buy a portable board that fits into a drawer.

PORTABLE IRONING BOARD:   No legs; 11″ x 24″ covered board fits into any open drawer: weighs 3½ lbs.; hangs on a nail. (About $17, Joan Cook)

ELECTRIC STEAMER:   Flashlight-size; takes tap water; steams out wrinkles and restores creases right on hanger. (About $20, Joan Cook)

## To *save steps*

If you wash less at a time, but wash more often, each load will be less bulky. So if you live on one level and don't have to carry your wash downstairs, you can kick it along in a castored plastic dishpan (see page 5) or roll it along on a castored cart (see page 27). Do the same with your ironing. Store it in a castored dishpan or in a basket that can easily be put on your castored cart.

To save carrying laundry downstairs, get a carpenter to cut a hole in the floor under one of the sinks on the first floor (make sure he isn't going to hit wires or pipes in the cellar ceiling) and install a laundry chute. Or just have him cut a hole large enough to shove dirty clothes through to the cellar and place a large box or basket (or even the washing machine itself) below the hole to receive the clothes as they fall.

## To *carry laundry with one hand*

Loop webbing or rope through the handles of your laundry basket, fasten with a knot or dog leash snap, and slip your arm through the loop. Or use a large canvas bag with handles such as:

BOAT AND TOTE BAG:   Of extra heavy white duck; red, blue, or green handles and trim; in 2 sizes (both from L. L. Bean)—6″ x 13½″ x 12″ high, weighing 16 oz. (about $11); 8″ x 17″ x 16″ high, weighing 26 oz. (about $12)

## BEDMAKING

It may be easier to use fitted sheets. But it is certainly easier to make one side of the bed fully, then move to the end of the bed and work your way up the other side. Fold your clean sheets so that they can be placed lengthwise across one half of the bed without waving them in the air.

### An easy method

1. Place a chair at foot of bed and pull covers back onto it over end of bed.
2. Remove pillows, pillowcases, and soiled sheets.
3. Spread undersheet lengthwise across half the width of the bed.
4. Lift top corner of mattress and place wastebasket on its side under the corner to hold it up.
5. Tuck undersheet in at head and part of side.
6. Change pillowcase and place pillow so that you can reach it when you've finished tucking in other side of bed.
7. Spread upper sheet, then covers; tuck in at side.
8. Progress down toward foot, smoothing and tucking.
9. Move up second side in same manner, placing pillow and drawing up bedspread.[3]

### To facilitate tucking in sheets

Use a shoehorn (see page 49) or any kind of flat wooden paddle with a handle, such as a wooden spatula if you have a sturdy one—or even a Ping-Pong paddle if it's not covered with material that sticks to a sheet.

## CHAIRS AND STOOLS

To do your work with less stress, try sitting more. And whenever you can, shove a footstool under your feet to keep your legs from getting tired. The best way to use a footstool is to bend your knees and plant your feet flat on the stool, pointing straight ahead. Try attaching a broom handle or long dowel to the side of the stool to help you reposition it when necessary.[4]

### Some available types

ONE-STEP STOOL: Metal, 10½" high, weighs 6 lbs., handle extends 9" above stool. (About $12, Sears)

SWIVEL STOOLS/DIRECTORS' CHAIRS: Send for Sears catalog for a complete list of the many models available.

RECLINERS, CHAIR-TABLES, GLIDERS, ROCKERS, COMMODE CHAIRS:   Catalogs available from Lumex, Skandi-Form, and Winco.

SELF-RISING ARMCHAIRS:   Consider renting or advertising for second-hand models in rehabilitation magazines, or send for catalogs from Abbey, Burke, Ortho-Kinetics, Rise-O-Matic, Sears, or Wheelovator. To compare: Sears' price for a 110-volt, 8′ cord, semiassembled, push-button chair in button-tufted velveteen upholstery (rust-colored), weighs 73 lbs., steel base and legs, 28″ x 26½″ x 38″ high—about $750 plus shipping.

### *To raise height of chair or table legs*

LEG-EXTENDERS:   Elevate 1½″–9″ diameter round, square, or rectangular legs up to 8″; 2 wing nuts to attach. (Easy Riser)

NARROW LEG-EXTENDERS:   Elevate square legs up to 1″ diameter, or round legs up to 1¼″ from 3″–7″; screw-clamps. (About $35 for 4, Help Yourself Aids)

## RUGS

---

Flat, tightly woven "kitchen" or "indoor-outdoor" carpeting is very durable, less expensive than pile, and easier for maneuvering wheelchairs. To keep loose rugs from slipping, use a double-faced adhesive tape. (About $4 per roll, Miles Kimball or Sunset House)

### *To spot-clean the professional way*

Using any mild detergent, shake well, scrub rug with suds that form on top of the solution, then rub with towel. (For pet-caused spots on rug, see hint on page 5.)

## CLOSETS AND STORAGE

---

### *To reach things on shelves*

Keep a reacher handy to pull things toward you. You can store a number of things on trays, in castored dishpans (see page 5), or in a basket or:

UNDERSHELF BASKET:   "Arms" slip over top of the shelf and basket hangs below; storage basket measures 19¾″ x 9¾″ x 6″ deep. (About $7, Lillian Vernon) Smaller baskets are listed on page 154.

### *To store things on floor of closet*

STACKING BASKETS:   Largest plastic baskets on the market measure 13″ x 20½″ x 9″; castors for legs of bottom basket are optional; white, beige, or brown. (Each basket about $9; 4 castors, about $9, Garden Way)

Similar baskets measuring 12⅛″ x 17½″ x 18″ *without* castors, brown, red, white, or yellow. (About $14 for 3, Spiegel)

### Back-of-door storage with pegboard

Pegboard can be a great space-saver.

LINE DOOR WITH PEGBOARD AND HANG:

Shoes, using elastic threaded from behind board

Cleaning equipment, tools, and sports gear (balls go in bags)

Gloves, mail, keys in small baskets

Tools, paint brushes, and the like, in fingers of old gloves

Cosmetics, tools, other small items in pegboard bins: 5 plastic bins, each 19¾″ long x 3½″ high x 4″ deep, with clips or pegs that hold the bins onto the pegboard-lined door. (About $30, Brookstone)

PEGBOARD TOOL RACK:   Nine inches long, for all small tools. (About $3, Miles Kimball)

PEGBOARD WRENCH RACK:   Nine and one-quarter inches long, holds 6 wrenches. (About $3, Miles Kimball)

PEGBOARD JAR SET:   Small clear jars. (10 for about $9, Miles Kimball)

### Alternatives to pegboard

Back-of-door hanging shelf units, in a variety of lengths, are available in hardware stores. You might also try the following:

BACK-OF-DOOR SHELF SYSTEM:   Eight vinyl-coated shelf racks; each 5″ deep x 18″ wide; comes with hardware to mount on solid or hollow 72″ doors. (About $40, Joan Cook) A similar system is 12″ wide. (About $40, The Pottery Barn)

BACK-OF-DOOR SHOE RACK:

*To mount with screws:* Steel loops; set holds 12 pairs. (About $11, Sears)

*To hang over top of door:* Hangs over doors 1⅜″ thick; steel loops. (Holding 15 pairs, about $16, Sears; holding 21 pairs, about $18, Sears)

### To store shoes in bottom of closet

CIRCULAR CHROME RACK ON CASTORS:   Rolls out and spins around for easy selection of shoes that hang by their heels on circular rods; holds 12 pairs. (About $17, Joan Cook) A similar rack that does not spin and holds 12 pairs men's, 18 pairs women's shoes costs about $15 at Sears.

### To reach clothes from a wheelchair

"INSTANT" LOW SUSPENSION ROD:   Just hook over existing high closet rod; will hang 32″ below high rod; adjusts in length from 27″ to 48″. (About $7, Sears)

## *To store tools on wall*

Try a 50″ steel track that comes with 6 sliding metal holders for tools, and brackets and screws for wall mounting. (About $9, Miles Kimball)

## *Under-the-bed storage*

The following are great space-savers.

FIBERBOARD BOXES: Have lift-off lids and side handles; 35½″ x 6¼″ x 18″. (Set of 3 for about $11, Sears)

CLEAR VINYL CHEST: Opens by zipper, 40″ x 6″ x 18″, can be folded. (About $10, Joan Cook)

## *Other storage units*

(See page 154 for under-shelf storage ideas.)

LOW WARDROBE: Solid pine, 44″ high x 33″ wide x 21″ deep; holds up to 50 garments. (Kit, about $150; finished, about $200; Yield House)

ROLLING SLACK TROLLEY: 28½″ high x 18″ wide x 13½″ deep. (Kit, about $45; finished, about $55; Yield House)

## *To open drawers and cabinets*

Put a handle in the center of a drawer or the bottom center of cabinet door. Then attach a leather or webbing loop to the handle to pull the drawer or door open with your forearm. The following suggestions are also helpful:

GLIDES FOR DRAWERS: Metal tracks to install for easy gliding. (About $10 for 24″ length; other lengths available; from Miles Kimball or hardware/department stores)

TO MAKE DRAWERS PULL IN AND OUT MORE EASILY: Pure silicone spray. (About $5 per can, Brookstone)

## LIGHTS, KNOBS, AND SWITCHES

POWER FAILURE LIGHT: Goes on automatically when power fails; plug into any wall outlet. (About $25, Brookstone)

TO EXIT BEFORE LIGHTS GO OFF: Get a wall switch with delayed action. (About $5, Help Yourself Aids)

WALL PUSH SWITCH: Outlet for lamp or appliance, plus wall on-off button. (About $5, Help Yourself Aids)

"TOUCHTRONIC":   Attach under light bulb so lamp can be turned on and off with a light touch. (About $24, Westek)

REMOTE CONTROL SWITCHES:   To operate with finger or by blowing (see page 183).

## Wall switch extenders

(See also Wall Push Switch above.)

Improvise an extender by using a reacher, long shoehorn, dressing stick, and the like to turn wall switches on and off. Or buy:

WALL SWITCH AID:   Wooden dowel with piece at end to fit over switch. (About $4, The Independence Factory)

PERMANENT WALL SWITCH EXTENSION:   Plastic strip 22" x 2", screws over switch; hangs down for seated person to push and pull. (About $5, Abbey)

## Knob turners

You can make your own knob turner. Tape or glue a small piece of wood across the knob or build up the knob itself with tape or a small piece of foam rubber. If the "knob" is a thin vertical piece of metal located in the center of an appliance dial or under the light bulb of a lamp, and must be grasped between forefinger and thumb to turn the appliance on or off, the following may help:

APPLIANCE KNOB TURNER:   A wooden handle with crosspiece for grasp; slotted to fit over lamp or center-of-dial knobs described above. (About $4, The Independence Factory)

LAMP SWITCH EXTENSION LEVER:   A 4-winged unit to replace lamp knob described above. (About $6, Help Yourself Aids)

# DOORS

## To get up to front door

Use a Portable Half Step, described on page 14 of this chapter, or a ramp (see page 215).

## To remodel doorways

(See also To Narrow Your Chair on page 212.)

TO WIDEN DOORWAYS:   Use MED hinges to set door flat back against the wall behind a door frame, freeing 1½"–2" of space. Uses same three-hole mounting as standard hinges and leaves no marks when removed. (About $25 per set, MED)

TO FLATTEN THRESHOLDS: Have them removed and the area covered with strip flat metal, wood, or polyethylene.[5]

BIFOLD DOORS: Doors fold in middle to glide toward you on nylon tracks when hook handle is grasped and pulled; leaves space wide enough for a wheelchair. (Sears or Stanley Tools—prices vary according to size)

## To open and close doors

Install spring catches so you can simply push the door open and shut. Or put a crutch tip on one end of a dowel and a leather loop large enough to fit over a door handle at the other end; to close the door, hook the loop over the handle and pull it closed; to open the door, push with the crutch-tip end. Make this or order a similar "Wheelchair Door Opening Aid" for about $4 from Independence Factory. Two other helpful devices are:

DOOR CLOSER: Spring-operated; for doors with pin hinges (hinges must extend 3/8" or more from door molding). To install, remove hinge pin, place pin through device, replace pin with device attached in hinge. (About $12, Brookstone)

PETRIK VERTICAL DOOR OPENER: Vertical bar that extends from door's center almost to floor; releases by touch. (About $380, Petrik)

## For better grasp of door handles

For round knobs, apply the rubber daisies used on bottoms of bathtubs to prevent slipping or see other ideas on page 31. Or order:

RUBBER EXTENDER: Snaps over round knobs (needs pressure for original installation), leaving keyhole free. (Use lever with arm, hip, elbow.) (About $10, Help Yourself Aids)

STEEL EXTENDER: Lever that screws to round knob; use as above. (About $12, Help Yourself Aids)

PLASTIC EXTENDER: Lever that extends 3/4" from a round knob; attach with special pressure tape. (Set of 4 with tape, about $10, Help Yourself Aids)

FOR LEVER HANDLES: Buckle a man's leather belt, put the loop over lever, and use wrist or forearm to pull up or down.

## Keys

Keys can be awkward to use. To make them easier to handle, insert a nail (tape the pointed end) through the hole of a key, or bolt or rivet the key to a small block of wood. Help Yourself Aids sells a plastic key holder with screws to hold 4 keys. It adds leverage for turning, measures 3" x 1" x 5/8", and costs about $10.

## STAIRS

Stairs can present an obstacle—consider replacing them with lifts, elevators, and ramps. If that is not feasible, here are some ways to conquer the stairs:

"SIT" UP THE STAIRS:   If your doctor approves, try sitting on the bottom step and pulling yourself up to the next one using the banister or a series of sturdy loops hanging from it (buckle leather belts over banister between balusters at intervals, and tape the buckles to prevent them from scratching your arm as you pull yourself along).

STAIR WALKER:   Consult your doctor first, and use with assistance. See page 185.

PORTABLE HALF STEP:   This is an aid you can make for yourself. Attach a cane to the side of a block of balsa wood half the height of your stair riser. Nail 1″ x 1″ pieces of wood at each corner of the bottom of the block for "legs," and glue nonskid material (see page 31) to bottom of each leg.[6] You might also hinge the balsa to the cane so that the block can be folded up out of the way. (To get up bus steps, make a similar device, but use a thicker block of balsa.) *Be sure to use either device only with a railing on the other side of you for safety.*

## SHOPPING

(See also Groceries on page 27.)

### Shopping equipment

BAG ON WHEELS:   A vinyl bag mounted on wheels; 22″ high (plus straps) x 12″ wide x 7½″ deep. (About $12, Sleepy Hollow Gifts)

HAUL-ON-WHEELS:   To haul groceries (garden trash and so forth); holds large trash bags, drums, cartons, and the like and can carry loads up to 100 lbs. Made of 8-lb. aluminum tubing and includes stair-climber bars. (About $35, Brookstone)

SHOPPING CART:   One handle; 14″ x 17″ x 22″ wire basket; wide-tread back wheels; front castors. (About $35, Fashion-Able)

COIN PURSE:   Leather oval with "tray" to slide coins into for easy pick-up (About $17, Ferry House)

SHOULDER BAG PIN:   Use to pin your shoulder bag to a coat shoulder to keep the bag in place. (About $4, Miles Kimball)

TO SIT WHILE SHOPPING:   See Gadabout Chair-Cane on page 188.

## MISCELLANEOUS

*Sewing*

You'll find some helpful tips in Chapter 21, Arts, Crafts, and the Workshop.

*Smoking equipment*

SMOKER'S ROBOT:   A chrome ashtray with 38″ tube at the end of which is a mouthpiece to puff through while the robot holds your cigarette and collects ashes in the ashtray. (About $12, Cleo) Replacement tubes cost about $1.50 (Cleo)

CIGARETTE HOLDER:   Moldable to fit any hand. (About $10, Cleo)

ASHTRAY-UTILITY TRAY:   A spring clip attaches this tray to wheelchair, bed, or other piece of furniture. Includes a removable coil for holding cigarettes. When coil is removed, ashtray becomes a pin tray. (About $6, Cleo)

*Hardware*

MAGNETIC PADLOCK:   There's no combination to remember; magnetic sensor bar, when held to lock, opens it. (About $5, American Foundation for the Blind)

LIGHT BULB CHANGER:   Fits all sizes of incandescent bulbs; a cone on 4′ aluminum tube; weighs 3 lbs. To operate, place cone over the bulb, pull handle down, twist to unscrew the bulb. Reverse the process to insert a new bulb. (About $35, G. E. Miller)

*To keep animals out of outdoor garbage pails*

Sprinkle ammonia on the ground around pails; it won't hurt the animals, but they won't like the smell. Or buckle together two leather belts. Thread the resulting long strap through the metal clamps at either side of the pail, then through the handle at the top, then buckle.[7]

## BARRIER-FREE HOUSING

Housing facilities designed for disabled people remove many obstacles. To find out where barrier-free, adapted housing facilities are located in the United States, write Rehabilitation Gazette, 4502 Maryland Ave., St. Louis, Mo. 63108. This magazine keeps continually updated files on such information. (See the Bibliography for other sources of information.)

Housing loans, rent subsidies, and general housing information can be found in Chapter 28.

# 2

# *How to Do a Lot Less in the Kitchen*

A great deal has been written about how to set up a kitchen if you are confined to a wheelchair or otherwise disabled. You are told to remodel your kitchen to create knee space of at least 24″ x 24″ when sitting to work at surfaces 27″–32″ high. You are also enjoined to install built-in lazy Susan cabinets, pull-out shelves and racks, side-by-side refrigerator-freezers, and other such devices.

All of these ideas are good. But suppose you already have a kitchen that is *not* set up this way. You then have two options. You can apply to Vocational Rehabilitation for funds to help you remodel. Or you can find ways of using what you have more effectively.

If you decide to make do with what you have, your challenge is to create a comfortable place to sit to work, to prepare food and transport it to and from the table efficiently, and to arrange easy-to-reach storage.

You can have all these features for far less than the cost of a couple of built-ins. You need two basic types of equipment. One is a *utility cart* that can be used to do just about anything from a sitting position and to transport food and equipment. The other vital piece of equipment is one or more sets of *stacking baskets* for easy-reach storage and moving more equipment or food from place to place.

Throughout this chapter, "O-H" follows items especially good for the one-handed. "L-V" follows those helpful to people with low vision.

## WORKING WHILE YOU SIT

### Utility cart

Here are two utility carts you might consider. The first measures 30" high and has 2" castors, two handles, and two 26" x 18" shelves, one of which folds out of the way for knee room when you sit. (About $110, MED) The second cart, available from Help Yourself Aids, is similar to the first but has larger castors (4½") and no handles (there's a knob at each end instead). It folds to 3" wide, has two shelves 21" x 16", and comes in black or gold. (About $75)

*Please note that neither this cart nor any other is a substitute walking aid. If you want to walk with it as your sole support, be sure your doctor or therapist thinks it's stable enough for you. If not, perhaps your doctor would approve your weighting it down with sandbags.*

### Other ways to sit to work at the right height

Use a chair with "leg extenders" or a high stool (see page 8); elevate your chair or wheelchair with extra cushions (see page 211); buy or rent an "elevating wheelchair" (powered to raise you to the right working height—see page 204); for working, use an adjustable table (see page 180) or a lapboard (see page 210) or hang a fold-down shelf on your wall at the right height for sitting.

If your utility cart is your main workplace, keep a flat tray handy for sliding things from too high shelves or counters to your work surface.[1]

If you already have a place to sit to work, but need a sturdy, inexpensive cart to transport dishes and other items, see Carts on page 27. These can also be used instead of stacking baskets.

## STORAGE

If you're in a wheelchair, you should remove as many of your below-counter cabinet doors as possible. For better grasp of cabinet door handles, reposition them horizontally at the bottom of the door.

### Stacking baskets

Consider these as substitutes for below-counter shelves. Each measures 20½" x 13" x 9" high, and is made of plastic. They are flat-bottomed to stack and put on castors for easy roll-out and access to supplies. (About $9 per basket, 4 castors to fit legs on bottom basket; about $8, Garden Way) Three stacked baskets stand 27" high, so they should—even with castors—fit under your counter. (Most counters average about 36" high.)

You can hook the whole stack with your cane or reacher and roll your supplies right to your wheelchair, to the table, or to wherever you're working.

You can also store these baskets at the back of your shelves and pull them easily toward you, with or without castors. Use them stacked high in any kitchen corner. (Or use the Castored Basket Cart described on page 27 instead.)

## Other kitchen storage ideas

Another way to reach things on the backs of shelves is to store them on trays. (Keep only lightweight things on trays or they can be dangerous.) Or put vertical dividers in cabinets to "file" items like trays and cookie sheets.

Whenever there are a few inches of space below a shelf, try an "under-shelf basket" (see page 154). This holds items underneath and toward the front of a shelf for easy access.

For bringing things into reach in the refrigerator, as well as on shelves, plastic lazy Susans (from any variety store—single- or double-tiered) are very convenient.

STACK-RACK HALF-SHELVES:   Folding, stacking; 18½" x 7¾" x 5½" high. (About $8, Lillian Vernon)

40-PIECE DINNER SET RACK:   Measures 18½" across, 10" deep. (About $10, Ferry House)

FRIDGE-FREEZER UNDERSHELF RACK:   Hooks to *wire shelves only* to create a bin 10½" x 10¾" x 5¾" deep. (About $7, Lillian Vernon)

BIG-BOTTLE RACK:   Similar to above, but contoured to hold two 5"-wide bottles. (About $7, Lillian Vernon)

POT-LID RACK:   To hang on wall or back of door; 17" x 19" at its widest. (About $6, Lillian Vernon)

FOLD-AWAY DISH RACK:   With tray; 22 V-shaped slots for draining dishes, 12 cup hooks. (About $13, Lillian Vernon)

HARDWOOD DISH RACK:   Hangs or stands to hold 30 dishes; slats of natural wood; 14" x 14" x 8½". (About $12, Lillian Vernon)

> *Matching Flatware Rack:* Measures 13" wide x 6" high x 2⅛" deep; to hang or stand. (About $8, Lillian Vernon)

> *Matching 3-Shelf Rack:* Measures 14¾" x 14¼" x 4¾". (About $12, Lillian Vernon)

OVER-SINK TRAY:   White vinyl-clad steel basket, 15" x 8½" x 2½" deep; arms to fit sink area up to 19". (About $8, Lillian Vernon)

Don't forget about pegboard and the other ideas suggested on page 10.

## A FEW GENERAL TIPS

### *To go from a sitting to a standing position*

Try putting a grab bar or parallel in front of the kitchen sink and another in the cooking area. These are also great if you don't need any help in getting up but tend to tire as you stand. These bars can be used with or without a safety strap around the lower back.[2]

### *Water*

To fill pans on the stove or counter or on your work surface, rather than in the sink, have a plumber install a retractable hose near a faucet or get one for watering plants (see page 148). (Also see To Pour Beverages and Water from Containers on page 23.)

### *If your sink is too deep*

Place inverted plastic baskets or even old coffee cans in the sink, or use an Over-Sink Tray or Stack-Rack Half-Shelves, described on page 18.

### *Aprons*

These are great for carrying a number of items with you. See page 190 for many varieties.

APRON HOOP:　Flexible plastic hoop to slide in and out of waistbands of aprons, eliminating behind-the-back tying (especially good for the one-handed). (About $6, Help Yourself Aids)

### *If reach is a problem*

Use long-handled barbecue tools.

### *To stabilize bowls, etc.*

Put them on a wet sponge cloth or paper towel, or buy one of the following:

PAN HANDLER:　Suction cups to anchor wooden frame that holds pot handles steady; for handles $1\frac{3}{8}''$–$5\frac{1}{2}''$ high. (About $8, Fashion-Able)

FOLDING PAN HOLDER:　Similar to above, but with folding steel legs. (About $20, Help Yourself Aids)

### *To see into pots*

Use a hand mirror.

### *To keep roasting pans clean*

Line pan (not rack) with foil.

### Cleaning up crumbs

"ASPIRAL": A 6" x 2½" plastic box; one side holds a revolving brush to whirl crumbs up into box. Pry the cover up with a knife and shake out the crumbs every few days. (About $5, The Pottery Barn) (O-H)

## BROILER-OVENS, STEAMERS, AND OTHER COOKERS

### Two helpful tips

TO INCREASE GRASP ON ANY KNOB: ( See ideas on page 13.)
TO PICK UP TOPS OF SKILLETS:   Use the tines of a large fork.[3]

On the appliances that follow, model numbers are given wherever possible to facilitate ordering from houseware and department stores. However, the items from the American Foundation for the Blind are especially adapted and must be ordered through the foundation.

### Portable electric countertop cookers

BROILER-OVENS

GE (T26/3126–004): Front slide controls; top-to-bottom opening; toaster with crumb tray. (About $55)

Toastmaster (5242): Color-coded buttons to operate; top-to-bottom opening; continuous self-cleaning. (About $80) (L-V)

Farberware Turbo (460R): Cool to the touch; self-cleaning; right-to-left opening door; broils on all sides at once; roasts faster than most models. (About $180)

TOASTMASTER HOT PLATE:   Front controls; model #6400 has a double burner (about $60); #6401 has a single burner (about $45).

HOOVER (B3009–2) BROILER/FRYPAN:   Easy-to-grasp top (with fork or hook); for broil and fry; bread-warming tray underneath. (About $80)

SUNBEAM (KM 901) FRYPAN:   To fry, bake, or roast: easy-to-grasp top, immersible, for use with Removable Control below. (About $50, American Foundation for the Blind) (L-V)

Removable Control for Sunbeam Frypan (KM 903): Notched, brailled temperature control with large print. (About $28, American Foundation for the Blind)

### Nonelectric stove-top cookers

(See also Small Portable Stove under Cooking for One.)

STEAMER FOR COOKING A WHOLE MEAL AT ONCE:   Aluminum pot with base 10" in diameter x 4½" deep with 2 stacking baskets, 3½" deep and

2½" deep, respectively. Boil or poach meat or fish in bottom pot; steam two vegetables separately above it. Total height 13", weight 3¼ lbs. (About $35, The Wooden Spoon) (See also Steamer)

PRESSURE COOKER MIRRO-MATIC (KM 123): Four-qt.; audible bouncing weights to indicate when desired pressure is reached; safety fuse to blow if vent pipe clogs. (About $40, American Foundation for the Blind) (L-V)

(See also mini-versions of frypan and pressure cooker under Cooking for One, below.)

OVEN: Nine inches x 4" high; to bake, toast, or warm food over electric burner. (About $9, Fashion-Able)

STEAMER: Eight-qt. pot plus steam basket, grain colander, and vented lid; made of heavy aluminum. (About $33, Joan Cook)

## COOKING FOR ONE

### Equipment

MIRRO TINY PRESSURE COOKER: Two-and-one-half qt.; 6" high; made of heavy aluminum, weighs 3 lbs.; pressure control and safety fuse; rack; recipe book; warranty. (About $42, Joan Cook)

MEASURING CUP TO COOK IN: Safe to use on burner, in oven, microwave oven, freezer; 1 cup with measuring marks. (About $12, Joan Cook)

TINY WHISTLING TEAKETTLE: Loud whistle; 4-cup; made of dishwasher-safe glass; sturdy handle; vinyl top with handle. (About $12, Joan Cook)

MINI-POTS: Nonstick, 7" frypan; 6" griddle; 1-qt. saucepan; all made of heavy aluminum with cool-grip handles. (About $26 for all three, Joan Cook)

SMALL PORTABLE STOVE: For use with nonexplosive fuel like denatured alcohol or shellac thinner (6 oz. burn for over 1 hour); feet to protect surfaces; handles on both sides. (About $15, Joan Cook)

TOASTMASTER TINY ELECTRIC FRYPAN: Eight-inch; level-adjustable heat control; immersible; see-through glass lid with large knob; warranty. (About $45, Joan Cook)

TRI-PAN: Cooks 3 foods at the same time in divided 10" square covered pan. (About $25, Miles Kimball)

### Mini-refrigerator

Install one of these at the right height to be reached easily from a wheelchair, for use without bending, or next to a bed.

MINI-REFRIGERATOR WITH FREEZER: Measures 19⅝" wide x 16½"

deep x 18½″ high; door opens left to right; freezer compartment (2 ice cube trays included); 2 adjustable shelves in refrigerator area; door has a bottle and egg rack; warranty. (About $170, Abbey)

Four similar models with variations are available through Sears. (About $220–$300)

## CARRYING ITEMS WITH ONE HAND OR WITHOUT HANDS

Use a flat-bottomed basket with handles at each end or cut oblong slits at each end of a sturdy open box. Thread a man's belt through basket handles or box slots, buckle the belt, and use it as a strap for carrying. The box can be used for carrying beverages if you put a damp sponge, towel, or wet paper towel under the glass.[4] Another alternative is to wear an apron with lots of pockets (see page 190). For no-hands carrying, see Picker Pocket and Harvesting Bag (page 146) or use a knapsack.

ONE-HANDED TRAY: Easy-grip offset handle; nonskid surface. (About $55, MED) (O-H)

PERSONAL MOBILITY AID: A 14″ x 18″ removable tray on vertical rolling shaft; contoured handgrip, 9½ lbs., 19¼″ overall width; wire basket available. Useful for transporting things but, although it's advertised as a mobility aid to take the place of one cane or crutch, *do not use this for ambulation* unless your doctor or therapist says it is safe to do so. (About $160, Anik) (O-H)

## OPENING CANS AND JARS

### Cans

ELECTRIC OPENER: Made especially for one-handed use. (About $70, Help Yourself Aids) (O-H)

E-Z TURN: A hand opener with less-effort cutter wheel; long handles give better leverage. (About $8, Help Yourself Aids)

SWING-AWAY (407): Moderate grasp required; large key rotates with heel of hand. (About $6, most houseware and department stores)

PULL-TAB POP-TOP CANS: Easy-grip handle, curved rod notched to hold pop-top ring as you pull. (About $4, Independence Factory)

### Jars

One helpful suggestion: Place the jar in a shallow drawer, pressing your hip against the drawer so that the jar is held firmly while unscrewed with one hand. (O-H)

A number of devices on the market will also help.

HANDYAID RUBBER GRIP:　A 5″ disk made of flexible rubber; use for better grip when unscrewing jars; also good as nonskid mat. (2 for about $4, Fashion-Able)

ZIM:　Wall-mounted; holds jar on bottle in its "jaws" while jar is hand-turned. (About $12, Help Yourself Aids) (O-H)

UNDERCOUNTER:　Attached by screws; press jar against gripper to turn. (About $10, Help Yourself Aids) (O-H)

LONG LEVER:　Band slips around lid; tighten via wrench action on long handles. (About $20, Help Yourself Aids)

## Cans or jars

ZIM TWIN:　Similar to Zim above, but also to open cans. (About $20, Help Yourself Aids)

# TO MIX AND POUR

## To drain hot water from pots

PAN STRAINER:　Perforated metal shield to fit over pot; spring-loaded to stay in place while you pour. (About $4, American Foundation for the Blind) (L-V, O-H)

LOCKLID SAUCEPAN:　A 3-qt., Teflon-lined porcelain pan; self-lock top; perforations on side of pot for pouring out liquid. (About $14, American Foundation for the Blind) (L-V, O-H)

## To pour beverages and water from containers

(See also the suggestions on filling pots on page 19 of this chapter and the Bowl with Stand below.)

TAP-A-GLASS DRINK DISPENSER:　One-gallon, heavy-duty plastic container with push-lever handle on spigot. Fill with water and fill pots or glasses right from counter or refrigerator shelf. (About $10, Starcrest of California)

MIXER-PITCHER:　For easy mixing of concentrated juices and other beverages without removing no-spill top; has easy-grip, up-down motion mixer attached to top of 2-qt. pitcher. (About $8, Help Yourself Aids) (L-V, O-H)

## To pour semisolid foods

SQUEEZE BOTTLES:　Easy-to-squeeze, 4 oz., about $3; 8 oz., about $3; 16 oz., about $4; all from Abbey. (L-V, O-H)

KETCHUP PUMP:   Pumps 1 teaspoon at a time with light palm or finger pressure. (About $3, American Foundation for the Blind) (L-V, O-H)

### To pour milk

To open cardboard carton, carefully saw off one corner. To pour more easily through the resulting hole, slip the carton into:

CARTON HOLDER:   Vinyl-coated rack holds ½ gallon; 2 side handles. (About $6, Abbey) (O-H)

### To mix and pour batter, etc.

BOWL WITH STAND:   A 3-qt. steel bowl and stand to hold it steady while mixing; lock stand into tilt position for scraping and pouring. (About $40, Help Yourself Aids) (L-V, O-H)

BOWL WITH HANDLE:   Three-qt., made of steel; use with wet paper towel or sponge cloth to prevent moving. (About $16, Help Yourself Aids) (L-V, O-H)

A similar device with a pouring lip and measuring marks costs about $13 from Fashion-Able.

### Mixers

For one-handed mixing, use a portable electric mixer with the Bowl with Stand described above, or place a damp paper towel or sponge cloth under a regular bowl to prevent it from sliding. There are standard mixers that can hold bowls in place for you, such as:

HAMILTON BEACH (021) COMPACT STANDARD ELECTRIC:   Steel bowls; 10-speed control (some hand strength needed); easy-to-use bowl control knob for less scraping. (About $95, houseware and department stores)

ELECTRIC MIXER SPATTER SHIELD:   Locks over 7″ and 10″ bowls; for all mixers except Kitchen Aid. (About $5, American Foundation for the Blind) (L-V)

## CLEANING, PEELING, CHOPPING, GRATING

BRUSH TO CLEAN VEGETABLES:   Fingernail-type nylon brush, mounted on suction cups. (About $6, Help Yourself Aids) (L-V, O-H)

### Peelers

MIRACLE PEELER:   Usable by quadriplegics; large handle, swivel blade. (About $6, Help Yourself Aids)

DOUBLE-EDGED PEELER:   Mounted in metal clamp to attach to table or cutting board; slide vegetable against peeler. (About $23, Abbey) (L-V, O-H)

## Choppers

AUTOMATIC CHOPPER:   Spring-action, palm-push; 4½″ diameter, 6 blades, open-bottomed container (put a board underneath). (About $8, American Foundation for the Blind) (L-V, O-H)

CHOPPING BOWL AND CHOPPER:   Diameter is 10½″, hardwood; can't tip; 4-bladed chopper. (About $10, Help Yourself Aids) (O-H)

## Graters

STAY PUT GRATER:   Suction cups to stabilize; bin catches food as grated. (About $6, Help Yourself Aids) (O-H)

# ROASTING AND CARVING

## To cut raw meat

Pop into freezer for an hour to harden slightly[5] and use:

ROCKER BUTCHER KNIFE:   Easy-grip handle, long curved blade. (About $14, Help Yourself Aids) (O-H)

## Roasting aid

MEAT THERMOMETER:   Notched at every 10°, with raised dots at 140°, 160°, and 180°; stay-cool dial to insert for quick reading; *do not leave in oven.* (About $25, American Foundation for the Blind) (L-V)

## Carving

Let meat stand 15–30 minutes after removing from the oven for easier carving.

ROAST HOLDER AND SLICING GUIDE:   Handles to grip roast; tines to guide knife. (About $11, American Foundation for the Blind) (L-V)

Help Yourself Aids sells a similar item, made of plastic, for about $10.

MAGNA KNIFE WITH DETACHABLE SLICING GUIDE:   Scalloped, no-sharpen blade, specify right or left hand. (About $18, American Foundation for the Blind) (L-V)

*Note:* Use the Roast Holder and Magna Knife with meat impaled on the one-handed carving boards described below.

MAGNA FORK:   Matches Magna Knife to make a complete carving set. (About $8, American Foundation for the Blind) (L-V)

AUTO-FORK:   For carving, serving, and eating; 8½″ long; squeeze tong handles to push metal plate along prongs to eject food. (About $5, American Foundation for the Blind) (L-V, O-H)

### One-handed cutting and carving boards

HARDWOOD: Measures 7″ x 14″ laminated; suction cups on bottom, nails to hold food, corner ledge. (About $12, Fashion-Able) (O-H)

FORMICA: Similar to hardwood model, but measures 8″ x 10″. (About $20, Help Yourself Aids) (O-H)

LARGE BOARD WITH RIM: Measures 12″ x 16″, laminated maple; slanted surface and a rim to catch juices; nails to hold food, corner ledge. (About $20, Help Yourself Aids) (O-H)

## COOKING AND BAKING

### To sift and measure

SUGAR METER: Measures dry ingredients; 12-oz. capacity; dispenses ½ teaspoon at a time. (About $4, American Foundation for the Blind) (L-V, O-H)

SIFTER: Long-handled, lightweight plastic, 1-cup capacity; squeeze handles together to sift. (About $3, Help Yourself Aids) (O-H)

E-Z READ JIGGER: Lucite with ledges to indicate ½, 1, 1½, and 2 oz. of liquid; to measure 1 cup, fill jigger 4 times. (About $3, American Foundation for the Blind) (L-V)

### To roll dough

Use a paint roller or:

ROLLING PIN WITH CENTER HANDLE: Horizontal handle; 2 interchangeable wooden rollers. (About $8, Help Yourself Aids) (O-H)

### For the oven

ITALIAN RACK-JACK: Notched 11″ wooden paddle for pulling out oven racks. (About $4, Miles Kimball)

MITTS:

Extra-Long: Protects forearms and hands. (About $16 a pair, Help Yourself Aids)

The Grabber: Extra-wide mitt, flexible thumb area; Teflon-coated. (About $5, Miles Kimball)

Casserole Paws: Wide quilted band to fit around casserole; mitts at each end. (About $8, House of Minnel)

*To turn and toss food or serve pasta*

DOUBLE SPATULA:  Detachable for single-spatula use; one side slotted. (About $5, American Foundation for the Blind) (L-V, O-H)

TONGS:  Scissors-style; one side is a large-tined fork. (About $5, American Foundation for the Blind) (L-V, O-H)

*Note:* Tongs can make excellent reacher-grabbers for picking things up, turning faucets on and off, etc.

*To wash up*

BOTTLE BRUSH:  Pair of 7"-high nylon brushes that screw into 6" suction base. (About $16; replacement brushes about $5; Help Yourself Aids)

ECONOMY DISH MOP:  Small, standing mop that attaches by suction to bottom of sink for washing glasses and dishes. (About $5, Help Yourself Aids)

# GROCERIES

(See also Bag on Wheels, page 14.)

*To keep meat, frozen foods cold in back of car*

INSULATED FOOD AND BEVERAGE BAG:  Measures 20" x 12½" x 9", made of zippered vinyl; handles all way around for added strength: (About $12, Miles Kimball)

Another Miles Kimball model is smaller, measuring 16" x 10" x 6½", with handles attached at top only. (About $7)

*Carts*

Be very careful about using any cart when walking, even if it is sturdy and weighted with sandbags; it can tip.

UTILITY:  (See page 17.)

CASTORED BASKET:  Three white vinyl-clad metal baskets (removable for separate use), each 10" x 14½" x 2½"; lift-off brown plastic tray on top; handle at each end of cart; castors; height of entire unit, 32½". (About $33, Lillian Vernon)

Vernon also sells a similar model for about $26: 25" high; no lift-off tray; each of 3 baskets measures 9½" x 15" x 3⅛".

METAL SERVING CART:  Castored, 29½" high; 2 enameled steel shelves each 17" x 24"; lift-off tray on top, handle at each end; walnut (about $38), gold (about $31), chocolate (about $31). (Sears)

A similar model, 32″ high, with 3 shelves, without lift-off tray, in white or chocolate costs about $21. (Sears)

For more information on cooking with a disability, see the Bibliography. One invaluable source of information is *Mealtime Manual for People with Disabilities and the Aging,* by Judith Lannefeld Klinger (see Bibliography). This gives a number of excellent, easy recipes and tips on all aspects of homemaking, particularly kitchen work, as these relate to specific disabilities.

# 3

## Getting a
## Better Grip on Things

### REACHERS

There are lots of ways to pick up things you can't pick up, reach things you can't reach, grab things that are ungrabbable—you probably have several great reachers in the house already.

Canes and dressing sticks make good reachers. Try screwing a large closet hook (the kind you hang your robe on) into the end of a plant stake, dowel, or broom handle. You can bend a wire coat hanger so that the triangular part becomes long and straight. Holding the straightened part, use the hook of the coat hanger (taped to eliminate rough edges) to pull things toward you.[1]

A child's garden rake or hoe (with the sharp surfaces taped) or a Chinese bamboo backscratcher can make excellent reachers.

To pick up stamps and similar items, attach a small piece of double-stick tape to any of the reaching implements described above.

To pick up pins and paper clips, glue a small magnet on the end of the reacher. You can also buy a magnet for about $1 from the American Foundation for the Blind, Inc. If you decide to buy a reacher, remember: The longer it is and the wider its jaw, the heavier it's likely to be. If your wrist gives you trouble, get a reacher with the handle angled at 45 degrees for less strain.

To lift clothes from your closet rod or to push a faucet on and off, keep a dowel with a notch at one end in the clothes closet; another in the bathroom; and one in the kitchen. Or, for turning taps on and off, also see tap turners on page 6.

### Reachers on the market

HOOK:   Extends your reach by 18"; easy-to-grasp contoured grip handle; magnet on the end. (About $6, Nelson)

RUBBER-GRIP REACHER:   Extends your reach by 30", weighs just 9 oz.; use to pick up tiny objects such as pins, as well as objects up to 4" in size, such as a cup or glass; requires normal hand pressure to operate. (About $25, Help Yourelf Aids)

UTILITY STICK COMBINATION:   Adds 24" to your reach; has loop on one end and several devices can be attached to the other—sponge, comb, reaching hook, grasping device, shoe horn, and magnet; attachments included. (About $52, Cleo)

GRAB-ALL REACHER:   Extends your reach by 30"; all metal; works best on large, bulky objects like food cans, books, etc.; requires normal hand pressure to operate; double tongs provide a stronger hold; has a magnetized tip. (About $14, Help Yourself Aids, Cleo)

ECONOMY REACHER AND DRESSING STICK:   Lengthens your reach by 24"; vinyl-covered push-pull hook on one end of the 27" hardwood shaft; small C hook at the other end. (About $8, Help Yourself Aids)

BETTER-GRIP WOODEN REACHER:   Adds 27" to your reach. This scissors-type reacher does just what its name suggests: it provides leverage for a strong grip between serrated rubber grippers. Made of lightweight, sturdy birchwood with a magnet at the tip. (About $16, Help Yourself Aids, Cleo, Nelson, G. E. Miller)

Similar Cleo model extends your reach by 33". (About $13, Cleo)

GIANT TONGS:   Increase your reach by 15". Lightweight, yet sturdy chrome-plated steel tongs feature oversized handgrips and serrated jaws to supply extra holding power. (About $10, Help Yourself Aids, Nelson)

EXTEND-A-HAND REACHER:   Lengthens your reach by 27". Probably the most versatile reacher on the market, it features a strong aluminum frame, trigger action to close the pick-up jaw (the harder you squeeze, the tighter the jaw holds), a pulling lug near the tip for pulling things toward you, a Velcro hook on the reacher handle, and a Velcro loop for attaching the reacher to your wheelchair or walker. Weighs just 7 oz. (About $28, Help Yourself Aids, Cleo, G. E. Miller)

EXTRA-LONG EXTEND-A-HAND REACHER:   Same as the above but adds another 5" to your reach (to bring the total length to 32"), while weighing only 2 oz. more (a total of 9 oz.). (About $30, Help Yourself Aids)

THE LONGEST REACHER OF THEM ALL:   Length is 4' 10½"; made of vinyl-covered tubular lightweight aluminum; handle must be squeezed to work the small or large grabbing claws. (Requires a good grasp, but only one hand.) (About $27, Brookstone)

GRABBER:   This 14"-long grabber has 4 small but strong spring-steel claws that spread when a plunger is squeezed (requires a good grasp but only one hand). What makes this grabber unique, aside from its ability to pick up small objects that have dropped into inaccessible places or to hold or start stubborn nuts or screws, is that it is made of coiled spring wire. So *it can be bent double or bent to fit around corners and obstructions!* Extends your reach by 14". (About $5, Brookstone) (O-H)

Similar model extends your reach by 24". (About $6, Brookstone)

NONSTOOP SHOEHORN:   Eighteen inches long; might be handy as a reacher if you need a shoehorn anyway. Also useful for tucking in sheets when making a bed. (About $4, Nelson) (Cleo makes a 24"-long model for about $6)

## FOR BETTER GRASP AND TRACTION

### To build grasp on handles of tools, utensils, sports equipment, etc.

Cover them with any of the following: masking tape, cloth tape, cushion grip tape, rubber bands, foam curler, practice golf ball, Dycem matting.

FOAM TUBING:   Has 1⅜" diameter; ⅜" hole in center; black. (About $5 per yard, Help Yourself Aids)

FOAM RUBBER SHEETING:   Measures ¼" thick x 36" x 60" (about $15); ½" thick x 36" x 60" (about $20); both from G. E. Miller.

DIP-IT-YOURSELF PLASTIC COMPOUND:   To increase grip, reduce vibration; dip handle into compound; dries in 24 hours; bright red or yellow. (About $8 per can, Brookstone)

### To increase grip on cup or glass

Cover with rubber bands or a terry cloth "sleeve" (available at hardware and variety stores). Or try:

DYCEM MATTING:   Pressure-sensitive backing; 16" x 36" sheets to be cut with scissors; useful for tool handles, etc. (About $39, Help Yourself Aids)

### To absorb vibrations while building grasp

Wrap power tools, steering wheels, bike or motorbike handlebars, sports equipment, hammers, axes, and the like with:

CUSHION GRIP TAPE:   More than 1/10″ thick; 14′ roll, ¾″ wide; orange or black. (About $8, Brookstone)

DIP-IT-YOURSELF PLASTIC COMPOUND:   (see above)

## To hold knitting needs, crochet hooks, rattail combs, etc.

Push implements through a foam hair roller (cut to size), or foam tubing (see above).

## For leverage on jars, taps, hoses, sports equipment

(For greatest ease in opening jars, see Zim Jar Opener on page 23.)

MYSTIC GRIP DISK:   Soft rubber disk 4¾″ in diameter; for ease in holding or turning taps, tops of jars, hose connections; fishing rods, etc. (About $3, at most variety stores or J. A. Industries, 440 Totten Pond Rd., Waltham, Mass. 02154)

## To hold plates, cups, typewriters, things on trays, etc., in place

Place on a damp sponge or damp sponge towel (or even a damp paper towel) or use:

LITTLE OCTOPUS SUCTION HOLDERS:   Disks, each having 24 tiny suction cups on each side. (3 disks for about $8, Help Yourself Aids)

DYCEM PADS:   Set under any item to hold it to hard surface; blue only. Eight-inch round pad (about $14); 10″ round pad (about $16); 10″ x 14″ pad (about $22); 8″ x 72″ sheet (about $29); 16″ x 36″ sheet (about $39); 16″ x 72″ sheet (about $47). (Help Yourself Aids)

DYCEM NETTING:   Use to coat shelves, countertops, etc.; creates nonskid surface; nylon netting (with ½″ square openings); 7½″ x 36″; straw color. (About $9, Help Yourself Aids)

## To texture walking surfaces for better traction

Coat stairs, ramps, and entrances with sand paint, or use:

ADHESIVE SCOTCH TREAD:   For any potentially slippery surface including tubs and showers; long strip 10′ x 1″ may be cut to correct lengths. (About $3, Help Yourself Aids)

# PART TWO

## PERSONAL CARE

4

# *Eat, Drink, and Be Merry*

Conforming to convention often comes so naturally that it doesn't occur to us there might be an easier way. Eating is a case in point. We're so used to the usual forks, spoons, and plates that we seldom stop to think, "If I got a different shape, might it be easier to handle?" With this in mind, you might want to just cast your eye over the items described below in case one or two might make your mealtimes more pleasant.

Please note that in the chapter Getting a Better Grip on Things, there are a number of suggestions on how to build up any utensils, including those for eating.

## PLATES, DISHES, AND FOODGUARDS

### *Plates and dishes*

SUCTION PLATE: Unbreakable, dishwasher-safe; 8⅜" plastic; has 3 suction cups and inner lip to keep food from sliding off; light gray. (About $13, Help Yourself Aids)

*Note:* For a double-acting grip to firmly anchor plates, bowls, order:

*Little Octopus Suction Holders:* (See page 32.)

HIGH-SIDED DISH: Has sides 2¼" high; measures 7¾" in diameter. (About $8, Help Yourself Aids)

SCOOP DISHES   (see also High-Sided Dish above, which is great for scooping):
>    *Oval:* Slopes low in front and high in back; dishwasher-safe. (About $13 for 8½"; about $18 for 11"; Help Yourself Aids)
>    *Round:* Same as above but round; comes in 8" size only, has nonskid rubber pad under it. (About $10, Help Yourself Aids)
>    *Partitioned:* Round; 9½" diameter; sides ¾" high; ½"-high partitions that divide food area into three sections; white plastic; dishwasher-safe in top rack of washer. (About $6, Help Yourself Aids)

COMPARTMENTED TRAY:   Unbreakable; has lid and 5 food compartments; outer walls 1⅜" high, divider walls 1" high; top-rack dishwasher-safe. *Use without lid in microwave oven.* (About $8, Help Yourself Aids)

## Food guards

PLASTIC:   Clips onto any size plate; provides rim to push food against. (About $12, Help Yourself Aids)

CLEAR PLASTIC:   "Invisible"; has grooves that snap onto plate rims; specify 6"–8" or 9"–11" plates. (About $7 for either size, Help Yourself Aids)

STAINLESS STEEL:   Has spring clips, prices and sizes same as above. (Help Yourself Aids)

SURE-GRIP:   Steel with rubber fastener to prevent plate from sliding. (About $8, Abbey)

## TRAYS

(See Compartmented Tray above for tray you can eat from.)

DYCEM:   Measures 18" x 13½"; coated with slip-proof surface. (About $15, MED)

*Note:* See also Dycem Matting, which comes in 16" x 36" sheets (page 31).

TRAVELER:   Can be picked up or replaced without removing holder; holder attaches in seconds to your wheelchair; goes over lap or swings to the side. (About $22, Nelson) See also One-Handed Tray and Personal Mobility Aid (page 22).

## BIBS

### Terry cloth

POCKETED:   Width is 14½", 15" long; Velcro neck fastener; 3" pocket; white. (About $8, Help Yourself Aids)

EXTRA-LARGE:   No pocket; 18″ wide, 27″ long, Velcro neck fastener; blue. (About $7, Vermont Country Store)

### Disposable
Clear plastic; trough sides and bottom to catch spills; 20″ wide, 24″ long; neck cutout for snug fit. (About $14 for box of 50, Help Yourself Aids)

## CUPS AND GLASSES

### Egg cups
WITH CLIP:   Clips to side of plate; metal. (About $6, G. E. Miller)

FREE-STANDING:   Plastic, with suction cup on bottom. (About $3, G. E. Miller)

### Cups
WHEELCHAIR CUP HOLDER WITH CUP:   Clip-on holder, 8 oz., large-handled plastic cup; cover with hole for straw. (About $8, Help Yourself Aids)

CONVALESCENT FEEDING CUP:   Eight oz., covered, no-handled cup with slanted mouthpiece for nonspill drinking. (About $8, Help Yourself Aids)

*Base for cup (above):* Prevents tipping. (About $9, Help Yourself Aids)

WONDER-FLO VACUUM CUP:   Similar to the feeding cup, but when you stop sucking (even while prone), the liquid stops flowing. (About $8, Help Yourself Aids)

SNORKEL CUP:   Open cup with built-in plastic straw; no handles. (About $6 for 3, Help Yourself Aids)

CUPS WITH HANDLES:

*No-Tip:* Eight-oz. plastic cup; slip-on, plastic spring handle. (About $8, G. E. Miller)

*Modified Drinking Cup:* Covered, 8-oz. nylon cup with 2 soft plastic handles. (About $10, Help Yourself Aids)

### Glasses
GLASS HOLDERS:

*Bilateral:* Put glass into adjustable center ring; glass then has sturdy handles on either side of it. (About $13, Help Yourself Aids)

*Wheelchair:* Adjustable; clips on. (About $5, Help Yourself Aids)

*Sure-Grip:* Adjustable holder; one foam-lined handle easily molded to any shape. (About $4, G. E. Miller)

NOSEY CUTOUT GLASS:   Glass with a cutout for nose; allows you to drink without tipping head or extending neck. (Specify 8 or 12 oz.; about $4 for either size, Help Yourself Aids)

GLASS WITH LID:    A 12-oz. plastic glass with lid for straws; openings near edge for drinking. (About $4, Help Yourself Aids)

### Straws and straw holders

Attach a pencil clip (the kind you hook onto a pocket) to your glass to hold a straw or buy:

STRAW HOLDER:    Fits across glass, clips to rim; has several-sized holes; holds straw at proper angle. (About $6, Help Yourself Aids)

REUSABLE PLASTIC STRAWS:    Eighteen inches, flexible. (About $6 for: 10 straws with 3/16" diameter holes, 10 straws with ⅛" holes, 5 with ¼" holes; Help Yourself Aids)

## FORKS, KNIVES, AND SPOONS

### Forks

AUTOMATIC FORK:    Eight and one-half inches; handles, when squeezed, cause metal plate to slide down and push food off tines. (About $4, American Foundation for the Blind)

SIDE-CUTTER FORK:    Adds moderate cutting ability to edge of fork; will not injure mouth; cuts most foods, but not all meats. (About $10, Help Yourself Aids)

### Knives

ROCKER KNIFE-FORK:    Two prongs at tip of curved blade. (About $18 for stainless steel blade model; about $3 for metal blade; Help Yourself Aids)

ROCKER KNIFE:    Without fork end. (About $7 for all-steel model; about $18 for hollow-handled steel; Help Yourself Aids)

ROLLER KNIFE:    Pizza-cutter type; stainless steel cutter wheel to roll back across food; guard to protect hand; large, curved plastic handle. (About $6, Help Yourself Aids)

### Spoons

SPORK:    Fork-spoon combination. (About $6 for 5", 6", or 7" size, Help Yourself Aids)

RUBBER SPOON:    Silicone rubber; easy-to-hold teaspoon; protects teeth and lips; dishwasher-safe. (About $9, Help Yourself Aids)

## UTENSILS WITH SPECIAL HANDLES

### Extension

Makes spoon or fork 15″ long when completely extended; has joint to angle utensil. (About $6 for holder only, utensil not included, G. E. Miller)

### Angled

FORK:   Stainless steel; plastic handle; specify right or left hand. (About $8, G. E. Miller)

SPOON:   Matches above fork. (About $8, G. E. Miller)

SHALLOW-BOWLED SPOON:   Nearly flat; specify right or left hand. (About $9, Help Yourself Aids)

### Built-up and weighted

BUILT-UP KNIFE, FORK, TEASPOON, SOUP SPOON:   Stainless steel with soft, nonabsorbent foam grips, dishwasher-safe. (About $8 each; about $25 for set of 4; Help Yourself Aids)

WEIGHTED:   An 8-oz. weight inside each plastic handle. (About $9 each for teaspoon, soup spoon, spork, fork, Help Yourself Aids)

### Swivel

ADJUSTABLE:   Keeps food level; prevents spills when wrist or finger motion is limited; adjustable stops control amount of swivel in either direction; dishwasher-safe; flat handles for easy fit into utensil holder. (About $10 each for teaspoon, fork, soup spoon; medium- and large-sized sporks about $1 more, Help Yourself Aids)

NONADJUSTABLE:   Same as above but with nonadjustable swivel stops; plastic handles. (About $10 each for teaspoon, soup spoon, spork, and fork, Help Yourself Aids)

### Miscellaneous

PALM-HELD:   Handles at right angles to allow them to be held in mid-palm; bendable to other angles. (About $6 each for teaspoon, long teaspoon, soup spoon; fork; about $16 the set of 4, Help Yourself Aids)

FINGER RING:   Soft-coated steel bands attached to handles; bendable to encircle from one to three fingers. (About $6 each for knife, fork, teaspoon, soup spoon; about $18 the set of 4, Help Yourself Aids)

## UTENSIL HOLDERS

UNIVERSAL CUFF:   Slips over hand; made of vinyl with Velcro closure and pouch to vary length of insertion of utensil handles; specify with or without elastic band. (About $6 for small, medium, or large, Help Yourself Aids)

HAND CLIP:   Spring action clip fits around palm to back of hand; utensil not included. (About $4, G. E. Miller)

QUAD-QUIP UTENSIL HOLDER:   Wooden base angles utensil away from palm; Velcro loop, thumb hole, large **D** ring. (About $6, Help Yourself Aids)

## MISCELLANEOUS

SANDWICH HOLDER:   Dishwasher-safe handle made for insertion into a utensil holder; plastic holder at end for sandwich. (About $10, Help Yourself Aids)

ARM REST:   Tilts forward and back, swivels from side to side; 8¾"-high base with holes to attach to table; 7¼"-half-round arm support. (About $25, Help Yourself Aids)

# 5

# Dress without Stress

When you are in a wheelchair or braces, on crutches, or otherwise constrained, the cut of your clothes can often make a difference between being smartly dressed and comfortable or disheveled and miserable. Here are a few ways to look crisp and feel great.

## CHOOSING CLOTHES TO FIT SPECIAL NEEDS[1]

### When on crutches
Too much underarm fullness will tend to "bunch," but anything that fits too tightly under the arm will split easily. Stretch fabrics are a good choice.

Reinforce underarms by resewing the seams or patching with extra fabric. To keep your shirt or top tucked in, sew rubber strips to the inside of the waistband of pants or skirts.

### When elbow or shoulder motion is limited
Choose front-opening or wrap garments, with raglan or kimono sleeves and pleats or gussets.

### When in a cast or wearing braces
Consider zippering the inseams of your pants. Also, sew tabs at the waist of your pants so you can use a hook or dressing stick to help pull them up.

*Mastectomy*

Choose garments with dolman or kimono sleeves and gussets.

*One-handed*

Sew cuff buttons on with elastic thread and leave them buttoned at all times, sliding hand in and out. Or use Velcro to fasten cuffs. Use a dressing stick to help you get into and out of your skirts or trousers. (See also Dressing Techniques.)

*Low vision*

Get Braille identification tags or make a code for yourself, sewing on one knot or a piece of lace for white, two knots or a bit of rickrack for blue, etc. (See also Hi-marks for identifying clothing, page 247.)

*In a wheelchair*

Avoid clinging fabrics and long jackets. Both tend to bunch up. Capes and side- or back-wrap skirts or dresses with a little fullness work well. Looser styles move with the body, but very wide, flappy, or cuffed pants can be dangerous because they catch too easily.

## DRESSING TECHNIQUES

There are many tricks that make dressing easier. The following tips were developed by disabled individuals.

*Coat or jacket*

Always put clothing on the disabled limb first. (Reverse this when undressing.) Lay the coat or jacket over your shoulders, over the back of a chair, or suspend it from a door frame on two hooks, each attached to a rope hanging from the top of the door frame.[2] Then put your disabled arm into the sleeve, pull the sleeve up as far as it will go, and hold the coat with your teeth or dressing stick. Swing the loose side around to the good arm and slide that arm into its sleeve. Sometimes shrugging helps position the coat or jacket more easily.[3] To keep a jacket sleeve from crawling up when pushing your arm into an overcoat, bend a paper clip to fit over the cuff button on your jacket. Slip a rubber band into the rebent paper clip. Put your thumb into the rubber band before putting your arm into the overcoat. This will hold your jacket down.[4]

*Shirt or blouse*[5]

TO PUT ON OVER YOUR HEAD:   Lay the garment on your lap or on a table. Put your arms into the sleeves, lean forward, raise your arms, and flip the garment over your head. Shrug or pull it into place. If the garment fastens in back, button it partway before putting it on, then put it over your head with the buttons in front, finish fastening, then turn it around to the back and insert your arms.

TO PULL OFF OVER YOUR HEAD:    Hook the thumb of the noninvolved hand over the inside of the opposite armhole and pull or shake out the involved arm. Repeat on the other side. Grasp the garment at the back of the neck and pull over your head. If your hands are weak, rest them on a table or the arms of a chair while working.

## Slacks

TO PUT ON:    It can be easier to put on slacks, hose, or braces by sitting against the headboard of your bed or with a wedge pillow at your back as you sit on your bed.

If one pants leg of your slacks keeps falling down while you hold the other, lean against the wall and let the wall hold them up for you.

To keep your belt from slipping while putting on your pants, clip a spring clothespin or bulldog clip to the end of the belt opposite the buckle, then clip the belt to the waistband of your slacks.[6]

WHILE SITTING UP:    If you can sit cross-legged, it helps you to keep your balance when dressing on the bed. Cross one leg, pull on one pants leg, then cross your legs in the opposite direction and pull on the other leg, pulling up each as far as your knee. Then when both legs are covered to the knee, lie down and arch your back or roll from side to side, and pull them up the rest of the way.

You can also sit in your wheelchair to do the job with your feet on the bed. Cross your legs while sitting in the chair.[7]

WHILE LYING DOWN:    Bend knees close to your body to insert your legs into the garment. Pull up each pants leg past your knees. Arch your back or roll from side to side. Use a dressing stick or suspenders to help pull up the pants.

TO TAKE OFF SLACKS WHILE SITTING UP:    Lift one side of the body with one hand or elbow, or cross your legs, and push the garment over the buttocks with the other hand or dressing stick. Repeat on the other side. Pull off the pants by the cuffs, one leg crossed over the other, or kick the garment off.

WHILE LYING DOWN:    Arch your back and work the pants down over your knees with your hands or a dressing stick. Lift the knees with your hand and the pants will slip off the legs.[8]

## Tying a tie[9]

Although pretied, snap-on ties are attractive and easy to put on, you can tie a good Windsor knot with one good hand, one disabled hand, and your teeth, if necessary. If your right hand is disabled, follow these instructions. If your left hand is affected, reverse the procedure.

1.  Put the necktie around the shirt and under the collar, with the wide end (which should be about 30″ long) on your left and the narrow end (which should be about 10″ long) on your right.
2.  Pull out a dresser drawer high enough to rest your arm and disabled hand on while seated.
3.  Hold the narrow end of the tie with your right hand, resting your elbow on the open dresser drawer.
4.  Put the long end under the short end, moving from left to right.
5.  Pull the long end over the short end and tuck the long end under the V that appears under the chin; pull the end through to the left.
6.  Put this long part under the tie and pull across the top of the tie and down under your chin toward the left.
7.  Cross the top of the tie to the right and come down under the chin to the opening; open the knot and spear the tie through the opening.
8.  Work the tie toward your chin as usual to make the tie look neat.
9.  To open, loosen tie from neck, pull through short end, and unravel long end.

### Putting on and taking off socks, stockings, and shoes

(See also Stocking Aids on page 47 and Shoe Aids on page 49.)

SOCKS:    You can sew tabs or loops on both sides of your sock cuffs and use your dressing stick to pull them up.[10]

STOCKINGS:    Get a wooden embroidery hoop wider than the widest part of your thigh, stretch the top of a stocking or one leg of your panty hose over it, and pull it over your leg with your dressing stick. Another suggestion: Cut a piece of foam rubber slightly larger than your foot. Put your stocking over your toes only, then push your foot against the piece of foam and keep pushing against it to work the stocking over your foot.[11]

SHOES:    Wedging your shoe against something firm, such as the wall, helps stabilize it and makes it easier to put it on. To take it off, hook the back of the shoe against a chair rung or foot stool and pull against it. Push one off with the toe of the other shoe.[12]

### Bras

Buy bras with Velcro or some other kind of front opening. Or if it hooks in back, hook it in front, then turn it around to the back before putting your arms into the straps. Or order a no-fasten, step-in bra from Fashion-Able.

## *Gloves*

If you can't get a regular glove on your hand, cut the foot off a wool sock and sew up its raw end. Use this as a glove.[13]

To put on gloves, lay the glove on a flat surface, push your hand into it, and "rub" the glove on.[14]

## CLOTHES TO ORDER BY MAIL

If you send for two excellent catalogs, many of your clothing problems will be solved. One is published by VGRS (Vocational Guidance and Rehabilitation Services) and is called *Wings of VGRS*. It is available from 2239 East 55th St., Cleveland, Ohio 44103, or by calling (216) 431–7800. This agency manufactures specially adapted garments and will further tailor any item to your special needs.

The other company is called Fashion-Able, which manufactures unique items such as water-repellent capes and custom jeans. Send for their catalog by writing Fashion-Able, Rocky Hill, N.J. 08553.

Among other items, *Wings of VGRS* carries back-wrap and wraparound dresses and skirts, zip-front, pullover, and front-opening dresses with Velcro, a great crutch bag (see Crutch Accessories, page 190), and a variety of wrap and zip-front slips. For men and boys, they carry back-opening and other robes, drop-front or back slacks, with Velcro or zipper-opening seams as optional feature.

Fashion-Able carries, in addition to its custom jeans (tailored just for you) and its front-zipping, hooded cape (which comes with or without fleece lining), a poncho blanket, knitted undershirts and knee warmers, a wraparound garter belt, a no-fasten step-in bra, shoulder protectors to ease shoulder strap discomfort, and a lovely, easy-to-slip-on shoulder shrug in 100 percent wool. They also carry several varieties of front-opening and step-in slips, camisoles, half-slips, bras, girdles, etc. For men and boys, there are slacks with a self-crossing fly and no buttons, zippers, or belts.

A quilted coat liner that buttons into any coat, made of quilted rayon acetate lined with orlon, with knit cuffs, is available from The Ferry House, 554 North State Road, Briarcliff Manor, N.Y. 10510. It comes in sizes 8–20 for about $18. (They send you the buttons, you sew them into your coat, then button in the warm liner.)

(For more clothing ideas, including extra-warm shirts and pants, long underwear, double-seated pants, knee-warmers, vests, slippers, and slipper-socks, see Chapter 7, Stay Cool/Keep Warm.)

## DRESSING AIDS

One of the best dressing aids you could own is a wooden dowel or broom handle with a cup hook at one end to help pull on your clothes, and a notch at the other end to remove clothes hangers and hang them up on your closet rod.

Another homemade aid is a wire coat hanger, stretched out so that the triangular part is long and thin. You hold the long end and use the hook as a reacher, and for help in getting dressed and undressed. Tape the hook's rough edges to prevent snagging of clothes.

An excellent aid is the 27"-long wooden Reacher Dressing Stick. It has a large vinyl-covered push-pull hook at one end and a cup hook at the other end. (About $3, Help Yourself Aids, Fashion-Able)

A 30½" Dressing Stick has a shoehorn and push-pull hook at one end, and a garter hook and a push-pull hook at the other. Two adjustable hand-loops in the middle of the stick give greater maneuverability. (About $17, Cleo)

The following devices will help you handle specific dressing jobs.

PAIR OF DRESSING STICKS (for skirts or pants): A pair of sticks, each 20" long, that have garter clips attached to tape extensions at the ends of the sticks. Attach the garter clips to the waistband of a garment and use the sticks to pull it on. (About $9 the pair, Abbey)

PANTS PUT "R" ON "R"S: A pair of sticks, each 26" long, with a spring device to automatically lock nonsnag pull hooks to the waistband. (About $17 the pair, MED)

BUTTON AIDS (see also Combination Buttoner-Zipper Pull):

To keep buttons from falling off, dab clear nail polish at their centers, both back and front.*

The following button aids are available from Help Yourself Aids:

Wooden handle (about $5)          Aid with pocket clip (about $8)

Knob handle (about $6)            One-handed (for cuffs, about $6)

* From *Mary Ellen's Best of Helpful Hints* by Pearl Higginbotham and Mary Ellen Pinkham. Copyright © 1979. Reprinted by permission of Warner Books/New York.

| | |
|---|---|
| Rubber handle (about $7) | Amputee (for cuffs, about $6) |
| Plastic ribbed-handle (about $8) | Square handle amputee (about $7) |

*Button Extender:* Eliminates buttoning shirt cuffs. (About $5, from Help Yourself Aids)
(Or achieve same effect by sewing buttons on with elastic.)

## Zipper pulls

SHORT:

*Ring Pull:* A 1″ diameter ring with a snap attached. Clip snap through hole in the zipper pull-tab and pull. (About $4 for package of 3, Help Yourself Aids)

*Shorty Pull:* A rounded shaft attached to a hook. Hook goes through the zipper pull-tab hole. Comes with regular or rubber handle. (Both about $6, Help Yourself Aids)

LONG:

*Cord Pull:* This 18″ plastic cord has a metal hook at one end that goes through a zipper puller pull-tab hole, while you grasp a ring at the other end and pull. (About $3, Help Yourself Aids, Nelson)

T *Handle Pull:* This 20″ wooden stick comes with 20 rings to attach to zipper pull-tab holes. One end of the stick is a T handle for pulling up a zipper; the other end is a metal Z that goes into the ring attached to the zipper. (About $10, Abbey)

COMBINATION BUTTONER-ZIPPER PULL: Made especially for quadriplegics, this is an easy-bend steel cuff coated with comfortable Plastisol contours to fit your hand. It has a wire button hook attached to the left side of the cuff, a wire zipper-pull hook attached to its right side. (About $10, Help Yourself Aids)

## Stocking and sock aids

(See ideas under Putting On and Taking Off Socks, Stockings, and Shoes, page 44.)

QUICKY HOSE PULL-ON: Two garter clips are attached to a 26″ handle to help pull on stockings. (About $7, Cleo)

FLEXIBLE SOCK AND STOCKING AID: Draw sock or stocking over the flexible plastic core and insert your foot. Attach garter clips to the tops of the hose, then pull long webbing strips to draw hose on. (Not for one-handed individuals.) (About $15, Help Yourself Aids)

TOTAL HIP SOCK AID:   A pair of 38½″ sticks with garter clips to attach to tops of hose, circular hand guards for firm grip, and plastic-covered hook on the end of each stick for push-pull. Garters release by simple downward push. Excellent for those who cannot bend. (About $18 the pair, Help Yourself Aids)

QUAD-QUIP SOCK MITTS:   Adjustable mitts that go over palms, with material to grip a loosely fitting wool sock and draw it over the foot. (About $7, Abbey)

## FOOT CARE AND AIDS

### Toenail clippers

NAIL CLIPPERS ON BOARD:   A sturdy pair of clippers attached to a board for greater leverage and ease in cutting toenails. (About $3.50, The Independence Factory)

EXTENDED NAIL CLIPPERS:   Long-handled clippers. (About $3.50, The Independence Factory)

### For foot comfort

POLYTUBE CORN PADS:   Washable, nonallergenic soft tubes that fit over and surround each painful toe to relieve corns, hammer toes, and ingrown toenail pain. Set includes one small, one medium, and one large toe tube. (About $5 the set, Fashion-Able)

TOE REGULATOR:   A washable pad (that can be cut to fit any shoe size) with loops attached to hold one toe (or two adjacent toes) straighter. Specify for left or right foot. (About $3.50 for one pad with loops, Fashion-Able)

UNDER TOE PADS:   Pads come molded to fit under the base of four small toes (fits area where four small toes meet the foot) to relieve bent-under (claw or hammer) toes. Comes in small (7½) and medium (8–10) for women; 9½ for men and large (10 plus) for both men and women. Specify left or right foot and size. (About $5, Fashion-Able)

TOE TOASTER:   Slip both feet into a heating pad shaped like the front of a slipper and surround your feet with heat. (About $13, The Ferry House)

(See also dry heat mitts/booties on page 61.)

### Odd or different-sized shoes

To buy just one shoe instead of a pair, or for unusual sizes, write:

Handicappers of America, R.R. 2, Box 58, Camby, Ind., or The National Odd-Shoe Exchange, 1415 Ocean Front, Santa Monica, Cal. 90401.

EXTRA LARGE OR LIGHTWEIGHT SHOES:   Write to King Size Company, Brockton, Mass. 22402.

## *To keep slip-on shoes on your feet*

If a slip-on shoe tends to slide off your foot, ask a shoemaker or leather shop to sew roller skate straps onto the back of your shoe. Buckle the strap around your ankle when you put it on. To remove, loosen straps to the last hole and slip your foot out.[15]

## SHOE AIDS

### *To get shoes on and off*

INSERT-A-FOOT SHOE AID:   A curved plastic shell that goes over the back of a shoe to allow the foot to slide in easily. Slips out easily after foot is in place. (About $8, Cleo, Help Yourself Aids)

INSERT-A-FOOT SHOE AID WITH HANDLE:   Same as above but with 25″ wooden dowel attached. The dowel has a hook on top to help pull up socks. (About $9, Help Yourself Aids)

### *Shoe horns*

PLASTIC:   Eighteen inches with a hole in the handle to insert a finger. (About $2, MED, Cleo, Help Yourself Aids)

STAINLESS STEEL:   Twelve inches, about $6, Abbey, Help Yourself Aids; 18″, about $6, Abbey, Help Yourself Aids; 24″, about $7, Abbey, Help Yourself Aids.

All these stainless steel horns have Plastisol handgrips for better grip and a dressing hook on the handle to help put on socks and garments.

FLEXIBLE ALUMINUM:   Twenty-four inches with spring action at end. (About $7, Cleo)

BENDABLE:   A 26″ horn can be bent to best angle; has a dressing hook. (About $8, MED)

EXTENDED HANDLE:   Thirty-three inches; has special angle and adjustable hand loops, also a dressing hook, for use with flail hand. (About $15, MED)

(See also Extended Double Shoehorn under Chapter 30, Make It Yourself.)

### *To fasten shoes*

WRAP-A-LACE:   Probably the easiest one-handed shoelace fastener available. You wrap the lace under a plastic buckle and lock in any of four slots to give desired tightness. To open the lace, unwind from the buckle and pull. Black or brown. (About $3 per pair, Abbey, Fashion-Able, Help Yourself Aids)

ELASTIC LACES:　Once laces have been threaded through all eyelets, retainers on each end prevent them from coming out and you can slip your foot in and out of shoes without relacing. White, black, brown. (About $3 per pair, Abbey, Cleo, Fashion-Able, Help Yourself Aids)

TYLASTIC SHOELACES:　Heavy-duty elastic shoelaces for those who want firmer support across the top of shoes; black only. (About $3, Help Yourself Aids)

ZIPPER SHOE FASTENER:　Plastic zipper, over which you thread laces that never again need to be undone. Simply zip shoe open or closed with laces intact. Black or brown; five or six eyelet. (About $4 per pair, Abbey, Cleo, Help Yourself Aids)

KNO-BOWS:　If it's hard to tie a bow on regular shoelaces, a pinch and pull tightens, a pinch loosens these. Black, brown, or white plastic knobs. (About $2.50 per pair, Cleo, Fashion-Able)

### Innersoles

NEOPRENE:　Made of molded, rubberlike ¼″ material that provides comfort while helping to distribute your foot pressure properly. (Spenco or order through surgical supply store)

FELT:　Tightly woven white wool felt, 3/16″ thick, increases warmth, absorbs perspiration, and cushions the foot. Small (6–7), medium (8–9), large (10–11), and extra-large (12–13). (About $10, L. L. Bean)

### Miscellaneous

ICE CREEPERS:　Prevent sliding on ice; steel calks riveted to steel cross-pieces; lightweight; easy on-off straps. (About $8 for women, about $11 for men, American Foundation for the Blind)

BOOT JACK:　Wooden. (About $3, The Independence Factory)

# Bathing and Grooming

You're wondering how there can be a whole chapter on bathing and grooming. New grooming aids, maybe—but what more is there to say about bathing? A tub is still a tub and a shower is still a shower and how often do inventive brains address themselves to such mundane things?

Perhaps not often, but recently. Among the many bathing and grooming devices are four outstanding new inventions, each more innovative than the last. One is a bathtub you can enter via a little door rather than stepping over the side. The second is an easy-to-use portable, inflatable tub to use right on the bed. The third is a graded-entry shower you can wheel straight into. Fourth is a cushioned shower-tub. All are described in this chapter.

## BATHING

### Tub and shower safety

Nonslip tape, such as the Adhesive Scotch Tread described on page 32, is essential for tub and shower bottoms, as well as for the edge of your tub if it has no safety rail. Use a suction rubber bathmat or the following in addition to the tape.

BATH MATE: Machine washable eggcrate foam pads; specify 20″ x 36″ tub pad or 24″ x 24″ shower pad with drain opening. (About $13 each, Starcrest of California)

Also use nonslip tape for tub and shower seats (especially built-ins), and for further safety and comfort, put a towel or a Bath Mate over the seat. Also use Bath Mates on the floor outside your tub or shower.

Chair and stool legs should have rubber tips for stability. Castored shower chairs should have brakes, but in case the brakes should start to fail, it's good to have sandbags handy to block wheels. Sandbags are also good for blocking wheels on rolling commode chairs.

Handrails are also vital for tub, shower, and toilet. (Never use the towel bar as a handrail, as it can easily pull away from the wall.) Vertical rails are useful for standing transfers and horizontal ones for sitting transfers.[1]

There is such a variety of handrails and ways of mounting them that you should see all the possibilities and get professional advice before deciding what to buy. Write Invacare or Lumex for their illustrated Bathroom Safety Aid Information, which shows all the options.

## Tubs

SAFE-T-BATH:   Five-foot fiberglass, 18″ off floor; watertight 30″ entrance door that opens 180 degrees so bather can sit on tub bottom, slide in, and close door; push-pull drain, double-lock. To install, move present faucets up about 18″ on wall, move tub in, and hook to drain pipe. Eight models available. (About $2,000, Safe-T-Bath of New England)

PORTABLE ON-THE-BED BATHTUB:   (See page 181.)

## Showers

ROLL-IN:   Measures 4½ sq. ft.; made of fiberglass; graded entry; 3 easy-to-install panels, a shelf, and an optional visual-thermometer shower head; folding shower door. (About $800, Braun)

CUSHIONED SHOWER-TUB:   Fully cushioned seat with backrest at wheelchair-seat height to sit while portable hand shower (see Bathing Accessories) sluices you. Especially for quadriplegics; installable over most tubs; 60″ x 30″ x 16″ high; grab bars. (About $950, Facetglas)

## Seats

Before making your choice of seats for sitting in shower or tub or for transfer in and out of them, be sure to get advice from your doctor or therapist. The bathroom is a hazardous place and no adjustments should be made without advice.

## To transfer in and out of tub[2]

Straight-backed chairs are best if you have trouble with sitting balance. If you don't, use sturdy wooden stools. Use one inside, one outside the tub with a transfer board covered with a towel in between. Or see Transfer Seats below. These are benches with two legs resting on the floor and the other two legs inside the tub. To make the seat stable, shorten the adjustable legs inside the tub. Whatever units you choose for transfer, be sure they have rubber tips on the legs and that you add nonslip tape to the seat.

## Tub seats

SAFETY SEAT: Vinyl-over-steel, no-back bench stretches width of tub; ends fit over sides of tub. (About $37, Abbey)

STOOL: No back; rubber-tipped legs; 9" high. (About $30, Abbey)

UTILITY CHAIR: Vinyl seat, with or without back; 15" high; rubber-tipped legs. (Without back, about $30; with back, about $40; Lumex; order all Lumex products through surgical supply stores)

ADJUSTABLE PADDED CHAIR: Made of heavily padded, park-bench-type slats (so water drains between them); adjustable-height back slats; adjustable rubber-tipped legs. (About $65, Lumex; order all Lumex products through surgical supply stores)

TRANSFER SEATS:

*Adjustable:* Put one set of legs outside tub, other set inside. Fiberglass seat; padded back bar; adjustable rubber-tipped legs; extra-long extension legs available. (About $58, Abbey)

*Padded Adjustable:* Slatted, padded park-bench-type; adjustable rubber-tipped legs; grab bar at one end. (About $110, Lumex)

## Shower seats

STOOL: Eighteen inches high; rubber-tipped, flared legs; chrome-finished steel. (About $30, Lumex)

TRANSPORT CHAIR: Seat is 19" high; suction cup legs or swivel 3" or 5" castors (2 swivel with brake; 2 fixed); optional accessories—armrests, footrest, white nylon back, commode seat for overstandard toilet or bedpan holder. (From about $65 for chair with suction cups, no accessories, to about $125 for castored chair with all accessories; Winfield or order through a surgical supply store)

BATH LIFT: (See page 217.)

## Bathing accessories

PORTABLE HAND SHOWERS: Suction wall bracket for mounting shower head anywhere within reach of the 5' vinyl hose; head snaps on and off bracket for wall or hand use; universal adapter for most tub faucets. (About $18, Help Yourself Aids)

WASH MITT:   Terry cloth; shaped like a mitten without a thumb; Velcro closure; small, medium, or large. (About $6, Nelson)

You can make your own wash mitt: Trace the outline of your hand, allowing ¼″ extra all around for the seam; then cut two pieces of terry cloth in that shape and sew them together.

LONG-HANDLED ROUND BRUSH:   Nineteen inches, offset plastic-handled nylon brush with bristles all around. (About $8, Nelson)

FINGER-RING BRUSH:   Flexible plastic, octagonal palm-held brush with top ring to slide finger through; for bathing or shampooing. (About $3, Nelson)

ADJUSTABLE BACK BRUSH:   Twelve inches, aluminum adjustable-handled brush. (About $14, Help Yourself Aids)

CURVED-BACK BRUSH:   U-shaped handle for reaching back and neck. (About $18, Help Yourself Aids)

WEDGE-SHAPED SPONGE:   Has 8″ handle. (2 for about $6, Help Yourself Aids)

EXTRA-LONG-HANDLED SPONGE:   Twenty inches, take-apart, offset aluminum handle with either 3½″ x 4½″ x 2″ sponge or 5½″ x 5½″ x 2″ sponge attached. (About $4 for smaller sponge, about $5 for larger, Nelson)

SOAP POCKET SPONGE:   Natural rubber sponge with pocket for bar of soap; 17″ offset plastic handle. (About $8, Nelson)

## Miscellaneous

FLOATING THERMOMETER:   Range from 66–106 degrees. (About $6, Help Yourself Aids)

WHIRLPOOL AND SITZ BATHS:   (See pages 62–63.)

BATH PILLOW:   Measures 9″ x 18″; waterproof; suction cups hold it to back of tub; gold, pink, blue, or yellow floral on white. (About $6, Abbey)

SHOWER CADDY:   A 2-shelf, white vinyl rack that hangs over shower for shampoo, etc.; hooks and bar for brushes; wash cloth; measures 21¼″ x 10½″. (About $9, Lillian Vernon)

BATH CADDY:   Fits over tub; has rack and tray for soap, sponges, etc.; white vinyl-coated steel wire. (About $10, Lillian Vernon)

BATH READER:   Made of aluminum tubing; clamps over side of tub; Plexiglas tray with ledge to hold book; tray 12″ x 7½″ with 2″ ledge. (About $42, Cleo)

# THE TOILET

## Raised seats

MOLDED:   White polyethylene; weighs 3 lbs.; adds 4″ to seat height; flange fits into toilet bowl. (About $35, Help Yourself Aids)

CONTOURED: Same as above except for high back, contoured seat, and front cutout. (About $37, Help Yourself Aids)

HIGH CONTOURED: Same as above but adds 6″ to seat height. (About $40, Abbey)

SLOPING: For hip and spine problems, leg in cast, or arthritic knee. One side level, other side sloped forward toward floor; adds 4″ to seat height; polyester. Specify left or right side sloped. (About $28, Abbey)

ADJUSTABLE: Regular, noncontoured toilet seat on chrome-plated brackets; adjusts from 3″ to 6″ high. (About $21, Sears)

PORTABLE: Similar to above, but nonadjustable; 4″ high, with optional white plastic shield that attaches to seat ring and extends to bowl; extra front bracket; 6″-high brackets. (About $29 for basic unit, Winfield or order through surgical supply stores)

## Guardrails

WITH LEGS: Aluminum tubing with plastic armrests, plastic-tipped legs; 27″ overall height. (About $21, Sears, Winfield)

LEGLESS: Arms mount entirely on toilet; attach by removing seat and installing between seat and bowl; armrests 12″ above bowl. (About $19, Winfield)

RAISED SEAT AND GUARDRAIL COMBINATION: Brackets raise existing seat 5″–6″ above bowl, arms 7″ above seat. (About $53, Abbey)

## Commode chairs

(See also Shower Transport Chair on page 53—has commode attachment.)

ALUMINUM TUBED: Seat height 17½″; plastic pail; nonslip rubber tips; uses 20″ x 20″ floor space. (About $50, Winfield)

ADJUSTABLE: Same as above but adjustable 19″–24″ in height. (About $55, Winfield)

CASTORED: Nonadjustable; no brakes; seat height 19½″. (About $60, Winfield)

## Portable commodes

BOX TYPE: Measures 13½″ x 13½″ x 15½″ high; wood-based white vinyl-covered box; boilable pail; hinged lid; weighs 12 lbs. (About $28, Sears)

FOLDING ALUMINUM TUBED CHAIR: Standard toilet seat; weighs 18 lbs., arms adjust 27¾″–32½″ in height. (About $65, Abbey)

## Upholstered armchair-commode combinations

PINE: Light pine; straight frame and arms; padded cream vinyl back and removable seat; plastic toilet seat height 18″; boilable pail and lid; measures 22″ x 21″ x 34″ overall height, weighs 26 lbs. (About $70, Sears)

HARDWOOD WALNUT-FINISHED: Same as above except for beige vinyl padding, contoured toilet seat height 17″, and measures 25″ x 26″ x 34½″. (About $190, Sears)

## Toilet aids

BIDET: Submersible pump fits into toilet tank and connects to warm water storage tank; under-seat warm water spray head operates with push-button control to cleanse perineal area. (About $150, Mentor)

TOILET FUNNEL AND TUBING: Directs urine flow into bowl. (About $4, The Independence Factory)

## Toilet paper aids

To make your own holder, straighten out a wire coat hanger, then bend several small spirals in the middle of it to hold pieces of toilet tissue. Tape the ends of the wire together to form a handle and hang it on a nail near the toilet. Or buy:

TISSUE AID: A 23″ handle has Plastisol-coated "fingers" at end to hold pieces of toilet paper; lever presses against side of bowl to release paper. (Also good for tampon insertion.) (About $40, MED)

SHORT TOILET TISSUE AID: Steel tongs with vinyl-coated end to grasp tissue; shaped to proper angle; held with scissorslike handles. (About $5, Help Yourself Aids)

## Bedpans

CONTOURED: Light blue plastic; boilable; 11½″ x 14½″ long. (About $10, Sears)

FRACTURE: Similar to above except low wedge-shaped front for moving in place without moving patient. (About $10, Sears)

## Urinals, leg bags, and other aids

MALE URINAL: Light blue plastic; cover helps prevent spillage; horizontal or vertical use. (About $7, Sears)

DAY AND NIGHT URINAL: Rubber sheath treated to remain odorless; one-way valve; for use with leg bag (see below). (About $33, Sears)

DRIP URINAL: Odorless rubber sheath; understrap, plug, and 12″ extension; for use with leg bag (below). (About $43, Sears)

LEG BAG: Vinyl; 20-oz. capacity; for use with Day and Night or Drip Urinal described above. (About $11, Sears)

LEG BAG DRAIN VALVE: Operated by pulling ring gently with one finger; closes automatically when ring is released. (About $10, MED)

COLOSTOMY POUCHES: Odor-barrier; special adhesive; double-channel air vent that, when pressed, allows only air to escape; adjustable in size of openings: 5″ x 8″ size, 5½″ x 8″ size, 6″ x 10″ size. (Price for all sizes about $5 for package of ten, Sears)

INCONTINENT PANTS: Plasticized rayon; waterproof; elasticized leg and waist; extra snap fasteners to prevent seepage; liner has 3 double layers of absorbent flannel plus a top layer of knit that remains dry after fluid passes through it. Specify small waist (22″–28″), medium (30″–36″), large (38″–44″), extra-large (46″–52″).

       Prices: About $11 for pants with liner
               About $7 for replacement liner
               About $8 for pants with 3 disposable liners
               About $6 for 25 disposable liners

All available from Abbey.

DISPOSABLE LINER: Snaps into place in pants; can be flushed; thick fluffy pad absorbs 16 times its own weight in liquid; made of the same paper used in infants' disposable diapers with moisture barrier. Specify small for waist sizes 22″–28″ only, standard for all other sizes listed above. (Abbey)

MED also offers a variety of urinary care items including catheters, intermittent catheters, catheter insertion trays, bladder irrigation devices, as well as suppository inserters and aids for rectal stimulation. Contact your nearest MED distributor for a free *MED Urinary Care Equipment Catalog.*

## GROOMING

Grooming has a lot to do with self-respect. When you know you look well, it makes you feel better about yourself. And feeling better about yourself—keeping your thoughts upbeat—is sometimes a tough job, but a vital one, particularly when you're alone all day.

Of course, there are days when everything seems more tiring, days when it may be vital not to overdo. On those days, you may find a few of the following items helpful.

### *Your hair—cleaning and styling*

HOMEMADE DRY SHAMPOO: When for some reason you can't wash your hair and it needs it, mix 1 tablespoon salt to ½ cup cornmeal, sprinkle lightly on hair, brush out dirt.* Other devices for shampooing your hair in bed can be found on page 182.

* From *Mary Ellen's Best of Helpful Hints* by Pearl Higginbotham and Mary Ellen Pinkham. Copyright © 1979. Reprinted by permission of Warner Books/New York.

QUAD-QUIP BRUSH: Fits into any hand; soft teeth for use as hair or shampoo brush; finger dividers; flared cuff; adjustable handle. (About $6, Help Yourself Aids)

FINGER-RING BRUSH:   (See description on page 54.)

BUILT-UP HANDLE BRUSH:

> *Foam:* Has 1½″ diameter handle; round brush. (About $10, Help Yourself Aids)
>
> *Extended Offset:* (About $5, The Independence Factory)
>
> *Long Extended:* Measures 25″, bendable aluminum; Plastisol hand-grip; nut to angle and lock brush into place. (About $10, Help Yourself Aids)

STRAP-HANDLE BRUSH:   Regular-length brush; soft comblike teeth; Velcro to strap brush to hand. (About $8, Help Yourself Aids)

COMBS WITH BUILT-UP HANDLE:   See same category under brushes. All combs are the same price except the Extended Offset Comb, which is priced at about $4. (The Independence Factory)

HAIR PICKS:   Also called "Afro picks." Specify large or small. (About $4, The Independence Factory)

ROLLERS:   For one-handed use, no clips or picks needed. Small (¾″ diameter), medium (1″), large (1¼″), bouffant (1⅝″). (About $10 per package of 12 of any one size, Help Yourself Aids)

SPRAY CAN AID:   Straps around can; lever for one-finger operation. Also for shaving cream, deodorant, or kitchen use. Specify large or small can. (About $4, The Independence Factory)

*Note:* With top-button spray cans, try gluing a small piece of wood across the top and press.

## Your teeth

TOOTHBRUSHES:

> *Built-up Handle:* (About $3, The Independence Factory)
>
> *Extended Built-up Handle:* (About $3, The Independence Factory)

DENTAL FLOSSER:   For one-handed use; refill available. (About $3 for flosser, about $2 for refill, Nelson)

ULTRASONIC DENTURE CLEANER:   Also for cleaning combs and other personal items via vibrating cleaning solution. Just put item in appliance and flick the switch. (About $60, Abbey)

## Your nails (for manicures)

SUCTION BRUSH:   Nylon; scrub your nails on brush anchored by strong suction cups. (About $4, Help Yourself Aids)

NAIL FILE PAD:   Emery paper pad held by suction cups. (About $6, Abbey)

## Nail clippers/scissors

ON A BOARD:   Board stabilizes clippers for one-finger operation. (About $4, The Independence Factory)

EXTENDED:   Held like scissors. (About $4, The Independence Factory)

FINGER GRIP:   Circular finger grips (one for thumb; one for forefinger) on standard clipper with file. (About $3, Abbey)

NAIL SCISSORS:   Palm-held, no finger action required, automatic release. (About $15, Abbey)

## Shaving

ELECTRIC SHAVER HOLDER:   Two Velcro straps attached to vinyl-coated handle that can be bent to fit hand; foam pad inside handle to minimize vibration; fits all electric shavers. (About $13, Help Yourself Aids)

GILLETTE TRAC II HOLDER:   Vinyl-covered Quad-Quip (or open) cuff. (About $7, MED)

SHAVING-CREAM SPRAY CAN AID:   (See Spray Can Aid on page 58.)

## Applying deodorant

See Spray Can Aid on page 58. Or use a cream on a long-handled sponge (see page 54), or roll-on deodorant, or:

EXTENDED DEODORANT HOLDER:   Built-up handle with circular pad at other end. (About $4, The Independence Factory)

## Makeup

(To apply creams, see ideas under Applying Deodorant.)

LIPSTICK HOLDER:   Extended. (About $4, The Independence Factory)

Q-TIP HOLDER:   Extended. (About $4, The Independence Factory)

STAND-UP MIRROR:   An 11" hands-free mirror on 11"-diameter base; swivels, tilts, telescopes from 36" to 5' high. (About $40, Fashion-Able)

## Miscellaneous

THE BOX:   Forty-four round and square slots molded into an 8" x 5" x 3" high vinyl box; holds cosmetics, scissors, desk supplies, etc.; white, yellow, or black. (About $17, Lillian Vernon)

AUTOMATIC TWEEZERS:   Squeeze slightly, sharp ends lock; squeeze more and eyebrow or sliver comes out without pulling. (About $9, The Vermont Country Store)

SCALE WITH WAIST-HIGH DIAL:   A 35"-high extension for easier reading of dial; rubber-covered 13" x 10" step-up platform; not portable; weighs 100 lbs. (About $110, Products for Low Vision, American Foundation for the Blind)

# 7

# Stay Cool/Keep Warm

There are a number of ways to make yourself more comfortable: whirlpool baths, massagers, instant hot packs, noise mufflers, body quilts, and foot warmers. Comfortable chairs and pillows are also key elements of comfort and they can be found in a couple of places in this book. Chairs are in How to Do a Lot Less around the House, and cushions are listed in Wheelchairs and All about Beds. (Two orthopedic back-ease cushions are described below.)

## CUSHIONS, MASSAGERS, HEATING PADS, COMPRESSES

### Cushions for your back

POSTURE: (The British House of Commons recommended this for the lower back problems of British pilots!) S curve to hug small of back and properly position spine; 12″ x 14″ foam; removable cover; *best for people under 5′8″*. (About $18, Joan Cook)

ORTHOPEDIC: Four inches thick at its base where it hits small of back, tapering to 1½″ at top; 18″ high x 17″ across; *excellent for tall people, and those with broad backs*. (About $18, Abbey)

## Massagers

THE BODY MASSAGER: Small wooden balls threaded in double row within 2 vertical cords. (About $10, Sleepy Hollow Gifts)

PROFESSIONAL-TYPE ELECTRIC MASSAGER: Person giving you a rubdown straps a motor, encased in a steel housing on a contoured plastic base, to the back of the hand. As he or she rubs your back with the palm, gentle or vigorous vibrations are transmitted to your skin. Unit measures 5¾" long x 3½" wide x 3½" high, weighs 2½ lbs.; 110–120 volts; 8' cord. (About $38, Sears)

CONTOURED BACK MASSAGER: Pad for use sitting or lying down. Massage or heat can be used alone or in many combinations of settings. 15½" x 3¼" x 31½" long; 110–120 volts; 7½' cord. (About $45, Sears) Neck attachment available for massage of neck and shoulders. (About $13)

A similar Sears model with neck attachment measures 18½" x 4⅜" x 38" long. (About $60, Sears)

## Electric heating pads

ELECTRIC MOIST PAD: Generates its own moist heat and drapes like a blanket over any part of your body. Comes with washable covers; 13" x 27", about $60; 13" x 13", about $53; 4' x 14", about $44; available from Abbey, Cleo, G. E. Miller.

DRY PADS:

*Regular:* Measures 12" x 15"; removable cover; lighted dial. (About $12, Cleo) Also comes in 12" x 24" size. (About $22, Cleo)

*Mitts:* For hands or feet. (About $22, Cleo)

*Booties:* For feet only; separate thermostats for each foot. (About $25, Cleo)

*Sinus Mask:* For upper facial area. (About $21, Cleo)

*Mini:* For neck, elbows, knees, ankles, etc.; removable cover. (About $18, Cleo)

## Hot/cold compresses

HOT-R-COLD MASK: Pliable plastic filled with harmless chemical that retains heat or cold. For heat: 5 minutes in boiling water. For cold: a short time in the refrigerator. (About $11, Cleo)

HOT-R-COLD PACK: Same as the mask, but for use on any part of body. (About $13, Cleo)

INSTANT HOT PACK: Squeeze inner bag until it breaks, then shake 8–10 seconds; wrap in towel to produce instant heat for several hours. Not reusable; 5¾" x 8¾". (About $33 per dozen, Cleo) Cleo also makes an Instant Cold Pack at the same price.

## SUN AND HEAT LAMPS

### *Table*

SUN LAMP:   Four-hundred-watt ultraviolet; 80 sq. in. reflector; eye-shields included; 13" x 7¼" x 11¼" high. (About $85; replacement bulb about $32; Sears)

### *Floor*

HEAT LAMP:   Has 50-watt infrared ring element; shield, flexible arm, 11" reflector; height-adjustable, 51"–72". (About $110; with tripod castored base, about $130; G. E. Miller)

A similar lamp tilts to any angle, extends over bed 22"; height adjustable, 44"–76". (About $160, G. E. Miller)

SUN AND HEAT LAMP:   Six-hundred-watt; 100 sq. in. reflector; 2 infrared rods plus ultraviolet tube; angle- and height-adjustable, 30"–51"; eyeshields. (About $185; replacement bulb about $40, Sears)

### *Miscellaneous*

GOGGLES:   Fit into eye orbits; 23 mm, smoke-green therapeutic lenses. (About $7, G. E. Miller)

## BATHS AND ATTACHMENTS

### *Paraffin bath*

PARABATH:   Compact, lightweight; stainless inside tank, 12" x 6" x 6" deep; quick-melt circuit; temperature ranges up to 125–129 degrees Fahrenheit; 110-volt; safety switch. (About $100, G. E. Miller)

### *Whirlpool baths*

PORTABLE:   Fits any tub; pumps about 50 gallons per minute; adjustable jet spray for massage to any part of body; all electrical parts on outside of tub; 110-volt; automatic timer 0–60 minutes. (About $222, Abbey)

SEARS PORTABLE MODELS:   One pumps about 42 gallons per minute (about $190), the other pumps about 32 gallons per minute (about $165).

COMPACT WHIRLPOOL:   For hands and feet; all electrical parts away from water; tub measures 21" x 14" x 5½" high; 6' cord. (About $60, Sears)

> *Whirlpool Attachments:* For use with all Sears over-the-tub whirlpools; hand-held hose with one head for general spray, another head for cupping over specific areas. (About $30, Sears)

SIX-GALLON PORTABLE:   Similar to Sears model, but larger; with jet stream action; measures 26⅜" x 12¼" x 16¾". (About $100, Abbey)

## *Sitz baths*

A sitz bath combines the features of a bidet and a conventional toilet. Individual using toilet is washed by a gentle spray installed inside the toilet.

REG-U-TEMP: Contour seat to take weight off affected area. (About $40, G. E. Miller)

The following accessories are also available from G. E. Miller: water mixer for separate hot/cold taps (about $12); 9′ extension hose with coupler (about $10); adapter for oversized faucets (about $7); snap coupler set (about $11).

PORTABLE: Similar to Reg-U-Temp, but with faucet connector, 10′ hose. (About $45, G. E. Miller)

SITZ FOR BEDSIDE USE: Tubular aluminum frame with steel water pan; drain valve, removable steel seat; 10′ cord with 3-pronged plug; auxiliary ground wire with clamp; castors, 2 with locks; 34″ high x 29″ wide x 28″ deep. (Without heat assembly, about $400; with heat assembly, about $440; G. E. Miller)

## *Steam baths*

PORTABLE PLUG-IN: Molded fiberglass; leakproof; 24″ x 36″ x 44⅞″ high; no special plumbing, just add water and plug in; 110 volt, 60 cycle, 1,000 watt; thermostat, timer, on-off switch; 6′ cord. (About $410, Sears)

NUSAUNA: Similar to above, but seat is adjustable to 3 heights; adjustable thermostat; neon pilot light indicates when cast aluminum generator is on; uses an average of 350 watts per hour. (About $500, G. E. Miller)

## SPECIAL CLOTHING FOR THE WHEELCHAIR USER

(See also page 42 of Dress without Stress.)

## *Knickers*

DOUBLE-SEATED: Mid-wale corduroy; Velcro fasteners below knee; long-wearing double seat; taupe, slate blue, navy; sizes 30–40 for men, 8–18 for women. (All sizes and colors about $50, Vermont Country Store)

REGULAR WOOL: Medium gray; single seat; sizes same as above. (About $41, L. L. Bean)

## *Ponchos*

RAIN: Light waterproof nylon; longer front, shorter back; slips over head; zippered front; drawstring hood; light blue, tan. (About $20, Gorman Products)

BLANKET-STYLE: Machine-washable acrylic; 50″ x 60″; unzip it and it's a lap robe; red or blue plaid; warm enough for outdoors. (About $22, Fashion-Able)

## Cape

FOR WHEELCHAIR OR WALKING:    Handsomely tailored, trench-coat-type; water-repellent poplin; cut just below waist in back for wheelchair users, but can be ordered same length front and back for walkers; hood, 17″ front zipper. For wheelchair users: with fleece lining, about $58; without lining, about $45. For walkers: unlined only; about $45. (Fashion-Able)

# CLOTHES AND OTHER ITEMS TO KEEP YOU VERY WARM

The following are all exceptionally long-wearing *and* warm, and therefore worth a little extra cash outlay.

## Pants

VERMONT WORK PANTS:    Made for 100 years for loggers and other outdoorsmen; full-cut, forest-green loden cloth; weighs 22 oz.; sizes 30–42 even; leg lengths 29″, 31″, 33″; finished and ready to wear; front pockets, button top, zipper front; for men. (About $38; waist sizes 44 and 45 cost about $5 extra; Vermont Country Store)

ICE-MAN'S PANTS:    Heavier weight (26–28 oz.) than the Vermont Work Pants; "Ice-Man's" because the heavy, water-repellent 80 percent wool, 20 percent nylon cloth was the only protection the ice man had; same sizes as above, except no 33″ leg length. (About $48; waist sizes 44 and 46 cost about $5 extra; Vermont Country Store)

INSULATED OVERPANTS:    The heaviest of all; cotton and nylon shell; specially quilted polyester lining for warmth without bulk; washable; 2-way zippers (opening from top *or* bottom) *running full length of outer seams*; weigh 22 oz.; elasticized waist and cuffs; for men and women; waist sizes XS (26–28), S (30–32), M (34–36), L (38–40), XL (42–44); tan, navy. (About $45, L. L. Bean)

### A very warm, soft shirt and a coat lining

CHAMOIS CLOTH SHIRT:    Cotton flannel thickly napped on *both* sides; softer than wool; machine-washable; extra-full cut; 2 flapped breast pockets; slips over the head; buttoned placket front; navy, slate blue, forest green, red, light tan. Men's: 14½–20, about $20. Men's long: 15–19, about $21. Women's: 6–20, about $20. (L. L. Bean)

ZIP-IN QUILTED COAT LINING:    Knit cuffs; sew buttons into your coat, then button to lining; sizes 8–20. (About $22, The Ferry House)

## Long underwear

WINTERSKINS: The best washable long underwear at the lowest prices; 2 layers with air space between; ribbed neck, cuffs, ankles, elastic waist; absorbent inner layer made of cotton and polyester; white or light blue. (Sears)

WOMEN'S TOPS: S (32–34), M (35–37), L (38–40), XL (41–43); wool and polyester outer layer about $15; acrylic and polyester outer layer about $13. (Sears)

WOMEN'S ANKLE-LENGTH PANTS: S (34–36), M (37–39), L (40–42), XL (43–45); wool and polyester outer layer about $15; acrylic and polyester outer layer about $13. (Sears)

MEN'S SHIRTS: S (34–36), M (38–40), L (40–42), XL (46–48); outer layer is 50 percent polyester, 50 percent acrylic; for 5'7"–5'11", about $14; for over 5'11"–6'3", about $15. (Sears)

MEN'S DRAWERS: S (30–32), M (34–36), L (38–40), XL (42–44); outer layer is 50 percent polyester, 50 percent acrylic; elastic waist, double-fabric fly and crotch, ribbed at ankles; for 5'7"–5'11", about $14; for over 5'11"–6'3", about $15. (Sears)

ANGORA THERMAL UNDERWEAR: The underwear that climbed the Himalayas and reached the summit of the tenth highest mountain in the world: Annapurna. So very warm and a cashmere look-alike; can be worn without outer clothing; cold-water washable; cream-colored; from Sears. Caution: Angora is very soft, but it can be itchy, although this blend—50 percent angora rabbit hair, 30 percent wool, and 20 percent nylon—may not be.

> *Tops:* Ribbed knit crew neck and cuffs; set-in sleeves; hemmed; S (34–36), M (38–40), L (42–44), XL (46–48); about $45.
>
> *Drawers:* Covered, knit-elastic waistband; double-fabric fly and crotch; S (30–32), M (34–36), L (38–40), XL (42–44); about $48.

## Warmers and socks

KNEE WARMERS: Made of 100 percent Australian stretch wool; 12" long; slip on like socks; flesh color; for men and women; specify regular or extra-large. (About $8 the pair, Miles Kimball)

SLIPPER SOCKS: Ragg wool (worn by Norwegians for centuries); leather soles, inner sponge soles; for men and women; state shoe size. (About $27, The Vermont Country Store)

## Ankle-hugging slippers

LUXURY COWHIDE: Cowhide suede uppers lined with acrylic pile; beige; composition sole; whole sizes only, medium width; men's 7–13; women's, 5–10. (Both about $22, Deerskin Trading Post)

## Moccasin slippers

MOCCASINS WITH ARCH SUPPORTS:   Hand-laced deerskin; suede lining; sponge rubber insoles; rawhide tie; tan; whole sizes, medium width; men (7–13); women (5–10). (Both about $26, Deerskin Trading Post)

PILE-LINED MOCCASINS:   Deerskin; pile lining; composition soles; rawhide tie; half and whole sizes; medium width; tan; men's (7–11, 12, and 13 in whole sizes only), women's (5–10). (Both about $27, Deerskin Trading Post)

# KEEPING WARM WHILE SITTING OR IN BED

## To keep warm in bed

BLANKET SHEETS:   Soft 100 percent cotton flannel replaces or goes over your sheet for no-shiver slipping into bed in winter, light protection in summer; about 10 percent shrinkage; single size (70″ x 90″, about $14), double (80″ x 108″, about $18); pillowcases come in regular size (about $14 the pair) and queen size (about $15 the pair). (The Vermont Country Store)

## To keep warm while sitting

BODY QUILT:   Front-zipping, polyester bag with arm and foot openings to leave hands free and feet free for walking; encases you in a 70″ x 32″ cozy cocoon; unzipped, it's a quilt for your bed. (About $30, Joan Cook)

## To keep warm while sitting and/or in bed

THE BUNDLER:   Like kids' Dr. Dentons; blanket-weight, 100 percent Acrilan; Wear-Dated by Monsanto; full-torso front zipper; detachable booties; for men and women; men's colors—light blue, red, chocolate, camel, navy; women's colors—pink, orange, yellow, light blue, red; men's sizes S (up to 5′6″), M (5′6″–5′9″), L (5′9″–6′), XL (over 6′); women's S (up to 5′2″), M (5′2″–5′4″), L (5′4″–5′6″), XL (over 5′6″). (Men's, about $29; women's, about $27 for regular or Baby Pink Drop-Seat Model; Adam York, 340 Poplar St., Hanover, Penn. 17331)

# MISCELLANEOUS

FOLDING LEGREST:   Elevates and supports legs properly; adjustable-angle; folds flat; 11″ x 9″; walnut-finished hardwood. (About $20, Whitaker Surgical)

## Noise mufflers

When tomcats howl, the wind whistles, horns honk, taps drip, and drains gurgle, you may be glad of the following:

EAR MUFFS: Adjustable to cup whole ear without pressure, shut out sound. (About $20, Wuensch Surgical)

SLEEP CONDITIONER: To generate "white sound" to lull you to sleep. (About $40). Similar models are Sound of Rain, about $80; or Surf and Rain, about $120. (Whitaker Surgical)

## Vaporizer and fans

COOL-MIST VAPORIZER-HUMIDIFIER: Adds moisture without heating room (dispenses cool moist air); 2 gallon; only one filling for 19 hours of use; 110-volt; 5' cord. (About $24, Sears)

MINIATURE FAN: Sits in front of you and cools face and neck; use on your desk, bedside table—anywhere; 6" high; angle-adjustable; plastic with grill in front of blade. (About $9, Jean Stuart)

SALTON PERSONAL FAN: Six inch, multiposition, 2-speed fan; place on table to cool any part of the body; 120 watt. (About $30, Salton Inc.)

# PART THREE

# HELP
# FOR SPECIFIC
# PROBLEMS

# 8

## *For the Disabled Parent*

### SOME GENERAL TIPS

As a hardworking parent, you should try to save as many steps and as much labor as possible. For example, stash little hidden caches of diapers (and plastic bags for disposing of them) behind furniture or in a cabinet in each room in the house. Then wherever your child happens to be when needing changing, you can do it right there. That bare space under your baby's dressing table can be used for storage by getting a couple of Under-shelf Baskets (see page 9).

When bathing or dressing the baby in his or her room, try to have all work surfaces at the same height. If you can't, at least place the furniture close enough together to slide the baby on a transfer board (see page 179) from dressing surface to bassinet to crib. Be sure you have enough knee room to allow you to work in a forward position.

For maneuverability, try a crib with castors or a castored car bed or an infant seat or car bed on a dolly. If you use a dolly, be sure that the device holding your child is well anchored.

# ADAPTING FURNITURE AND EQUIPMENT

## *Crib*[1]

If you are in a wheelchair, you may find it hard to lower the side of the crib with the toe-trip bar. The mattress height may also be awkward for you. Procedures for remedying both these situations are outlined below.

TO ADJUST TOE-TRIP BAR:

1. Remove front side of crib by removing the 2 rod guides and latching plate.
2. Saw off the angular-lock part of the latching plate and smooth down.
3. Replace the plate.
4. Reverse side of crib when replacing it so trip bar operates by being pushed inward.

TO ADJUST HEIGHT OF MATTRESS　(use same procedure for carriages and bassinets):

1. Cut two stringers slightly less than crib length and three-fourths the desired elevating distance.
2. Cut three cross ties slightly less than crib width and the same width as stringers.
3. Cut ¼″ notches in the stringers and panels to the midline of each panel.
4. Sand each piece, shellac, then paint.
5. Cut plywood platform slightly smaller than bottom of crib.
6. Sand, shellac, and paint.
7. Interlock cross ties and stringers.
8. Place platform on top of stringers and then place the mattress on the platform.

# DRESSING

## *For dressing your child while seated*

FOLDING UTILITY CART:　Measures 26″ x 18″ x 30″ high; 2″ castors; lower shelf folds out of the way while upper shelf is used; handles to push cart. Top shelf could be padded with foam rubber for dressing the baby. (About $60, MED)

(See also For Disabled Children, page 77.)

## BATHING

(For more information, see chapters Bathing and Grooming and For Disabled Children.)

### To shampoo without hurting baby's eyes
Put petroleum jelly on the baby's eyebrows and eyelids. Soap will run sideways instead of downward!*

### To keep a baby smelling sweet
If your child bubbles often, to eliminate the sour odor, moisten a cloth, dip it in baking soda, and dab at the dribbled area on the clothing. The odor will disappear.*

## FEEDING

There are a number of helpful devices to make mealtimes easier. You'll find some of them listed on page 78 in the chapter For Disabled Children.

### To eliminate spills before they happen
Cut an opening in the center of a sponge and insert the cup or glass you want to use. The sponge keeps it from tipping over and absorbs any overflow. (Reprinted from *Mary Ellen's Best of Helpful Hints*.)

## CARRYING YOUR CHILD

### No hands
You must have good balance to use this next item or the child's weight will pull you down.

SNUGLI CHILD CARRIER: Inner pouch for child, outer pouch with zipper for storage; back and neck support for *you*; for use as backpack, front pouch, or nursing sling; washable corduroy, adjustable padded shoulder straps; weighs 1 lb. 3 oz.; camel or blue. (About $50, L. L. Bean)

* *Mary Ellen's Best of Helpful Hints* by Pearl Higginbotham and Mary Ellen Pinkham, copyright © 1979. Reprinted by permission of Warner Books/New York.

## SAFETY

Here are a couple of devices to make cabinets and outlets childproof.

CHILDPROOF LATCHES: For insides of cabinet doors. (About $2 each, Kindergard)

SAFETY OUTLET COVERS: To make electrical outlets childproof; squeeze both sides, insert plug, and close cover. (About $5, hardware stores)

## MISCELLANEOUS*

### *For the sick or injured child*

IF YOUR CHILD HAS TROUBLE SWALLOWING A PILL: Place the pill in a teaspoon of applesauce and see how easily it goes down.

TO REMOVE A SPLINTER: Soak the area in cooking oil (unheated) for a few minutes to make it easier to remove the splinter. Also, apply an ice cube to numb the area.

### *Clothing tips*

TO KEEP A BABY FROM SLIPPING ON HARD SURFACES WHEN WEARING THE FIRST PAIR OF SHOES: Glue a very thin strip of foam rubber to the soles of the shoes. When foam is worn, scrape off the remains with a razor blade and apply a new piece.

TO HELP YOUR CHILD MAKE IT THROUGH THE WINTER IN LAST YEAR'S JACKET: Sew knitted cuffs (available in notions departments) to the sleeves.

TO KEEP BUTTONS ON YOUR CHILD'S CLOTHES: Touch the center of each button (front and back) with clear nail polish to seal the threads.

The next chapter, For Disabled Children, provides additional tips and sources of information and equipment to make child care a bit easier.

---

* All of the hints in this section reprinted from *Mary Ellen's Best of Helpful Hints* by Higginbotham and Pinkham.

# 9

# *For Disabled Children*

Since you can't be too careful in your choice of equipment for your child, you will need a picture and full details for each possibility within a given category before you and your doctor make final choices. Therefore, this chapter lists manufacturers only. It is suggested that you send for brochures or catalog tear sheets from *all* the manufacturers within each relevant category. This is one way of ensuring that you and your doctor will have full opportunity to make detailed comparisons.

You might also want to note that there is an organization that will help to provide for disabled children in the event of their parents' death, retirement, or permanent disability. If you'd like information about their services, write to the New Hope Foundation, Inc., Suite 630, 6100 N. Keystone Ave., Indianapolis, Ind. 46220.

## FURNITURE AND EQUIPMENT

### *Walk, crawl, and stand aids*
CRUTCHES:   G. E. Miller
WALKERS:   Abbey, Cleo, Invacare, G. E. Miller, J. A. Preston
STAND AIDS:   Abbey, Ortho-Kinetics
STAND-IN TABLES:   Abbey, Cleo, Hausmann

CRAWLERS AND SCOOTERS:   Abbey, Cleo (crawlers only), J. A. Preston (scooters only)

## Chairs and seats

WHEELCHAIRS:   Abbey, Invacare, G. E. Miller, Ortho-Kinetics, J. A. Preston, R. J. Reynolds (build it yourself for the very small child—see page 241)

SLING SEATS:   Ortho-Kinetics (castored for transporting, bathing, lifting, relaxing); J. A. Preston (with suction feet)

TRAVEL AND FOLDING CHAIRS:   Abbey, Cleo, Ortho-Kinetics (also usable as car seat and stroller), J. A. Preston

FLOOR SITTER CHAIRS:   Abbey, Hausmann, J. A. Preston

FLOOR SITTER CART:   Cleo has two models, one for self-propulsion or for being pulled, the other a heavy-duty orthopedic cart with hand brakes.

ORTHOPEDIC CHAIRS:   J. A. Preston

CAR SEATS:   Abbey, Ortho-Kinetics

FEEDER SEATS:   J. A. Preston manufactures the seats in 2 sizes: small for infants to 36″, large for children to 48″. The seats are contoured for posturally correct sitting position. For lap, floor, table, wheelchair, sofa, or car seat use.

## Tables

STAND-IN TABLES:   (See page 75.)

CUTOUT TABLES:   Abbey, Hausmann, J. A. Preston

THE ABLE TABLE:   (See page 180.)

## Desks

LAP DESKS:   (See page 181.)

ON-THE-BED FOLDING TRAY:   Doubles as a writing surface. (About $20, Abbey) (see page 181)

TURNTABLE DESK:   For over wheelchair or bed (see page 180)

SCHOOL DESKS:   J. A. Preston (or use their cutout table as a child's desk)

## Recreation equipment

TOYS, GAMES, AND EXERCISE GEAR:   Abbey, J. A. Preston

TO CHOOSE OR MODIFY TOYS:   Write for *Let's Play Games*—an illustrated, 62-page booklet of games for disabled children—from the National Easter Seal Society, 2023 West Ogden Ave., Chicago, Ill. 60612. Another helpful source is the 16-page pamphlet *Adapting Toys* by C. Edward Wethered, which explains how to modify battery-operated toys. Write to Communication Outlook, Artificial Language Laboratory, Computer Science Dept., Michigan State Univ., East Lansing, Mich. 48824.

You can also send a battery-operated toy to be modified with a special switch to the Toy Modification Service, operated by Prentke Romich Co. (see address in Sources of Equipment and Information at the end of the book). (Approximate cost of modification—about $25)

Catalogs are available from Abbey and J. A. Preston. (See addresses at the end of the book.) Or send for the following: *Choosing Toys and Activities for Handicapped Children, Toys for Children with Speech, Hearing and Language Difficulties,* and other pamphlets available from Toy Libraries Association, Sunley House, 10 Gunthorpe Street, London E1 7RW, England. The entire 11-pamphlet series costs about $11 by surface mail or about $17.50 by airmail.

SELF-OPERATING TAPE RECORDER:   Simplified operation. (J. A. Preston)

TRICYCLES:   Abbey, Cleo (hand-propelled), Hand-operated (see page 160)

For further recreation equipment, see the chapter Sports and Games. Much of this equipment is adaptable for children.

## DRESSING

To learn all there is to know about dressing your child, send for the invaluable 64-page booklet called *Self-Help Clothing for Children Who Have Physical Disabilities,* published by the National Easter Seal Society, 2023 West Ogden Ave., Chicago, Ill. 60612. The booklet tells you how to teach dressing skills, what kinds of fabrics and styles are best for specific disabilities, and how to adapt every garment to every conceivable need. (See also the chapter Dress without Stress in this book.)

## BATHING*

When bathing an infant, use a Bathinette or, if bathing the child in the sink, use an infant seat with suction cups or a rubber suction mat under it. If you prefer not to strap the child in, put a folded towel inside the seat to prevent slipping; if you are using a sling seat, there is even less danger of slippage.

When the child is past the baby stage, but too small for the tub, try bathing him or her in the sink with a piece of foam rubber or a rubber

---

* Ideas for bathing from *Mary Ellen's Best of Helpful Hints* by Pearl Higginbotham and Mary Ellen Pinkham, copyright © 1979. Reprinted by permission of Warner Books/New York.

suction mat under the child. You can bathe the child this way either in the infant seat or without it. (See Chapter 6, Bathing and Grooming, for aids and ideas.)

CHILD-SIZED COMMODES:   Abbey, Cleo, Invacare, G. E. Miller

## EATING

### Self-feeding utensils, child-sized

DRINKING CUP:   J. A. Preston (See page 37 for other nonspill cups.)

THREE-IN-ONE EATING UTENSIL:   Fork, spoon, and knife in one; functional handle; from J. A. Preston

TEETH PROTECTOR SPOON:   Plastisol-coated; from Help Yourself Aids

SWIVEL SPOON:   Nonadjustable; built-up handle; Help Yourself Aids (baby and junior sizes) and J. A. Preston

ADJUSTABLE SWIVEL SPOON:   Junior only, Help Yourself Aids

### Other equipment

SUCTION AND SPECIAL-RIM PLATES AND BOWLS, TRAYS, ETC.:   (See Chapter 4, Eat, Drink, and Be Merry.)

FEEDER SEATS:   (See page 76.)

AUTOMATIC FEEDERS   (for the severely disabled):

Abbey (carries 4 extraordinary inventions; write to Abbey for complete descriptions)

J. A. Preston (has 2: a head-operated food scoop and an arm-controlled swivel device for the child with upper-extremity weakness)

PLATE POSITIONER:   Abbey

SPOON FEEDER:   Plastic control-flow bottle with spoon attached for feeding semisolid foods; available from J. A. Preston

You'll find additional mealtime tips and equipment listed in Chapter 4, Eat, Drink, and Be Merry.

## SOURCES OF ADDITIONAL INFORMATION

For an extensive reading list on child care, write to the National Easter Seal Society and ask for their pamphlet *Books and Pamphlets for Parents and Teachers of Children Who Have Disabilities: A Basic Reading List* (2023 West Ogden Avenue, Chicago, Ill. 60612).

## Special catalogs of equipment for disabled children

*Abbey Medical Equipment Catalogue* includes a section for disabled children. (See Appendix: Sources of Equipment and Information.)

*Preston Equipment for Health Care and Rehabilitation,* free from J. A. Preston. A guide to equipment for health and rehabilitation, including special materials for children.

*Products for People with Vision Problems.* New York: American Foundation for the Blind, Inc., 1980. A comprehensive source of information about special aids and devices for people with visual impairments. Describes more than 400 products. (Free)

*Preston Materials for Exceptional Children: Special Education Catalog,* free from J. A. Preston. A wide range of materials for the remediation of learning and other disabilities for use in special education classes and at home.

## Organizations for the parents of disabled children

"Closer Look," The National Information Center for the Handicapped, 1201 16th St., N.W., Washington, D.C. 20036.

Coordinating Council for Handicapped Children, 407 S. Dearborn St., Chicago, Ill. 60605.

# 10

# For People with the Use of One Arm or Leg

Throughout the book, you'll find equipment and ideas that will prove helpful if you have the use of one arm or leg. This chapter offers a few more ideas, and the Bibliography lists a number of helpful sources.

## FOR PEOPLE WITH THE USE OF ONE HAND

### Hand exercising equipment

Both Abbey and Cleo carry many kinds of hand, wrist, and arm exercisers, including various kinds of putty. (There is also Silly Putty, sold in toy and variety stores, which some therapists recommend for hand-squeezing exercise.) Please consult your doctor before deciding which equipment to purchase.

### Equipment for left-handed use

A shop called Left Hand Plus, Inc. (P.O. Box 161, Morton Grove, Ill. 60053, [313] 966–3033) carries writing aids, scissors, cooking and eating utensils, books of instructions for left-handed guitar-playing, sports, and crafts, as well as children's sports equipment and books. Send for their catalog.

You may also want to write for the following catalogs:

Aristera Left-Handed Products, 9 Rice's La., Westport, Conn. 06880.
Left Hand Plus, Inc., P.O. Box 161, Morton Grove, Ill. 60053.
Left Hand World, P.O. Box 26316, San Francisco, Calif. 94126.
Lefty's Survival Manual (from Aristera—address above).
The Left Hand, 140 West 22nd St., New York, N.Y. 10011.

## IDEAS AND EQUIPMENT
## FOR PEOPLE WITH THE USE OF ONE LEG

### *To get things from room to room that won't fit into an apron or crutch bag*

SHOPPING BAG ON WHEELS:   Made of leatherlike vinyl, on castors; 22″ high plus carrying straps; 12″ wide x 7½″ deep. (About $12, Sleepy Hollow Gifts, P.O. Box 2327, Falls Church, Va. 22042)

A PLASTIC DISHPAN MOUNTED ON CASTORS:   Put lightweight things (or a small amount of water for scrubbing) in this and you'll have no trouble kicking it from room to room. Make it yourself or order one from Help Yourself Aids. (About $12)

# 11

*Notes on Strokes*

## A STROKE IN THE FAMILY

To learn how to help a relative or friend after a stroke, invest in the book *A Stroke in the Family* by Valerie Eaton Griffith. Griffith developed the lessons explained in her book to help an actress recover from nearly total aphasia. These lessons have since changed the nature of stroke therapy as they allowed a new form of rehabilitation to emerge: amateur stroke therapy.

Aphasia is defined as an impairment of one or more of the basic communication skills: listening, understanding, speaking, reading, writing. It *can* often be cured—if caught quickly enough—by the friends and relatives of the stroke patient.

A few samples of Griffith's step-by-step lessons follow,[1] but only a few: Be sure to buy the book. Its carefully laid-out lessons will be invaluable to your patient's recovery, and can be easily followed even by someone completely unacquainted with speech therapy.

### For relatives

"Don't try and teach the patient yourself. You'll resume your old prestroke relationship with him/her far more easily and will be freer to get on with your own work if you let friends do the teaching.

"Remember that a person who has had a stroke has not reverted to childhood. He is emotionally adult. . . . So never talk down to him. . . . But [keep it] light. . . . Be encouraging and laugh with him.

"Start his lessons quickly."

Although most doctors say that no further improvement takes place after two years, Valerie Griffith discovered that improvement can definitely continue, though more slowly, well beyond that point.

"Lastly, get the patient out and about as much as possible. This is a tremendous stimulus to recovery, the need for which cannot be over-stressed."

### For the friend/teacher

"Think of the patient as he was before the stroke. What sort of man was he? What was his job? What were his interests? What were his strong points, his weaknesses?

"Flit from subject to subject. . . . The stroke patient will [concentrate better] if he continually has new subjects to work on.

"Vary your approach. For example [if a person has trouble with the alphabet . . . can't even remember one letter of it, try getting him to look at a globe and find some familiar spot. Something may suddenly click.]

"Try to get [him] interested in anything from gardening to pets, from painting to music. Explore his hobbies.

"[Try] a few games [to] establish communication [and] also help you find out a good deal about how much the patient can manage."

### For both relatives and teachers

"[Don't] deny him the right to despondency. . . . Be gentle in helping him dispel these moods. . . . Provide some of his 'favorites' saved for a rainy day . . . invite a good friend in for a visit, take him to a film.

"[To build his] self-confidence . . . encourage him to do every single thing he is able to do for himself, from cleaning his shoes to stirring the soup. . . .

"Always bring him into a conversation or decision . . . leaving him loads of time to get across what he wants to say.

"Try leaving him on his own with a child. Children . . . seem to have a magic touch with a stroke patient."

## THE NORTHEAST ASSOCIATION OF POST STROKE CLUBS, INC.

In 1971, Julius Lombardi, a stroke victim, founded the Northeast Association of Post Stroke Clubs, Inc., an organization (headquartered at 119

Arrow Street South, Schenectady, N.Y. 12304) dedicated to helping stroke victims and their families meet others in similar circumstances and together find solutions to their physical and emotional problems.

Finding friends who share their difficulties can eliminate one of the feelings common to all stroke patients—isolation, even ostracism from the more easily communicating community.

The Northeast Association is now composed of more than 15 clubs. All of the clubs offer information and techniques for therapy, professional speakers, films, etc. The present clubs are located in Schenectady, Plattsburgh, Glens Falls, Saratoga Springs, Troy, East Greenbush, Albany, Amsterdam, Binghamton, and Utica, N.Y.—and in Bennington, Vt.

For further information about these clubs, or to learn how to start one in your area, write to Julius Lombardi at the address given above.

Lombardi has also written an excellent pamphlet entitled *Handy, Helpful Hints for the Handicapped,* available from the National Easter Seal Society, 2023 West Ogden Ave., Chicago, Ill. 60612. Also available from the Easter Seal Society is a pamphlet called *Understanding Stroke,* and another on stroke clubs (see the Bibliography).

# 12

## Speech and Hearing Aids

Like a kindergartner being introduced to Disney World, the mind boggles when first exposed to the magic of today's communication devices. They span all price ranges and come in different forms: scanner boards, speech synthesizers, devices that convert print to speech, and so on. More about them later. First, a word about Teletypewriters (TTY) for the deaf and the National Crisis Center at the University of Virginia. Using your TTY, you can call the center, toll-free, 24 hours a day in an emergency and they will dispatch police, fire, and rescue squads from your community—or give emergency medical advice from their trained professionals standing by. The number is (800) 466–9876 (for Virginia only, [800] 522–3723).

TTYs, whose cost is tax-deductible, come in several forms (they are grouped under the designation TDD, or Telecommunicating Devices for the Deaf). All are typing devices used in connection with your regular telephone service and billed at the regular phone rate—and all require that both the user and the receiver have similar devices. Some convey their information to the receiver via a paper printout. Others print it on a TV-type screen or one-line calculator-type display. Some are portable with handsets that can be put into the cradle of a public telephone and used anywhere in the country. And sets are available with printouts in Braille. All cost in the neighborhood of $190–$500.

For further information on TTYs and to learn where to obtain one in your area, contact Telecommunications for the Deaf, Inc., 814 Thayer Ave., Silver Spring, Md. 20910, (301) 587–1788.

## AIDS FOR THE NONVOCAL PERSON

The aids described below by no means cover the range of what is available. A few of the more reasonably priced items are given in each category. But communication aids are one of the few areas today in which prices often go *down*! Technology is constantly expanding—rather, exploding—so fast it is difficult to keep up with all the new advances that frequently lower production costs.

The best way to keep up with the advances in communication aids is to subscribe to the quarterly newsletter *Communication Outlook*, which regularly describes all the newest aids in detail. It also gives valuable information on obtaining used devices, on jobs, and on communication workshops. Subscriptions are $10 per year ($12 outside North America) from Communication Outlook, Artificial Language Laboratory, Computer Science Dept., Michigan State University, East Lansing, Mich. 48824.

Another source is the book *Non-Vocal Communication Resource Book*, available for $12.50 from Trace Research and Development Center, University of Wisconsin, 314 Waisman Ctr., 1500 Highland Ave., Madison, Wis. 53706. It is an illustrated digest of nonvocal communication aids.

### To fund your communication aid

Write for *Guidelines for Seeking Funding for Communication Aids*, free from Zygo Industries, Inc., P.O. Box 1008, Portland, Ore. 97207. This publication gives histories of how individuals in Wisconsin obtained funds. Another helpful source of information is *Funding of Non-Vocal Communications Aids: Current Issues and Strategies* (about $3.50), published by Trace Research and Development Center (see address above). This gives a 4-step procedure to obtain funds.

### Speech synthesizers

FORM-A-PHRASE:   An 8-track pretaped speech cartridge embodying 128 words or phrases, available in male, female, or child's voice. (You may also order a custom cartridge set up with the phrases of your choice.) Controlled by push-button calculator-type keyboard or marker that is moved by hand, foot, headpointer, or mouthstick. (About $650 for Main Unit; $25–$400 additional for Control; SciTronics)

TRS–80 VOICE SYNTHESIZER:   Plug-in box to be used with Radio Shack's home computers (which run from $700 to $999) to produce electronically synthesized speech with unlimited vocabulary. (About $450, Radio Shack, VOTRAX)

PHONIC MIRROR HANDIVOICE:

> *HC 120:* Hand-held or standing calculator-type keyboard with 900 words, plus the alphabet; potential for user to create new words.
>
> *HC 110:* Lapboard-style with 128 individual squares to be pressed via optional switches; creates 400 words and phrases, plus capacity for new words; available often with financing if recommended by a health professional. (About $2,595 for either model, H C Electronics)

ELECTRONIC ARTIFICIAL LARYNX: For use with the telephone (see page 124).

## Paper tape printer

CANON COMMUNICATOR: Battery-operated, hand-held calculator-type keyboard (available with keyboard overlays for motor-impaired people); 26 alphabet keys plus number shift lever to produce paper tape printouts. (About $600, including battery pack and charger, 20 tape rolls, lasting about 3½ hours each, keyboard overlays, armbelt with extension belts, neck strap, and case, Telesensory Systems)

## Scanner communicators

These are lighted boxes, the surface of which is divided into squares, onto which messages may be entered with overlays, decals, or wax pencils. When various switches are activated, the chosen message lights up on the box's surface.

ILLUMINAID: Make-it-yourself, battery-operated, portable box with 10 buttons and corresponding light bulbs; space near each light for messages printed on tape or made with a label-maker. (Approximate cost $35, includes cost of battery charger; for free instructions, write Jack Atzinger, Public Information Dept., The Cleveland Electric Illuminating Co., P.O. Box 5000, Cleveland, Ohio 44101)

SCANNER COMMUNICATORS (All from J. A. Preston):

> *Scan 100:* Has 100 squares with horizontal, vertical, and diagonal scanning. (About $700). Available with treadle-switch (about $50), finger-elbow switch (about $100), or calculatorlike device with attention alarm (about $200). Also pressure, tape, sip-and-puff, and button switches available.
>
> *Scan 40:* Forty squares; horizontal-only scanning, treadle switch. (About $395) Pressure, tape, sip-and-puff, and button switches also available.
>
> *Scan 8:* Switch on front panel. (About $190)

*Accessories:* Blissymbol and word message decals available for *all* Preston scanners (about $9 each); acetate overlays for Scan 100 and 40 models (5 for $5).

Other Scanner Communicators with special switches and overlays are sold by Possum, Inc., and Prentke Romich Co.

## Eye-gazing communicators

ZYGO: Sixteen squares; overlays; light and audible alarm to indicate message choice; optional breath, touch, etc. switches; technique must be taught by trained personnel; 3 models available—free-standing, table rest, or C-clamp. (About $550, contact Abbey at [800] 421–4126 for information.)

EYE TRANSFER: Coded transparent board; sender sits on one side to gaze at numbers/letters while recipient of message sits on other side of it to register the numbers and letters the sender's eye movements indicate; also usable with head-pointer or mouthstick. (About $140, Abbey)

## Communication boards/cards

Many people make these themselves by printing messages or pasting pictures on a large piece of cardboard within squares to which the user can point. Or buy:

TALKING PICTURES: Box with 110 cards illustrating daily necessities; 10 vinyl envelopes for pictures, ring to hold envelopes together; cord to tie ring and pictures to bed, wheelchair, belt, wrist, etc.; cards have pictures with words in English, Spanish, German, French, and Italian, representing room, bathroom, health aids, food, clothing, people, and miscellaneous. (About $15, Crestwood)

These pictures could also be pasted on a large piece of plywood and propped near the user.

THE COMMUNICATOR: Battery-operated pointer that moves as switch is pressed, stops when switch is released; operable with headstick; interchangeable boards with numbers, colors, felt objects, letters—all arranged in a circle. (About $230, G. E. Miller)

COMMUNICATION BOARD: For hospital use; 26 pictures of needs such as nurse, eyeglasses, razor, slippers, TV, etc. (About $26, Cleo)

HEAD POINTER: Adjustable, designed for use with manual communication boards. (About $18, Cleo)

## Symbol communications

BLISSYMBOLS: A set of 100 visual symbols based on meaning rather than sound; combinations of symbols form sentences to permit nonvocal people to communicate without necessarily having learned to read; available in different forms for various means of usage. For information, contact EBSCO Curriculum Materials, P.O. Box 11521, Birmingham, Ala. 35202, (800) 633–9263.

### Electronic aid control systems

These powered-wheelchair-based control systems come with tape recorder, typing, computer scanner, etc. Interfaces and links permit wireless control of devices from wheelchair or bed. (Romich, Beery, Bayer)

## HELPFUL DEVICES
## FOR PEOPLE WITH HEARING PROBLEMS

### To enhance your hearing aid

PHONIC EAR PERSONAL FM SYSTEM:   To use with hearing aid when competing room noise is present; sound is transmitted to your ear through telecoil of hearing aid via a receiver. The person addressing you wears a transmitter. (About $360 for receiver without microphone; about $400 with microphone; about $410 for transmitter; H C Electronics)

### Closed-captioned equipment

TELEVISION:   This is similar to foreign movie subtitling except that the captions are on TV sets equipped with a special decoding device. In March 1980, ABC, NBC, and PBS began broadcasting 16 hours of weekly prime time captioned programming, with more hours projected for the future.

To get in on this, order one of the following:

TELECAPTION TV ADAPTER:   Permits any size and make of TV set to display captioned versions of network shows; hook to antenna, then connect easily to set; walnut-grained 6 15/16″ x 4 7/16″ x 9 1/16″ deep; 120 volt; 8′ cord. (About $270, Sears)

TV WITH BUILT-IN TELECAPTION:   A 19″ color TV with built-in decoding circuitry. (About $540, Sears)

FILM:   Write Captioned Film Branch, Bureau of Research, Off. of Education, U.S. Dept. of Education, 330 C St., S.W., Washington, D.C. 20202.

### TV/radio listening equipment

See also Radio and TV Receivers on page 104 and In Touch (a radio information service) on page 152.

DIXON TV/RADIO HEARING AIDS:   Control, earphone receiver, and transformer to connect to TV/radio extension outlet. (About $85 for standard model; about $125 for superpowered model; Hal-Hen)

MARVEL INDUCTOR:   Induction plate with connecting clips that attach to speaker terminals of TV/radio; place a body hearing aid on induction plate or fit induction plate between ear-level/eyeglass hearing aids and head; specify ear level, eyeglass, or body hearing aid. (About $30 for monaural; about $35 for binaural; Hal-Hen)

AMPLITEL LOOP INDUCTION:   Induction loop; 60' cable attaches to radio/TV and loops around an area; earpiece to listen through loop; or listen to amplified sound within room without earpiece. (About $120, Hal-Hen)

### Stereo amplifier

STEREOPILLOW:   Two speakers inside pillow; 30' cable attaches to speaker output of hi-fi amplifier, allowing listener to hear music without hearing aid or headphones. (About $80 for 20" x 13" x 6"; about $125 for 27" x 20" x 6", Yeaple)

## MULTIUSE DEVICES FOR THE DEAF

BUZZER:   Place under pillow and attach to any signaling device. (About $25, Vibralite)

VIBRATOR:   Mounts on head/baseboard of bed and shakes bed when activated by any signaling device. (About $32, Vibralite, Applied Communications)

### To signal by sound

MULTIPURPOSE SYSTEM:   Magnetic pick-up coil attaches to phone, doorbell, etc. (About $100 for basic unit, accessories available, Applied Communications)

### To signal by light

SONIC ALERT:   Control unit with memory plugs into lamp and creates various rhythmic patterns of light. (About $350, Sonic Alert)

### To signal by light or vibrator

NUVOX (BABY) SENTINEL:   Portable power outlet with built-in microphone to which you attach your own lamp or vibrator. (About $175 without lamp or vibrator, Hal-Hen)

### To signal by sound, light, or vibrator

PORTABLE ALARM ALERT SYSTEM:   Pillow vibrator, microphone, doorbell pickup, all used with battery-operated control unit; order each separately or as kit, complete with light signal that uses house current; picks up any sounds, including alarm clock, burglar alarms, phone, baby, etc. (About $425 for complete kit; about $180 each for control unit or light signal; other accessories also available; Hal-Hen)

## PHONE AMPLIFIERS

(See also For No-Hands Phoning and For Hearing Loss on pages 123 and 124 of Phoning without Fuss.)

DELUXE NUVOX PORTABLE: Battery-operated, place on phone receiver with or without a hearing aid to amplify conversation; carry in pocket or purse; battery and case included. (About $30, Hal-Hen)

FONE-A-LERT: Battery-operated loudspeaker with 40′ of wire; suction cup attaches to side of phone with speaker in another room or outside house; creates sound when phone rings or may be used as doorbell signal; battery included. (About $28, Hal-Hen)

## ALARM SYSTEMS

### Burglar alarm system

DELTA ALERT ULTRASONIC SYSTEM: Plug into any wall outlet, then attach light or alarm to it; ultrasonic sound waves will radiate 300 sq. ft. area to activate light or alarm when intruder enters; adjustable timing control. (About $130, H. G. Grantham)

### Fire or gas leak detector

EARLY WARNING FIRE DETECTOR: Detector plugs into an outlet, receiver into another, with lamp plugged into receiver; when smoke or gas is present, light turns on. (About $230 for total unit, H. G. Grantham)

### Wake-up alarms

BED VIBRATORS:

GE *Vibrating Alarm Timer:* Heavy-duty bed vibrator, premounted on board with four holes for attaching to bedframe or springs and for plugging into timer. (About $100, Hal-Hen)

*Auto Digital Vibrating Alarm Clock Kit:* Digital clock, heavy-duty bed vibrator premounted on board with four holes; switch at front of clock turns on alarm and any other equipment plugged into clock. (About $120, Hal-Hen)

PILLOW VIBRATOR:

*Electro Alarm Clock Kit:* Lighted clock with pillow vibrator attached;

doorbell attachment also available. (About $110 for clock and vibrator; about $50 for doorbell accessory, Hal-Hen)

LIGHT-AND-VIBRATORS:

*Edison Digitimer Clock:* Digital clock into which lamp or bed vibrator can be plugged. (About $60, H. G. Grantham)

*GE Clock Radio:* Clock can be preset to play music only or music and alarm, with or without lamp or bed vibrator; lamp and vibrator not included but may be plugged into back of unit. (About $80, H. G. Grantham)

*Lamp Flasher Button:* Insert between socket and light bulb to make a regular lamp flash up to 85 times per minute. (About $3, hardware or electrical supply stores)

LIGHT-AND-BUZZER ALARM CLOCKS:

*Standard Moonbeam Flashing:* Alarm light flashes from clock; buzzer alarm goes off 10 minutes later; clock glows in dark. (About $30, Hal-Hen)

*Digital Moonbeam Flashing:* Similar to above but with lighted digital numbers; can be set for flashing light only or for light and buzzer. (About $60, Hal-Hen)

# MISCELLANEOUS

*For information on sign language and interpreters*

Write Registry of Interpreters for the Deaf, Inc., P.O. Box 1339, Washington, D.C. 20013.

*For tax information*

Call the Internal Revenue Service on a toll-free TTY number: (800) 428–4732 all over the United States, except for Indiana: (800) 382–4059.

*For information on the law as it pertains to the deaf*

Write National Center for Law and the Deaf, Gallaudet College, 7th St. and Florida Ave., N.E., Washington, D.C. 20002.

*Auto insurance for the deaf*

Contact Ms. Marilyn Rest, Marsh and McLennan/Chicago, 222 S. Riverside Plaza, Chicago, Ill. 60606. Phone: (312) 648–6173. TTY: (312) 648–6158.

*National Theatre of the Deaf*

(See page 153.)

# SOURCES OF
# ADDITIONAL INFORMATION AND HELP

## *Organizations*

American Speech and Hearing Association, 9030 Old Georgetown Rd., Washington, D.C. 20014.

Canine Companions for Independence, P.O. Box 446, Santa Rosa, Cal. 95402, (707) 528–0830.

Hearing Dogs, American Humane Association, 5351 S. Roslyn St., Englewood, Colo. 80110.

Helen Keller National Center, 111 Middle Neck Rd., Sands Point, N.Y. 11050, (516) 944–8900 (Voice or TTY). A rehabilitation center.

National Association of the Deaf, 814 Thayer Ave., Silver Spring, Md. 20910, (301) 587–1788. Rehab and TTY Information, magazine: *The Deaf American.*

National Center for Law and the Deaf, Gallaudet College, 7th St. and Florida Ave., Washington, D.C. 20002.

National Crisis Center, University of Virginia. TTY no.: (800) 446–9876. For Virginia: (800) 522–3723. For emergency help.

National Theatre of the Deaf, 305 Great Neck Rd., Waterford, Conn. 06385, (203) 443–5378. TTY no.: (203) 443–7406.

Registry of Interpreters for the Deaf, Inc., P.O. Box 1339, Washington, D.C. 20013. Sign and interpreter information.

Telecommunications for the Deaf (TTYs), National Association of the Deaf, 814 Thayer Ave., Silver Spring, Md. 20910, (301) 587–1788.

## *Books*

For a complete, 27-page bibliography, write for *Catalogue of Publications,* National Association of the Deaf, 814 Thayer Ave., Silver Spring, Md. 20910.

You can also write to the National Easter Seal Society for their complete, up-to-date bibliography, *Speech, Language, and Hearing Rehabilitation: An Annotated Checklist of Recent Books and Pamphlets* (2023 West Ogden Avenue, Chicago, Ill. 60612).

# 13

# For Diabetics and
# Those with Impaired Vision

The walrus in Lewis Carroll's *Alice in Wonderland* talked about "ships and shoes and sealing-wax and cabbages and kings." These are about the only items *not* found in The American Foundation for the Blind's catalog entitled *Products for People with Vision Problems*. The catalog contains more than 400 excellent low-cost aids, including special insulin syringes and needle guides, canes, clocks, watches and timers, household products, magnifiers, cards and games, reading, writing, recording, Brailling, and calculating equipment (even talking calculators), medical products, audible balls, sewing equipment, tools, and instruments.

## FOR DIABETICS

"C-BETTER" SYRINGE MAGNIFIER: Small, plastic, snap-on magnifying device for syringe; 2X magnification; snap-on wires can be adjusted for proper fit; user must be able to read typewriter print and viewing must be done through center of magnifier to prevent distortion; one size fits all. (About $7, American Foundation for the Blind)

## EXCITING AIDS FOR GENERAL VISION PROBLEMS

There is more hope today than ever before for people previously classified as "blind." Approximately 75 percent of all so-called blind people have some vision, and there are brand-new aids to promote functional sight. In addition to devices such as closed-circuit television reading devices, there are new forms of high-powered lenses as well as combinations of telescopic lenses (used for distance vision) and microscopic lenses (used for near vision). For further information, write American Optometric Association, 7000 Chippewa St., St. Louis, Mo. 63119 (or call [314] 382-5770).

Other low-vision aids—items marked L-V—are found in this book under How to Do a Lot Less in the Kitchen, Fatigue-Free Gardening, and Arts, Crafts, and the Workshop.

### Detecting light

LIGHT PROBE: Called by American Foundation for the Blind "a significant improvement over past light probes"; has a variety of audible pitches to distinguish reflectivity of surfaces; probe detects presence of print and light, so usable for typing and switchboard work, or detecting on-off position of light. (About $50, San Francisco Lighthouse for the Blind Store)

### Telling time

THE TALKING CLOCK: A 4½" x 2⅜" x ⅞" digital clock with voice-synthesizing system that tells time audibly; press a button and clock speaks up to tell you the time; will also tell time automatically every few minutes or half hour—or wake you up, then remind you 5 minutes later, "It's now 6:05 P.M. Please hurry." (About $90, Sharp Electronics Corp.)

### Reading machines

Reading machines convert inkprint characters into images blind people can recognize. For further information on these devices, write to the Library of Congress, Washington, D.C. 20542, and request *Reference Bibliography 77–2*, "Reading Machines for the Blind."

OPTACON: Allows you to read print by converting the visual image to a vibrating tactile image that can be felt with finger; training courses available. (About $4,000, Telesensory Systems)

*Optacon Accessories* (all from Telesensory Systems):
Calculator Lens Module (About $175)
Cathode Ray Tube Lens Module (About $350)
Magnifier Lens Module (About $175)
Typewriter Lens Module (About $1,100)

STEREOTONER: Converts images of printed and typewritten characters into tone patterns recognizable to a trained user. (About $1,350, Mauch Laboratories)

KURZWEIL READING MACHINE: Converts print to spoken words; any printed material may be placed face down on the surface of a scanner that transmits images to a small computer contained in the machine; the computer recognizes letters, groups them into words, and reproduces the pronunciation of each word electronically. (About $20,000, Kurzweil Computer Products)

Check Kurzweil for latest price on this (it might go down) and on:

KURZWEIL TALKING TERMINAL: Same as above, but attachable to any computer terminal. (About $3,700, Kurzweil)

DIGIVOX: Stores typed words in computer memory, then reads them aloud, letter by letter, allowing for corrections by blind typist. (About $2,500, PMI)

## Closed-circuit television reading devices

These devices are designed to magnify printed material electronically. Their major components are a mounted camera, a self-contained light source, a lens capable of magnifying print to various sizes or one fixed to individual specifications, and a monitor (TV screen).

ELECTRONIC VISUAL AID: Has 17" fixed or adjustable monitor. Apollo Lasers, 2124, Model 2B (vertical camera), $1,695 or $1,770; 4124, Model 4A (horizontal camera), $1,640 or $1,715; 610 (2-camera split-screen combination), $2,500.

LVA 500: Equipped with self-supporting scanning table, 14" monitor, and horizontal camera. (Pelco Sales, Inc., $1,595)

OPTISCOPE ELECTRO CC5000: Has 17" monitor and typewriter capability. (Stimulation Learning Aids, Ltd., $995)

PORTAREADER: Has 12" monitor and typewriter capability. (Apollo Lasers, 5100, $1,100)

SCHMIDT READER: Portable unit with 19" monitor. (Edutrainer, Inc., $1,095)

STANDARD READ/WRITE SYSTEM: Has 19" monitor. (Visualtek, RS-6, $1,795)

VISUALTEK'S COMMUTER: Has 9" monitor. (Visualtek, $995)

VISUALTEK'S MICROVIEWER: Allows visually handicapped persons to view microfiche and microcards through enlarged images. (Visualtek, $695)

VISUALTEK'S MINIVIEWER: Has 12" monitor. (Visualtek, $1,250)

NATIONAL INSTITUTE OF REHABILITATION ENGINEERING: Will design closed-circuit television systems based on the evaluation of an individual's visual loss or a recommendation from his or her eye doctor.

## Accessories for closed-circuit television reading devices

ELECTRONIC LINE MARKER OR ELECTRONIC WINDOW:　Allows user to view one line at a time. (Apollo Lasers, $75; Visualtek, $55)

HEIGHT EXTENDER FOR MINIVIEWER:　Visualtek, $40

MICROFICHE ATTACHMENT:　Apollo Lasers, Model 2B, $250

MONITOR STAND:　Provides for tilt and height position adjustments of monitor. (Apollo Lasers, $110; Visualtek, $85)

MOVABLE TABLE FOR MINIVIEWER OR COMMUTER:　Visualtek, $95

SCAN ADAPTER:　For across-the-room viewing. (Apollo Lasers, $30)

TYPEWRITER ACCESSORY:　Allows reader to view his or her own typing. (Apollo Lasers, Model 2B, $55; Visualtek, $75)

For further information on closed-circuit television reading devices, request *Reference Bibliography 77–1*, "Closed-Circuit Television Reading Devices for the Visually Handicapped," from the Library of Congress, Washington, D.C. 20542.

# BRAILLE PAPER AND WRITING EQUIPMENT

## Braille eraser

AMERICAN PRINTING HOUSE FOR THE BLIND:　1–0027 (wood), $0.12; 1–0028 (teflon plastic), $0.85.

HOWE PRESS:　wood for stylus, $0.25; wood for brailler, $0.30; aluminum with Teflon plastic, $1.15.

## Braille paper

BROWN MAGAZINE PAPER:　Available in three ½-pound packages; each pound has 45–55 sheets, depending on size; several sizes are available. American Printing House for the Blind, 1–0423 (11″ x 11″), $1.50 per package.

PAPER FOR INTERPOINT SLATE:　American Printing House for the Blind, 1–0413, $1.50 per package.

PLASTIC BRAILLE PAPER FOR UPWARD WRITING BRAILLE SLATE:　Solar Products Company, $8.50 per ream.

PUNCHED BRAILLE PAPER:　For use as filler for 3-ring notebooks. American Printing House for the Blind, 1–0448, (11″ x 11″), $1.50 per package; other sizes are available.

TRANSCRIBING PAPER:　Other weights and sizes are available. American Foundation for the Blind, WS 398 (8½″ x 11″, heavy), $6.95 per ream; American Printing House for the Blind, 1–0453 (8½″ x 11″), $5.00 per ream; Howe Press (8½″ x 11″, heavy), $5.10 per ream.

## Braille slates

A stylus is included with each slate.

DESK SLATE:   Mounted on a solid board to provide a flat writing surface; 4 lines.

> *American Printing House for the Blind:* 1–0002 (41 cell), $9.30; 1–0003 (37 cell), $9.00; 1–0006 (27 cell), $8.65.

> *Howe Press:* 140 (40 cell), $11.50; (27 cell, jumbo dot), $13.50.

POCKET SLATE:   Other types are available. American Foundation for the Blind, WS315 (19 cell, 6 lines), $10.05; American Printing House for the Blind, 1–0009 (28 cell, 4 lines), $5.10; Howe Press, 1 (27 cell, 4 lines), $4.85.

E-Z READ SLATE:   Braille can be read without removing paper from slate; several sizes are available. (Howe Press; 27 cell, 4 lines, $5.00)

INTERPOINT SLATE:   For writing Braille on both sides of paper. American Printing House for the Blind, 1–0007 (23 cell, 4 lines), $5.75; 1–0011 (19 cell, 4 lines), $5.40.

UPWARD WRITING BRAILLE SLATE:   Characters are written in exactly the same manner in which they are read. (Solar Products Company, $4.80)

## Braille stylus

AMERICAN FOUNDATION FOR THE BLIND:   BS39, $0.45.

AMERICAN PRINTING HOUSE FOR THE BLIND:   1–0020 (large); 1–0022 (small), $0.15.

HOWE PRESS:   Standard, $0.25; pencil with Teflon eraser, $1.50; jumbo pencil, $2.50.

## Braille writers

PERKINS BRAILLER:

> *American Printing House for the Blind:* 1–0085, $150. Standard. Available on quota accounts only.

> *Howe Press:* Standard, $150; unimanual for persons with use of only one hand, $165; electric, $300; jumbo dot, $195.

EXTENSION KEYS FOR PERKINS BRAILLER:   Permits Braillist to operate all 6 keys simultaneously with one hand. American Printing House for the Blind, 1–0086, $12.25, available on quota accounts only; Howe Press, $13.

LAVENDER BRAILLEWRITER:   American Printing House for the Blind, 1–0083, $115.

## Braillon thermoform paper

AMERICAN PRINTING HOUSE FOR THE BLIND:   1–0469, $24 per ream. Available on quota account only.

AMERICAN THERMOFORM CORP.: Measures 11″ x 11″ standard, $28.50 per ream. Other sizes are available.

For further information about Braille paper and writing equipment, request *Reference Circular 77–1,* "Braille Instruction for Writing Equipment," from the Library of Congress, Washington, D.C. 20542.

## Script guides

CHECK STENCIL: Template for filling in necessary information on checks. A blank check must be submitted since each stencil is made to order. (American Foundation for the Blind, MC171, $3.95)

CHECKWRITER: Device consisting of hinged aluminum plates with guides corresponding to the blank lines on a check. Has Braille cells that enable user to imprint information needed to identify check when it is returned from the bank. Braille cells are also used to keep records on check stub. Available to other banks at cost, as well as to any legally blind person with no account at Chemical Bank. (Chemical Bank, price not given)

ELASTIC LINE WRITING GUIDE: Designed for partially sighted individuals; guide opens to hold 8½″ x 11″ paper. (Fred Sammons, Inc., BK4073, $13.95)

ENVELOPE ADDRESSING GUIDE: Plastic mask with apertures corresponding with "to" and "from" areas of a standard envelope. (American Foundation for the Blind, WS412, $0.75)

FREUND LONGHAND WRITING KIT: For teaching script writing to blind persons, particularly signature writing. (American Printing House for the Blind, 1–0333, $17.50)

GROOVED FIBRE WRITING CARDS: For use by blind persons when writing with a pencil. (Howe Press, $0.40)

MARKS SCRIPT GUIDE: Composed of a clipboard, for standard 8½″ x 11″ paper, and a carriage made of metal rods with ¾″ slot. (American Foundation for the Blind, WS295, $14.95)

PERFECT LETTER TRAINER: Block and script letters, raised and indented with Palmer Method Type sheet; 20-gauge plastic. (Touch Aids, Inc., $3.50)

PLASTIC SCRIPT GUIDE: Raised lines serve as guides for script writing. (American Foundation for the Blind, WS296, $2.25)

RAISED LINE CHECKBOOK: For personal checking accounts; blank checks must be submitted; can also be used for instruction. (American Printing House for the Blind, 1–0350, $1.95)

RAISED LINE DRAWING KIT: Lines can be felt on the top surface of the paper as they are being drawn. (American Foundation for the Blind, WS293, $12.95.) Similar kit also sold by Howe Press.

SCRIPT LETTER BOARD: Capital and lowercase letters are incised into rigid board for blind students practicing movements for script writing. (American Printing House for the Blind, 1–0406, $3.75)

SCRIPT LETTER SHEETS: Capital and lowercase letters are embossed on white Braille paper for blind persons learning script writing. (American Printing House for the Blind, 1–0404, $0.04 per sheet.) Similar letters also sold by Howe Press.

SENSORY QUILL: Raised line drawing and writing instrument for the visually handicapped. For use in teaching blind persons handwriting skills, map designing, and geometric representations. Uses standard Braille on paper. (Mechstat, Inc.; individual unit, $295)

SIGNATURE GUIDE: Metal or plastic mask with aperture corresponding to standard signature area; has rubber backing to reduce slippage. (American Foundation for the Blind, WS294, $1.05; WS267, $0.35; American Printing House for the Blind, 1–0353, $2.00; Howe Press, $0.50)

DOUBLE SIGNATURE GUIDE: Can be placed on back of check for endorsement or opened out for writing on any signature line; washable plastic. (Sped Publications, $0.50)

SIGNATURE STAMP: Individual must send 3 samples of signature. (Dialogue with the Blind, $8.25)

SIGNATURE TRAINING BOARD: Pressed wood, deeply engraved with student's name in 3 sizes; includes check signing guide. (Touch Aids, $14.00)

# IDENTIFICATION AND LABELING MATERIALS

## Markers

For use by blind persons in locating public facilities such as elevators, restrooms, public telephones.

BRAILLE PLAQUE/PLATE: Braille or raised letters or numbers are embossed on stainless steel with epoxy or permanent adhesive backing. (Truxes Adhesives and Chemicals Company, $1.50–$2.50)

BRAILLETTERS: Heavy plastic Braille characters can be mounted into a clear plastic track (chase) to form any desired legend. (Scott Plastics Company, request price quotation)

INTERNATIONAL SYMBOL OF ACCESS PLAQUE/MARKER: Indoor or outdoor markers are available in plastic, aluminum, or steel; pressure-sensitive decals are also available. (Ability Building Center, Inc., request price quotation)

## Labelers

BRAILLE TAPEWRITER (LABELER): Includes 45 Braille characters; uses ½″ vinyl, magnetic labeling tape; can also be used as a standard alphabet labeler. (American Foundation for the Blind, BTW400, $33.95; with alphabet dial, $39.90)

FISHBURNE ALPHABET EMBOSSER: Enables blind persons who do not know Braille to write symbols using the Fishburne alphabet; lesson cassettes and training alphabet also available. (Adult Blind Engineering, $15.00)

LARGE PRINT LABELER: Embosses letters and numerals ½″ high on ¾″-wide tape; the raised symbols can be felt. (American Foundation for the Blind, LPW33, $39)

VOXCOM: Audio (voice) labeling device for use by visually handicapped persons when Braille or other conventional labeling methods are not appropriate. Consists of a standard cassette recorder with a special, removable card recorder adapter. Short messages, labels, or notes are either recorded on cards prestriped with magnetic recording tape or on folders, credit cards, or other similar materials bearing the self-adhesive tape. (Voxcom Division of Tapecon, Inc., $105)

## Labels

BRAILLABELS: Plastic sheets with pressure-sensitive backing; can be embossed using a Braille writer or a Braille slate. (American Thermoform Corporation, $8.25 per package of 12 sheets)

CASSETTE LABELS: Each label is 1¼″ x ½″ and includes the number in Braille and in large print; will produce labels on custom order. (Creative Services for the Blind, 101, $0.02 each for 100 or more of one number)

DYMO TAPE: American Foundation for the Blind, BC1 (vinyl), $3.95 per unit; BC7 (aluminum), $2.50 per roll.

LABELON TAPE: Pressure-sensitive; can be Brailled with slate. (American Foundation for the Blind, MC150, $1.20; MC151, for 2 Braille lines, $3.95)

MAGNETIC LABELING TAPE: American Foundation for the Blind, BC324, $3.50; BC35 (for large print labeler), $9.75 per roll.

PLASTIC STICK LABELS: Pressure-sensitive adhesive Braille labels that can be permanently attached to records or other objects. (American Foundation for the Blind, MC145, $1.50)

## Currency identification

PRINT IDENTIFIER AND LIGHT SOURCES: Unique tone patterns help user to identify values of paper currency; battery operated. (American Foundation for the Blind, MC900, $100)

## CALCULATORS FOR
## VISUALLY HANDICAPPED PERSONS

Calculators are designed for voice and/or Braille output rather than, or in addition to, visual displays. All have basic functions of addition, subtraction, multiplication, and division; most have additional functions as well.

AFB BRAILLE CALCULATOR: Five-function electronic calculator supplied with an 8-digit visual display and standard Braille output. (American Foundation for the Blind, MAS200, $375)

SPEECH AND TALKING CALCULATOR: Six-function electronic calculator with independent memory, automatic constant, and sign change; 24-word vocabulary. Telesensory Systems, Inc., $395; American Foundation for the Blind, $395.

## LIGHTING AIDS, LAMPS, AND ENLARGERS

### Glare shields

Glare shields enhance the utilization of residual vision by minimizing the interference of extraneous light. These aids may be obtained from local stationery stores or made from opaque materials such as dark poster board.

C.F. PRENTICE TYPOSCOPE: Black fiber 7" x 2¼" with 4½" x ⅛" slot. (Superior Optical Company, $4.00/10)

SPORT VISOR: Fits over regular glasses; 3" depth. (Gambit Corp., $1.25)

VISORETTE: Fits over regular glasses; 1¾" depth. (Gambit Corp., $1.25)

### High-intensity lamps

High-intensity lighting provides glare-free illumination and sometimes reduces reading difficulties for partially sighted readers.

INCANDESCENT AND FLUORESCENT LAMPS: Tensor Corp., $15.

PENDANT-LAMP. Designed to fit around the neck to give close-up, non-glare illumination. (Aqua Survey and Instrument Company, $21.95)

### Night vision aid

For retinitis pigmentosa patients and others who are unable to see adequately in dim light; hand-held. (National Institute of Rehabilitation Engineering, $995)

### Optical enlarger

(*Magnifiers* are listed on page 115.)

OPTISCOPE ILLUMINATED ENLARGER SYSTEM: Stimulation Learning Aids, Ltd., Model C, $399.

## POSTAL AIDS

Part 138 of the Postal Manual, based on Public Law 91–375, provides for free mailing of certain matter by blind or physically handicapped persons. Other persons and organizations are also granted free mailing privileges for sending matter for use by blind and physically handicapped persons under specific conditions.

### Mailing containers

BRAILLE CONTAINER: Made of fiberboard; for books. (American Printing House for the Blind, 1–0241, $4.15; 1–0242, $4.25; 1–0243, $4.25)

BRAILLE MAILING TUBE: Cardboard; primarily for Braille letters. (American Printing House for the Blind, 1–0410, $2.60)

PLASTIC CASSETTE CONTAINER: American Printing House for the Blind, 1–0262 (for 4 cassettes), $1.00; 1–0263 (for 6 cassettes), $1.10.

CARDBOARD CASSETTE CONTAINER: Dialogue with the Blind, C–1 (for 1 cassette), $0.20; R–5 (for 2 cassettes), $0.25; R–7 (for 6 cassettes), $0.35.

OPEN-REEL TAPE CONTAINER: Fiberboard; 7″ diameter only; sizes to hold from 1 to 6 reels of tape. (American Printing House for the Blind, $2.00–$2.25)

CARDBOARD OPEN-REEL TAPE CONTAINER: Dialogue with the Blind, R–3 (for 3 reels), $0.25; R–5 (for 5 reels), $0.25; R–7 (for 7 reels), $0.35.

TALKING BOOK (RECORDED DISK) CONTAINER: Plastic or fiberboard; request order numbers and descriptions; 10 different sizes available. (American Printing House for the Blind, $1.50–$2.25)

### Mailing labels

"FREE MATTER FOR THE BLIND AND PHYSICALLY HANDICAPPED" LABELS OR STICKERS: American Printing House for the Blind, 1–0411, $1.20 per 100; Dialogue with the Blind, $1.00 per 100, $5.00 per 500.

### Rubber stamp

NAME AND ADDRESS STAMP: Dialogue with the Blind, 1 line, $1.45; 2 lines, $2.25; 3 lines, $3.00; 4 lines, $3.75.

"FREE MATTER FOR THE BLIND AND PHYSICALLY HANDICAPPED" STAMP: American Foundation for the Blind, MC410, $1.10; Dialogue with the Blind, $1.50.

## RADIO AND TV RECEIVERS

### Special receivers

Special receivers may be required to listen to radio reading services for the blind and physically handicapped. For a listing of these radio services, request *Reference Circular 76–1*, "Directory of Local Radio Services for the Blind and Physically Handicapped," from the Library of Congress, Washington, D.C. 20542.

### TV-Radio receiver

TV-Radio receivers pick up the sound portion of television broadcasts as well as AM and FM radio broadcasts. Several brands of these receivers may be purchased from local radio and television dealers.

G.E. PORTABLE TV-RADIO:   American Foundation for the Blind, MC611, $43.95 net.

## SOURCES OF ADDITIONAL INFORMATION

### General information

*American Council of the Blind*, 1211 Connecticut Ave., N.W., Washington, D.C. 20036. Runs a problem-solving service called the National Blindness Information Center. Call (800) 424–8666, toll-free.

*American Foundation for the Blind*, 15 West 16th Street, New York, N.Y. 10011, (212) 620–2000. Has regional consultants in Washington, D.C., Chicago, Atlanta, Denver, and San Francisco, as well as in New York—to answer questions and direct you to receive help. They also have a library, publish a number of books and periodicals as well as "talking books," disseminate information about government programs, and press for new legislation from their Washington office. Send for their catalog, *Products for People with Vision Problems*, which offers over 400 excellent aids at low cost.

*American Printing House for the Blind*, 1839 Frankfort Ave., Louisville, Ky. 40206. Publishes and distributes talking books and books in Braille, in large type, as well as embossed.

*New Eyes for the Needy*, 549 Millburn Ave., Short Hills, N.J. 07078. Collects and distributes used eyeglasses, providing them free to the needy.

*National Association for Visually Handicapped, Inc.,* 305 East 24th St., New York, N.Y. 10010, (212) 889–3141, and 3201 Balboa St., San Francisco, Cal. 94121. Acts as an advocacy group and information center for partially seeing persons.

*National Federation for the Blind,* 1800 Johnson St., Baltimore, Md. 21230, (301) 659–9314. Affiliates in most states. Advocacy group that gives referral information.

## Guide dog associations

*Guiding Eyes for the Blind,* Yorktown Heights, N.Y. 10599.

*The Seeing Eye, Inc.,* Morristown, N.J. 07960.

# 14

# *How a Pet Can Help*

Dogs are wonderful because they don't care whether the world thinks you're adorable or dreary, darling or dismal, gregarious or grumpy, wise or crazy. Whatever you are, your dog will love you anyway.

Dogs are being used more and more in nursing homes and mental hospitals, not only to provide companionship, but as a form of psychotherapy. The results are extraordinary. Bedridden people get out of bed for the first time in years to walk dogs; once isolated and self-pitying people start to communicate; one brain-damaged man spoke for the first time in 26 years when a dog was brought to him. A study made by a pair of psychobiologists showed that out of 50 hospitalized psychiatric patients, 47 improved with "pet-facilitated psychotherapy."

For you at home, happily free of the above problems but having to cope with daily chores, a pet can help in the following areas.

## VISION PROBLEMS

We all know about "seeing eye" dogs and how magnificently they serve their masters. Anyone in the United States or Canada who would like to qualify for ownership of a dog may write to The Seeing Eye, Inc., Morristown, N.J. 07960 for an application form. If you qualify, you will be asked to report within approximately 1 to 4 months for training. Don't forget, cost of and upkeep for guide dogs are tax deductible. Also, travel expenses to the place of training are paid by The Seeing Eye.

## HEARING DIFFICULTIES

Several organizations train dogs to perform services such as alerting people to sounds (a baby crying, the phone or doorbell ringing, etc.). Two of these organizations are Hearing Dog Program, American Humane Association, 5351 S. Roslyn St., Englewood, Colo. 80110, which provides dogs free of charge to hearing-impaired people who live alone or with others who are hearing-impaired, and Canine Companions for Independence, P.O. Box 446, Santa Rosa, Cal. 95402, (707) 528–0830. Again, all guide-dog-related expenses are tax deductible.

## FOR ALL KINDS OF DISABILITIES

### Dogs

Canine Companions for Independence (address above) and Handi-Dog, Inc. (5332 E. Rosewood Ave., Tucson, Ariz. 85711, [602] 326–3412) are nonprofit organizations that train dogs to perform a variety of services. These dogs help to free people from dependence on paid attendants.

### Monkeys

Work has been done with a capuchin (tiny "organ grinder's") monkey at Tufts New England Medical Center in Boston. The monkey has been taught to do a number of things in response to signals from a laser beam pointer (fetch objects, turn keys, turn lights on and off, etc.). Because of the remarkable dexterity and intelligence of monkeys, they can do things like turn pages, play records, and the like—impossible tasks for other animals. However, monkeys are temperamental and apt to be destructive if left alone; their clever little hands can literally tear your furniture and draperies apart in a short time. They are also, initially, very timid and therefore hard to train until you have won their confidence.

### Horses

There are more than 200 therapeutic riding centers in the United States and Canada that generate spectacular improvements in the health and outlook of disabled people. Not only are there obvious benefits in terms of mobility and sense of achievement, but the motion of a horse stimulates muscles never otherwise used. Particularly if you are in a wheelchair, your doctor may prescribe riding as important therapy.

Each center, under the aegis of North American Riding for the Handicapped Association, Inc., has instructors who are proficient in physical therapy and orthopedics as well as horsemanship. The horses are carefully selected for their docile temperaments and trained under rigid safety standards, and each new rider is accompanied by 2 people who walk beside him or her and a leader who guides the horse.

If you are interested in the program, contact the regional director of the North American Riding for the Handicapped Association nearest you for information:

Mrs. Marjorie V. Kittredge, Brookview Rd., Boxford, Mass. 01921

Ms. Virginia H. Martin, Borderland Farm, Warwick, N.J. 10990

Mr. Alexander Mackay-Smith, Chronicle of the Horse, Middleburg, Va. 22117

Mrs. Lida L. McCowan, Cheff Ctr., RR 1, Box 171, Augusta, Mich. 49012

Mr. John A. Davies, St. James Farm, 3S 261 Winfield Rd., Warrenville, Ill. 60555

Mrs. G. Kenneth Baum, Walnut Ridge Farms, Rte. 1, Stilwell, Kans. 66085

Mrs. Gerald Joswick, 3443 Alta Vista Dr., Fallbrook, Cal. 92028

Mrs. Dorothy Ames, 68 Almond Dr., Thornhill, Ont., Canada L3T 1L2

## PET ACCESSORIES

3-IN-1 GROOMING BRUSH:   Self-cleaning, plastic-bristled brush for pets on one side, surface to remove pet hair and lint from clothing and upholstery on other side. (About $5, American Foundation for the Blind)

FLEXPORTS:   Mount in a door or on a wall; consists of circular opening filled with interlocking plastic triangles through which dog or cat pushes to let itself in or out; sizes of openings from 6″ x 8″ to 16″ x 24″; made of wood or lightweight or heavy aluminum, with or without additional covers for security, weatherproofing, and pet control. (From about $35 to $190; contact Turen, Inc., Box 270, Lebanon, N.H. 03766, [603] 448–2990)

AUTOMATIC DRINKING FOUNTAIN:   Attaches to any standard exterior plumbing outlet; refills as your pet drinks; includes 2′ hose, couplings, bracket pipe, valve, and bowl. (About $25, contact Turen, Inc., at above address)

PET FOOD-AND-WATER BOWL HOLDER:   With handle to make it possible to lift feeding bowls to and from floor without bending; directions given for making one yourself in the booklet *Aids and Adaptations*, available for $2.50 from The Arthritis Society, 920 Yonge St., Suite 420, Toronto, Ontario M4W 3J7, Canada.

DOG RUNS: Various models of overhead pulley runs or ground-based retractable wire units. (Prestige Products)

# PART FOUR

# COMMUNICATION

# 15

# *Reading*

The best way to travel into another world without leaving your chair is to read. And it needn't always be done with your eyes. A wide variety of books and magazines recorded on tape and record and cassette players are all available free from your local library though Talking Books. Inquire at the library or write Talking Books, National Library Service for the Blind and Physically Handicapped, Library of Congress, Washington, D.C. 20542.

If you cannot read large print or are unable to hold a book and turn pages, you are probably eligible for Talking Books. To qualify, you need a statement describing your condition from a doctor, nurse, optometrist, ophthalmologist, staff member of a health institution, or a librarian.

In addition, a company called Choice Magazine Listening, 14 Maple Street, Port Washington, N.Y. 11050 offers subscriptions to a series of 8 records, each of which includes 8 hours of articles, fiction, and poetry culled from such magazines as *The New Yorker, Harper's, Fortune, Esquire,* and *Sports Illustrated.*

## BOOK HOLDERS

*For table, lapboard, or bed tray*

WIRE: Shaped like the triangular part of a coat hanger; has legs; folds flat. (About $4, Cleo, Help Yourself Aids, MED)

WOODEN: Two flat pieces that lock together. (About $4, MED)

ADJUSTABLE: For sitting or lying flat; angle and height adjustable; has straps to hold down pages; folds flat. (About $25, American Foundation for the Blind)

DELUXE BOOK HOLDER: Adjusts from flat to nearly vertical; bridges the gap between a mechanical page turner and a frame bookholder because spring-loaded levers keep pages level as thickness of book changes; black metal. (About $27, Cleo)

NEWSPAPER AND MAGAZINE STAND: Overhangs table edge or sits on table top for 52- or 68-degree angle; has rods and clips to hold pages down. (About $40, Help Yourself Aids)

*For reading from a supine position*

READING TABLE: Stands by itself on the bed; has rods to hold pages; aluminum, adjustable support frame that adjusts in height from 8″ to 17″; tilts 180 degrees. (About $35, Abbey)

NELSON BOOK HOLDER: Can be mounted on side of bed or chair or overhead; adjusts in angle; has plastic fingers to hold pages; can also be used as easel or mirror holder or for reading while sitting. (Suction cup mount about $30; C-clamp mount about $48; overhead mount about $85; Nelson)

*Free-standing book holders*

SHAFER READING STAND: Floor pedestal holder; adjusts in angle for reading from a sitting, standing, or supine position. (About $90, American Foundation for the Blind)

STANDING NEWSPAPER HOLDER: Floor stand adjustable 36″–60″ from floor; has clips to hold any size newspaper. (About $85, Maddak)

## PAGE-TURNERS

*Manual*

Use the eraser of a pencil, buy a rubber finger cover, or dip a finger into Tacky Fingers (available at stationery stores or from Evans Specialty Co.) to help turn pages.

BATON: For hand use, as mouthstick, or attachable to arm or leg with strap; pattern for making strap-holder and mouthpiece is included; adjusts in length 11″–16″. (About $13, Help Yourself Aids)

EXTRA-LONG BATON:   Length adjusts to 20″; includes pattern for head-support strap. (About $12, Easy Reading Aids—see Sources of Equipment and Information for address)

PAGE AID:   An 11″ curved aid; has spring clip to fit hand; plastic with foam rubber tip. (About $9, Maddak)

MOUTH-HELD PAGE AID:   Lightweight plastic with serrated rubber tip. (About $12, Maddak)

## Mechanical

LAKELAND AUTOMATIC PAGE TURNER:   Electrical turning action controlled by foot, elbow, head, or by flexing a muscle. (About $350, Maddak)

AUTOMATIC PAGE TURNER:   Has 2 microswitches to turn pages forward or backward with a light touch; operates on D batteries. (About $420, J. A. Preston)

TOUCH TURNER:   Operable by finger, eyebrow, or breath; powered by D batteries; turns pages in either direction. (From about $300 to $400, depending on type of switch required, G. E. Miller)

## MAGNIFIERS/LIGHTS

CHEST REST MAGNIFIER:   Has cord to hang around neck, leaves hands free. (About $16, Fashion-Able)

TENSOR BOOK LIGHT:   High-intensity light that clips to table or book; multiposition. (About $13, Tensor Book Light)

## Hand-held

RECTANGULAR MAGNIFIER:   With handle and 2″ x 4″ lens. (About $16, Help Yourself Aids)

ROUND MAGNIFIER:   In 2″, 3″, 4″, or 5″ lens size with handles. (About $7 for the 3″ size, Swift Instruments)

FLASHLIGHT:   Operates on C or D batteries. (About $16, Bausch and Lomb)

PURSE-SIZE FLASHLIGHT:   Battery included. (About $7, Fashion-Able)

ILLUMINATED MAGNIFIER:   Has 2″ x 4″ rectangular lens with 110-volt bulb. (About $12, Bausch and Lomb)

## Larger magnifiers

MAGNIFYING BAR:   Can be placed directly over several lines of print. (About $5, Swift Instruments)

PAGE MAGNIFIER: Sheet that fits over an entire page of print. (From about $6 to $10, several sizes, Edmund Scientific Co.)

### Stand magnifiers

ADJUSTABLE: Adjusts front to back and side to side; can be removed for hand use or folded flat. (About $17, Help Yourself Aids)

ILLUMINATED STAND MAGNIFIER: Has 2″ x 4″ lens; 7-watt lamp. (About $20, Bausch and Lomb, Fashion-Able)

LARGE-FIELD ILLUMINATED: Battery or electrically operated. (About $22, Edmund Scientific Co.)

## PRISM GLASSES

BEDSPECS: Ophthalmologist-approved, gives adjustable angle vision for reading, watching TV while supine; usable over glasses. (About $33, G. E. Miller, Help Yourself Aids)

RECLINING VIEWER: Has 5″ mirror that can go over glasses; reflects image at about 45-degree angle. (About $7, Help Yourself Aids)

# 16

# *Writing and Typing*

Instead of writing everything down, consider occasionally taping your material. It's much more fun for a friend to hear your voice than to get an ordinary letter. And things you don't want to forget can be preserved just as easily by "jotting them down" orally.

But if you prefer to write most of the time, there are lots of ways to increase grasp on your pen or pencil.

## TO INCREASE WRITING GRASP

Try wrapping your pen or pencil with tape or twisting rubber bands around it. Or insert it into a practice golf ball, foam curler, foam tubing, a piece of child's modeling clay, or:

MAKE-IT-YOURSELF HOLDER: Shape a 1½"-wide strip of elastic around your thumb, then pin the elastic. Now pin elastic around a pen or pencil, then around your forefinger. Sew down each loop where it is pinned, remove pins, and you have a permanent writing aid.

Or try using the world's fattest pen:

EASY-GRIP BALL-POINT PEN: With twice the diameter of a normal pen (1½"). (About $4, Fashion-Able)

## WRITING AIDS

WOODEN PENCIL-HOLDER:   Block of wood shaped to fit palm of hand; has hole for inserting pen or pencil at proper angle. (About $4, The Independence Factory)

BUILT-UP PENCIL AND CRAYON HOLDER:   Set of 6 wooden holders; 1" diameter; holds pens, pencils, crayons, or brushes. (About $30 for 6 with a rack to hold, Help Yourself Aids)

WRAP-AROUND PENCIL HOLDER:   Thumb loop, leather index finger cuff, and long Velcro strap to be wrapped around fingers, palm, or wrist. (About $7, Cleo)

SARONG PENCIL HOLDER:   Pouch for holding pencil; strap to wrap around fingers. (About $6, Cleo)

SIDE-WINDER PENCIL HOLDER:   Holder shaped to fit palm of hand; may be slid into utensil holder to position pencil for writing; specify right or left hand. Order utensil holder separately. (About $7, Cleo)

   *Utensil Holder:* Elastic band with Velcro pouch for inserting fork, spoon, or Side-Winder Pencil Holder above. (About $7, Cleo)

WRITING FRAME:   Bow-shaped wire tripod to support fingers on right or left hand; finger motion is needed to grasp pencil. (About $7, Abbey, Cleo)

THE TABLE WRITER:   A series of swiveling rods designed to compensate for hand, wrist, forearm, elbow, or shoulder problems; comes with instruction manual. (About $100, G. E. Miller)

MOUTHSTICK WITH QUICK CHANGE:   Mouthstick with toolholders to allow switching from pen to paintbrush to page-turner; holders have spring to hold them on mouthstick rod; may be tightened into place with an Allen key (device similar to a screwdriver). (About $140, MED)

MAGNETIC WRIST HOLD-DOWN:   Holds down wrist with magnetic force; writing panel and strap included. (About $35, Help Yourself Aids, G. E. Miller)


## PAPER HOLDERS

The best paperholder is a clipboard. Next best is a printer's lead die (1" square and very heavy—ask your local printer for one). Or order:

ONE-HANDED WRITING BOARD:   Has clamps at top and rubber feet to prevent it from "walking"; specify right- or left-handed use. (About $8, Help Yourself Aids)

CLIP CADDIE:   Clipboard of simulated leather with compartment below it to hold supplies; black or red. (About $11, Fashion-Able)

# GENERAL WRITING TIPS

## To reduce writing friction
Sprinkle talcum powder across the paper.

## To draw a straight line
Use a yardstick instead of a ruler and place weights on either end. (Idea courtesy of Julius Lombardi.)

# TYPING

IBM sells reconditioned typewriters to disabled people at reduced prices. Olivetti, Royal, and Smith-Corona all make machines with large type. IBM and Olivetti also sell Orator elements for conversion of their machines to large type.

## Typewriters
OLYMPIA ELECTRIC TYPEWRITER FOR THE HANDICAPPED: With continuous-feed paper attachment, paper cutter, cushioned armrest, elevated keyboard. (Cost of standard typewriter plus about $175, Olympia)

IBM SELECTRIC: Has revolving printing head rather than a carriage; oversized carriage knobs, cartridge ribbon. (Check your local typewriter store or write to IBM, Armonk, N.Y. 10504 for possibly obtaining a reconditioned machine.)

DVORAK ONE-HANDED TYPEWRITER: Portable electric; specially arranged right- or left-handed keyboards; one-hand cartridge ribbon. (About $390, Typewriting Institute for the Handicapped)

## One-handed typing
See machine above, which comes with its own type-with-one-hand manual. Or if you wish to learn to type with one hand on a machine with a conventional keyboard, order:

TYPE WITH ONE HAND: Manual to teach either a right- or left-handed person the "home position" for using one hand to type. (About $6, Cleo)

JULIUS LOMBARDI SUGGESTS: If you have only one or two good fingers, use only capital letters when typing. (Idea reprinted with permission.)

## Typing accessories
FOR BETTER LEVERAGE ON CONTROLS: Attach spring clips to on-off switch of electric typewriter, also to paper bail, etc.[1]

FOR EASY CORRECTION: Typewriter ribbon that is half correction tape (top), half regular ribbon; adaptable for nearly all typewriters. (About $5, check your local stationers or write Eaton Allen Corporation, 67 Kent Avenue, Brooklyn, N.Y. 11211)

## Keyboards

KING KEYBOARD: An enlarged (25" x 13") keyboard to be used with an IBM Selectric typewriter that has a Solenoid Bank; keyboard slanted 12° and light-pressure keys are 1⅓" in diameter; has adjustable time control to avoid printing accidentally touched keys. (About $950; Solenoid Bank about $950). Contact TASH, Inc., c/o Sunnybrook Medical Center, 2075 Bayview Ave., Toronto, Ontario M4N 3M5, Canada.

TARGET MASTER KEYBOARD: Puff-pointer to be used with an IBM Selectric typewriter that has a Solenoid Bank. Aim pointer at key and puff lightly into mouthpiece to activate one of the solenoids mounted above the typewriter keys that then prints desired character. Entire keyboard may be activated with head movement of less than ⅔" from center position. (About $1,100; Solenoid Bank about $950) Contact TASH, Inc. (See address above.)

## Typing sticks

Try typing using the eraser end of a pencil to punch the keys. Or order:

MED TYPING STICK: Has adjustable plastic handle to fit the flail hand; may be used with or without Keyboard Shield (see below). (About $6, MED)

## To control unwanted finger movements

KEYBOARD SHIELD: Fits Smith-Corona electric portable typewriters; recesses keys slightly to allow hand to rest on typewriter; specify whether for regular or cartridge-ribbon machine. (About $48, MED)

SPASTIC HOOD: For Coronamatic 2200 (Smith-Corona), also certain Royal machines. (About $35, Royal, Smith-Corona)

## To insert paper

BIRD BEAK: A mouth-held device; grasp paper, using tongue to open gripper, insert paper in machine, return aid to elevated rack. (Bird Beak and rack about $40, Cleo)

## For arm support while typing

Rest your arms on a wedge-shaped pillow placed in your lap, or even on a hard-cover loose-leaf notebook—also wedge-shaped, but less comfortable.

Other ideas: Attach a wedge of wood to the front of your typewriting table; attach a low shelf to the back of a narrow table to hold your typewriter while you rest your arms on the higher narrow table in front of you; if shoulder rotation control is a problem, try putting boards inside your wheelchair arms for *you* to rest on—inside of boards should be made of Formica to reduce friction.[2]

# 17

# *Phoning without Fuss*

If you love to talk on the telephone, but find certain aspects of it inconvenient; if you sometimes wish you could combine talking with other activities, free of all the fuss with cords, receivers, etc., take heart—your problems are virtually solved. Not only are there gadgets currently on the market to simplify phone use, but there are also a number of exciting devices offered by the phone company to compensate for speech and hearing loss, to allow for hands-free phoning, even to enable you to go to school by phone.

## PHONE EQUIPMENT NOW ON THE MARKET

### For easier dialing

GIANT PUSHBUTTONS:   Convert touchtone phone buttons to larger size with wider spaces between each. (About $11, Help Yourself Aids)

LARGE-PRINT DIAL:   Converts standard dial to larger print. (About $2, American Foundation for the Blind)

(See also Single Button Phone, Speakerphone, and Touch-a-matic under Products offered by AT&T.)

## To hold receiver

QUAD-QUIP HOLDER: Bendable Plastisol-paddle handle to slip over hand; Velcro closure for attachment to receiver. (About $6, Help Yourself Aids)

FREE-STANDING HOLDER: Lampholder, one end clamps to desk, the other holds receiver in air; ask local phone company for lever switch for phone. (About $30 for 22″, 25″, or 29″ holder, MED; about $40, for 45″ holder, Cleo)

## For no-hands phoning (almost)

DROP-IN AMPLIFIER: Battery-operated speaker system for voice amplification. (About $30, Help Yourself Aids) Compare with Speakerphone under Products offered by AT&T below.

MURAPHONE: Remote-control device for pressing button, talking outdoors or inside up to 400 feet from phone. (About $115, Sun-Tel Co., 3308 Midway Dr., San Diego, Cal. 92110, or call [714] 223–5566) (Compare with next item and with Speakerphone.)

## For easier dialing and no-hands phoning

LITE TOUCH: Pushbuttons operable with lightest touch possible or with mouthstick; on-off push bar; calibrated volume mechanism, so usable from anywhere in room; mute bar for private conversation. (About $120; about $3 for adapter for use of unit as desk phone; about $9 for wall-mount unit, MED)

## To send large print or Braille telegrams

Contact your local Western Union office—$2 for 25 words plus $1 for each additional 25 words.

## Miscellaneous

THE DO-EVERYTHING BEDSIDE PHONE: Touchtone; lighted digital clock, alarm; one-button emergency dialer; silencer; no pick-up or dialing for 12 numbers stored in memory; automatic redialing for 10 minutes if line is busy (warranted by General Telephone and Electric). (About $230, Joan Cook)

SILENCER: Fingertip control; "off" switch for blessed silence while caller hears your phone "ring" normally (no busy signal). (About $13, The Vermont Country Store)

# PRODUCTS OFFERED BY AT&T (BELL TELEPHONE) AT MONTHLY RATES

(Call your local phone company office for details.)

### For speech loss

ELECTRONIC ARTIFICIAL LARYNX: Substitutes electronically controlled vibrations for vocal cord vibrations by placing instrument against throat. (Offered for about $85 rather than by monthly rate)

### For hearing loss

BONE CONDUCTION RECEIVER: Transmits vibrations to inner ear, bypassing part of normal hearing process.

CODE-COM: Flashing light signals convert sound into sight.

WATCHCASE RECEIVER: Enables a third person to help a deaf person converse by phone.

TONE-RINGER: Special frequency ringer that most people with impaired hearing can hear.

EIGHT-INCH GONG: Very loud bell in bass frequency range.

SIGNALMAN: Enables any lamp to flash on and off when phone rings.

For blind and deaf person: small electric fan blows gentle air toward person when phone rings.

### For simpler operation

SPEAKERPHONE: Push button to operate loudspeaker.

TOUCH-A-MATIC: Sixteen- or 32-number memory phones.

ONE-NUMBER DIALER: Automatic dialing of preprogrammed numbers. (See also page 183 for Silent Companion and Microalert.)

TOUCH TONE: Buttons for easier dialing.

TRIM-LINE: Illuminated dial; button to hang up—both mounted on receiver.

SINGLE-BUTTON: On-off switch for people who can't hold receiver; use with holder (through phone company or see Free-Standing Holder under To Hold Receiver).

HEADSET: Plugs into jack-equipped phone.

### To go to school by phone

TELE-CLASS SERVICE: Allows home- or hospital-bound students to participate in classes by using headsets and local phone network.

# PART FIVE

# TRAVEL, HOBBIES, SPORTS, AND GAMES

# *Travel*

If you've been considering a holiday alone, think about a tour instead. Okay, maybe you lack the herd instinct and loathe early-morning heartiness and good cheer. But consider the advantages.

You're bound to find a friend (or 30 or 40) if you join a tour for people with similar physical problems. Travel specialists who arrange tours are also bound to anticipate—and unsnarl in advance—many of the travel snags you'd be likely to encounter if you were traveling alone.

A few agencies that specialize in arranging tours for the disabled are:

Ability Tours, Inc., 729 Delaware Ave., S.W., Washington, D.C. 20024

All State Tours, 26 Court St., Brooklyn, N.Y. 11242, (212) 858–5404

C. I. Mobility Services, 250 Janaf Plaza, Norfolk, Va. 23502

Centers for the Handicapped, 10501 New Hampshire Ave., Silver Spring, Md. 20903

Evergreen Travel, 19424 44th Ave., West, Lynnwood, Wash. 98036, (206) 776–1184

Flying Wheels Tours, 143 West Bridge St., Owatoona, Minn. 55060, (507) 451–5005

Getz International Travel Agency, 640 Sacramento St., San Francisco, Cal. 94119

Handicabs of the Pacific, Inc., Wheelchair Taxi & Tour Co., P.O. Box 22428, Honolulu, Haw. 96822

Handi-Tours Calladine & Baldry, Ltd., Yorkdale Plaza, Suite 153, Toronto, Ontario, M6A 219, Canada

Pinetree Tours, Inc., 3600 Wilshire Blvd., Suite 1516, Los Angeles, Cal. 90010

Rambling Tours, P.O. Box 1304, Hallandale, Fla. 33009, (305) 921-2161

Tours for the hearing-impaired to Europe, California, and Hawaii include an interpreter: Mary Lou Hudson, 74 Shirlwin Dr., Granite City, Ill. 62040

Travel Teck, Inc., 33 Dartmouth St., Malden, Mass. 02148

Further names and addresses of tour agencies are available by writing to SATH (Society for Advancement of Travel for the Handicapped), 26 Court St., Brooklyn, N.Y. 11242. SATH also provides information on transportation and lodging.

Another organization set up to provide information on travel for the disabled is Mobility International, 2 Colombo St., London SWI 8DP, England. This is a clearinghouse for information on travel in Europe, North America, and the Middle East. Mobility provides specific contacts for exchange visits. (Further travel information center addresses are given at the end of this chapter.)

## FLYING

If you decide to travel alone and wish to make all the arrangements on your own, be sure to write for a booklet that, for about $1.25, reports the policies of 22 airlines toward handicapped people. Write National Easter Seal Society, 2023 West Ogden Ave., Chicago, Ill. 60612 and ask for *Airline Transportation for the Handicapped.*

For information on 69 accessibility features in more than 200 airports throughout the world, plus tips on arranging for special on-flight facilities, write for the free booklet *Access Travel: A Guide of Accessibility of Airport Terminals;* available from Consumer Information Center, Dept. 619–F, Pueblo, Colo. 81009.

### The pitfalls of flying

A recent *New York Times* article warned that while Airline A may be happy to take you to Chicago, Airline B may refuse to fly you and your wheelchair on from Chicago to San Francisco. This is why it is so important to research the policies of each airline through the Easter Seal booklet *well in advance*. You'll want to ensure that *each* airline on *each* leg of your journey is briefed well ahead of time about your needs, limitations, any special diet, and so on.

If you are carrying a powered wheelchair and respirator, for example, there may be an immediate snag. Airlines (with the exception of United, which *will* carry wet-cell batteries) will carry neither your oxygen tank nor your wet-cell batteries for powered chairs.* American Airlines and TWA (and perhaps others) will sell you a tank of oxygen for about $40 per flight. Maddeningly, if forced to change planes, you are also forced to pay an additional $40 for the second plane. Also, your doctor has to advise the airline on flow rate and the duration of oxygen use at least 24 hours before a domestic flight and 48 hours before an overseas flight. (See Converters for Respirators, page 130.)

While most airlines are big hearted enough to let you board if you are in a *collapsible* wheelchair, they will then immediately snatch it away from you and store it somewhere in the baggage area; so if you need it to get to the lavatory, you're out of luck—unless you can use a walker or have someone help you to the bathroom. The airlines advise you to avoid liquids for 5–6 hours and refrain from eating too much before a flight.

### For anyone who is refused by a commercial airline

There *are* recourses. One is to call the Civil Aeronautics Board, (202) 382–7735, and ask for help. Failing this, call the Air Medic at the toll-free number (800) 423–2667 and ask *their* help. They can make arrangements —either through the commercial airlines or through other facilities—for anybody to be transported anywhere, whether he or she needs a registered nurse, stretcher care, ground transportation at both ends, or whatever. They charge commercial airline fares, plus the cost of the nurse and special service.

The other flying ambulance service, called North American Air Ambulance, also at a toll-free number, (800) 257–8180, handles emergency situations, as it is a group of flying intensive care units. It carries all the necessary medical equipment and a certified flight nurse. It will also carry a member of a patient's family without extra charge. Anyone rejected by a commercial airline will be accepted, provided the patient's doctor says he or she is fit to travel. North American Air Ambulance will fly anywhere in this hemisphere at a flat rate (call for the latest information), plus

---

* Some people have found that airlines will accept their motorized wheelchairs with sealed-gel batteries. For information on where to obtain such batteries to meet aircraft regulations, contact Flying Wheels Tours (address on page 127).

the cost per hour of whatever medical technicians and extra special equipment might be required during the flight. The agency says the cost of travel often works out to less than the cost of staying home and paying for full-time registered nurses!

### Preflight checklist
- Call the airline well in advance to book your reservations and explain your limitations, any special equipment you will be carrying or might need, plus any special assistance you need at arrival and departure. At this time, prebook a wheelchair for boarding and debarking and/ or for use in the terminal if you are not carrying your own.
- Check whether you're allowed to travel alone.
- Check what medical clearance, if any, the airline requires.
- Reserve a seat with more legroom or near a toilet or both!
- If you have a guide dog, make sure there are no restrictions on it at your destination. Great Britain and Ireland, for example, require that any animal be quarantined for 6 months at the owner's expense.
- Be sure that you arrive at the airport at least one full hour before boarding time so that you can be preboarded.

### For free escort service within terminals
Contact the airline or Skycap Service Company free escort. (You can identify your escort by an armband bearing the symbol of access.)

### Converters for respirators
United Airlines has manufactured 3 free converters for respirator usage by their own or other airlines. Contact United Airlines' San Francisco Airport Engineering Facilities. Phone: (415) 876–4747.

## GUIDEBOOKS

At the end of this chapter you will find a list of addresses of organizations that provide guidebooks and lists of accessible facilities in Australia, Austria, Belgium, Canada, Denmark, England, Finland, France, Germany, Holland, Italy, Norway, Portugal, Scotland, Spain, Sweden, and Switzerland.

For the United States, there is a guidebook to end all guidebooks on accessibility. Called *The Wheelchair Traveler*, it is available for about $4.95 from its author, Douglass R. Annand, Ball Hill Road, Milford, N.H. 03055. Published in 1978 with yearly updates, it rates 3,200 hotels, motels, restaurants, and tourist attractions on access, transportation within each area as well as to and from airport, prices, and other services. It also gives tips on more efficient travel by wheelchair, and lists addresses of where to write for guidebooks to 97 cities in the United States and Canada, plus Aruba, Curaçao, Mexico, Newfoundland, Nova Scotia, and Puerto Rico.

Rehabilitation WORLD, 20 west 40th Street, New York, N.Y. 10018 publishes an *International Directory of Access Guides.* The directory lists addresses for obtaining guidebooks for cities in Australia, Canada, England, France, Germany, Ireland, Norway, Scotland, Spain, Sweden, Switzerland, the United States, and Wales.

## WHAT NOT TO FORGET
## TO TAKE (OR DO) BEFORE ANY TRIP

*Extra supply of special medication(s)* in case they are unavailable at your destination.

*Sturdy leather man's belt or coat hanger* to twist around the rear extensions of your chair to narrow it for access to narrow doorways. Or, if you prefer, a *wheelchair narrower* (see page 212).

*Portable ramp,* such as the model listed on page 216, for getting over curbs or short steps. Or a half-step, like the one described on page 14, to help you up steps, into buses, etc. The half-step consists of a cane with a balsa wood block attached to the bottom of it.

*If traveling by car, join an auto club* and get the national number to call in case of a road emergency.

*Rubber-tipped cane or reacher* for pulling in papers from the back of your car's trunk.

*Foam-padded wooden box* to rest your elbow on while driving.[1]

*Sturdy dowel,* 50" long, to keep in the trunk to hold its lid open, especially on windy days.[2]

*Length of wood,* 24½" long and 1" wide, notched at the end, to unlock the passenger door from the driver's seat.[3]

*Small suitcase with your medication and your most needed clothes and equipment* to carry with you at all times in case your luggage is lost.

*Extra clothes hangers.* In hotels and motels, they are generally affixed to the rod, making it difficult to reach clothes while in your wheelchair.

*Folding luggage carrier on wheels:* Weighs only 4 lbs., yet capable of holding up to 150 lbs. Open, it stands 34" high with a 9½"-wide base. Made of heavy-duty steel, it folds to a compact 9" x 3½", has a 5½"-wide handle. (About $25, Help Yourself Aids)

*Tensor Book Light:* small, high-intensity lamp that can be clipped to a table or book; multiposition. (About $13, Tensor Book Light)

## AUTOMOBILE TRANSPORTATION

AVIS RENT-A-CAR: Rents cars with hand controls. Three weeks advance notice required. Call toll-free (800) 331–1212 for domestic reservations and (800) 331–2112 for international reservations.

HERTZ RENT-A-CAR: Rents cars with hand controls in large cities in the United States. Ten days advance notice required. Call toll-free (800) 654–3131.

NATIONAL CAR RENTAL: Rents cars with hand controls. Three days advance notice required. Call toll-free (800) 328–4567.

## SPECIAL ACCOMMODATIONS

### *Major hotel/motel chains with accessible rooms*

Call ahead to be sure of ramped entrances, room, bathroom, and restaurant accessibility for the hotel/motel in the cities or towns where you plan to stay. Accessibility can vary from place to place. But in general, the following are accessible chains.

Best Western: United States and world
Holiday Inns: United States and world
Howard Johnson's: United States
Hyatt: South, Southeast, and West Coast
Quality Inns: United States
Ramada Inns: United States and world

### *House-swap: It's rent-free!*

If you'd like to live in a house in the place of your dreams for a few weeks, a house owned by someone with a similar disability so that it would contain the same basic equipment as your own home, write King of the Road Vacation Exchange, 117 Poland Rd., Danville, Ill. 61832. This organization was founded to promote house swaps among disabled people.

# SOURCES OF ADDITIONAL INFORMATION

## *Travel information centers in the United States*

American Foundation for the Blind, 15 West 16th St., New York, N.Y. 10011. Issues identification cards to visually handicapped persons who must travel with a sighted companion. The card enables a traveler to receive reduced fares on trains and buses. Full details about this program are contained in the brochure *Travel Concessions for Blind Persons*, available free on request from the American Foundation for the Blind.

IAMAT, International Association for Medical Assistance to Travelers, 350 Fifth Avenue, New York, N.Y. 10001. Arranges medical care in foreign countries from English-speaking physicians at a set fee. Members receive an identification card and a directory of IAMAT physicians.

Moss Rehabilitation Hospital, Travel Information Service, 12th Street and Tabor Road, Philadelphia, Pa. 19141. Maintains a free information center for handicapped persons on where to go, how to get there, and where to stay in the United States and abroad. No travel arrangements are made.

National Easter Seal Society for Crippled Children and Adults, Information Library, 2023 West Ogden Avenue, Chicago, Ill. 60612. Supplies handicapped travelers with listings of current access guides to hotels, theaters, shopping, and tourist attractions.

SATH, Society for the Advancement of Travel for the Handicapped, 26 Court Street, Brooklyn, N.Y. 11242. Serves as a clearinghouse for information about accessible domestic and international transportation and lodging facilities. Publishes *Bibliography of Materials Concerning Travel for the Handicapped*.

## *Bus transportation*

Continental Trailways and Greyhound Lines have plans under which a disabled traveler and a companion may travel for the price of a single ticket. They also have new barrier-free terminals.

CONTINENTAL TRAILWAYS: For information contact local terminals or Continental Trailways, 1500 Jackson Street, Dallas, Tex. 75201, (214) 655–7895.

GREYHOUND LINES: Greyhound has Silver Eagle coaches that accept motorized wheelchairs. For information contact local terminals or Customer Relations, Greyhound Lines, Greyhound Tower, Phoenix, Ariz. 85077, (602) 248–5276.

*Train transportation*

The booklet *Access Amtrak: A Guide to Amtrak Services for Elderly and Handicapped Travelers* is free on request from Amtrak, National Railroad Passenger Corp., 400 N. Capitol Street, N.W., Washington, D.C. 20001.

*Ship transportation*

Prospective travelers should contact passenger lines about any requirements for medical certification and physical accessibility of shipboard facilities.

*Travel information in foreign countries*

Physically handicapped travelers may wish to contact the following organizations for disabled persons to obtain guidebooks and lists of accessible facilities in the countries they plan to visit.

INTERNATIONAL:

Mobility International, Central Bureau of Educational Visits and Exchanges, 43 Dorset Street, London, W1H 3FN, England. Provides information about travel for physically handicapped persons. Branches situated throughout Europe promote exchanges among handicapped persons from various countries.

AUSTRALIA:

Australian College of Occupational Therapists, 295 Queen Street, Melbourne, Victoria 3000

Council of Social Services of Western Australia, 76 Murray Street, Perth, W.A. 6000

Australian Council for Rehabilitation of the Disabled, Cleveland House, Bedford and Buckingham Sts., Surry Hills, Sydney, New South Wales 2010

AUSTRIA:

Oesterreichische Arbeitsgemeinschaft für Rehabilitation, Barichgasse 28, 1030 Vienna

BELGIUM:

Croix-Rouge de Belgique, Chausse de Vieugat 98, 1050 Brussels

CANADA:

Canadian Paraplegia Association, 520 Sutherland Drive, Toronto, Ontario M4G 3V9

DENMARK:

Society and Home for the Disabled, Borgervaenget 7, DK–2100 Copenhagen

ENGLAND:

Royal Association for Disability and Rehabilitation, 25 Mortimer Street, London, W1N 8AB

FINLAND:

ISRD Finnish Committee, Insurance Rehabilitation Agency, Kalenvankatu 20, 00100 Helsinki 10

FRANCE:

Association pour le Transport et le Tourism des Malades et des Handicapes (ATTMH), 19–21 rue Bertrand-de-Goth, 33000 Bordeaux

GERMANY:

Deutsche Vereinigung für die Rehabilitation Behinderter e.V., BRD 69– Heidelberg-Schiervach 1, Zechnerweg 1A

HOLLAND:

Nederlandse Vereniging voor Revalidatie, Eisenhowerlaan 142, The Hague 2078

ITALY:

Italian Society for Rehabilitation of the Disabled, Clinica Orthopedica e Traumatologica Delia, Universita di Roma, Rome

NORWAY:

Norsk Revmatiker Forbund, Professor Dahlsgate–32, Box 5668, Oslo 2 (Oslo has a barrier-free underground rail system.)

PORTUGAL:

Santa Case de Misericordia de Lisboa, Centro de Medicina de Reabilitação, Alcoitão, Estoril

SCOTLAND:

Edinburgh Committee for the Coordination of Services for the Disabled, Simon Square Center, Howden Street, Edinburgh 8

SPAIN:

Fraternidad Católica de Enfermos, Domicilio Social, Montserrat 30, Madrid 8

SWEDEN:

Handikappinstituet, Fack, S–161, 03, Bromma 3

SWITZERLAND:

Association Suisse des Invalides, Froburgstrasse 4, 4600 Olten 1

# 19

## Control of Your Car

On one of those days when not much is going on—or too much is going on and you'd like to get away from it—it's nice to just get into your car and go. For some people, it's not that simple. There may be a need for adaptations to make your car drivable (if you're a veteran, the Veterans Administration can help with this and also with purchasing a car), or you may need special driving lessons, which takes money. However, your local or state division of Vocational Rehabilitation may be able to help you by providing or paying for driving lessons if you are in a wheelchair. Or write Driver Safety and Training Program, c/o Physical Therapy Dept., Institute of Rehabilitation Medicine, New York University Medical Center, 400 East 34th St., New York, N.Y. 10016.

### Before starting driver training

Check with your doctor. It may not be the right time. (A stroke, for example, sometimes leaves perceptual problems requiring therapy before the patient can drive again.)

You should also call the Motor Vehicle Bureau for their *Driver's Manual*, which gives test requirements and sample questions. Also ask whether there are any special automobile adaptations or other special requirements necessary in relation to your disability.

*To help you until you are able to drive again*

Local organizations in many communities with volunteers will gladly drive you on trips to the doctor, hospital, or even shopping. Two of these are the Junior League and FISH (Friends for Immediate and Sympathetic Help). Sometimes special cab services are also available. Check your Yellow Pages or write HandiCabs at HandiRamps, Inc., 1414 Armour Blvd., Mundelein, Ill. 60060.

## A FEW GENERAL TIPS

*To haul a wheelchair into a car*

There are a couple of ways to handle this challenge. One is to get a portable ramp (see page 216 of Ramps, Lifts, and Elevators) to help roll your chair up to the car door, then follow the instructions on page 141 of this chapter on how to lift your chair into the back of a car without a device.

The other way is to obtain a device, and some good ones are listed on pages 141 and 142. The only problem you will then face is having to pay for it. But if your need for a car is job-related, you may be able to get it free from Vocational Rehabilitation. If it is *not* job-related, try some of the other organizations suggested in Chapter 28. Don't forget, too, that some states give tax breaks to disabled drivers.

*Some tips from a disabled driver[1]*

TO LOCK AND UNLOCK PASSENGER DOOR FROM DRIVER'S SEAT: Keep a length of wood 24½″ long and 1″ wide, notched at the end.

TO HOLD LID OF TRUNK OPEN ON WINDY DAYS: Keep another stick 50″ long and 1¼″ wide in the trunk.

TO PULL THINGS FORWARD THAT HAVE SLID TO BACK OF TRUNK: Keep a cane in the trunk and use the curved end to pull things forward.

TO SUPPORT YOUR RIGHT ARM WHILE DRIVING: Pad a small wooden box by gluing sheet foam to it. Place it on the seat at your right side.

## GENERAL CAR ACCESSORIES

*To get in and out of the car*

See The Wilson Transporter and Transfer Boards on page 179. See also Travel Lift on page 218.

ASSIST HANDLES: For frame above door or front corner post of car; aid in moving from wheelchair to car; 5″ long (about $12), 15″ (about $15), 15″ with web loop for forearm (about $17), web loop alone (about $12). (All from Nelson)

### Car door openers

PUSHBUTTON: Curved end; enlarged handle. (About $4, The Independence Factory)

UNIVERSAL: To open all types of inside and outside door handles. (About $16, Maddak)

### Car seats and cushions

(See also Cushions for Your Back on page 60.)

AIR SEAT: Inflatable, bucket-type cushion to conform to body contours when inflated. (About $25, Colson)

AIR-COOLED SEAT: Plugs into dashboard cigarette lighter to circulate cool air through seat and back of seat. (About $32, Hammacher Schlemmer)

SWIVEL: Ask your car dealer about having existing seat adapted to swivel 90 degrees.

### Miscellaneous

WIDE-ANGLE MIRROR: Measures 13″ x 3″; snaps over present rearview mirror. (About $9, Starcrest of California)

GAS CAP OPENER: Enlarged wooden handle; curved end to fit around gas cap. (About $5, The Independence Factory)

## ROAD EMERGENCIES

AEROSOL CAN TO INFLATE AND REPAIR FLAT TIRES: A 7″ nozzle attaches can to tire valve. (About $9, hardware stores, Brookstone, Hanover House)

### Help signals

FLAG: Says "Need Aid—Handicapped." (About $10, Gresham Driving Aids)

SIGNAL: Stick out window; says "Help." (About $12, Henniker's)

INTERNATIONAL DISTRESS SIGNAL: Red reflecting warning triangle. (About $10, Clymer's of Bucks County)

## HAND CONTROLS FOR CAR OR VAN

There are a number of manufacturers of hand controls (see page 142 for a list). Before you order anything, be sure the unit you are considering fits your model of car and that you have the power equipment required to make the unit adaptable. (In other words, read the fine print before ordering.)

Drive-Master makes an inexpensive set of well-tested controls that fit all American and most foreign cars, can be self-installed, and do not require power brakes and power steering (although these make driving much more comfortable). This company will recommend the controls you need (many of them about $30) when you write or call explaining your problems. (See Appendix for address.)

## Brake extenders and control

AUTO-MATE:   Adjustable, self-installable; push-pull handle attaches to brake; fingertip operation. (About $80, Nelson)

PARKING BRAKE:   Similar to above, but for parking, not regular brake; attachable without drilling holes. (About $21, Nelson)

BRAKE/ACCELERATOR COMBINATION CONTROL:   Lever; self-installable to right or left side of steering column; shipped assembled. (About $140, Drive-Master)

## Signals and shift

RIGHT-HAND DIRECTIONAL SIGNAL LEVER:   Clamps to existing directional signal lever to convert it to right-hand use. (About $18, Nelson)

LEFT-HAND SHIFT LEVER:   Clamps to existing shift lever to convert it to left-hand use. (About $20, Nelson)

## Ignition starting aids

(See also information on key aids and holder on page 13.)

IGNITION LEVER:   For all cars with ignition on steering column; pull lever to start car. (About $13, Nelson)

## Steering wheel extensions

KNOB:   Fits all wheels. (About $16, Nelson)

QUAD BAR:   Fits across wheel; push-button-removable. (About $23) Specify any attachments (all from Nelson):

Knob (about $12)
Yoke for inserting palm (about $18)
Bendable, open-topped yoke (about $18)
Post: 1″ diameter, 3½″ high (about $16)
Ring-type: ⅞″ diameter for hook or other prosthetic device. (about $16)

## Miscellaneous

DIMMER SWITCH:   Fastens to steering column; dims auto headlights; no interference with present dimmer. (About $18, Nelson)

## FOOT CONTROLS

Cameron Enns, who lost the use of his arms, has developed a set of custom-made controls for steering with either leg, provided you have one good leg and foot and sufficient strength in the other foot (or hand) to operate accelerator and brake, and *if* your car, van, or truck has automatic transmission, power steering, and power brakes.

Cameron Enns also manufactures the following foot-operated equipment: brake and accelerator extensions, ignition switch, gear selector controls, knee-operated door openers, turn signals, and more. All of the following equipment might also be helpful.

### *Accelerator extenders*

BUILT-UP ACCELERATOR EXTENDER: Adjustable from 1"–6" by cutting easily with hacksaw. (About $18, Nelson)

LEFT-FOOT ACCELERATOR EXTENDER: Attach to floor with self-tapping screws, telescoping crossbar for adjustable mounting, detachable, folding. (About $32, Nelson)

### *Brake extenders*

BUILT-UP: Adjustable like the Built-up Accelerator Extender above. (About $20, Nelson)

### *Converting the Volkswagen Rabbit to foot controls (ideal for the armless driver)*

Die-A-Matic can supply the following equipment: foot-operated steering, radio, warning lights, and windshield wipers operated by foot or knee. Contact Die-A-Matic, Inc., 4004 Fifth Rd. N., Arlington, Va. 22203.

## VEHICLES YOU CAN DRIVE FROM YOUR WHEELCHAIR

CANOPIED VOLT COLT: A powered, moving platform onto which you drive your chair; platform then raises to 5"; adjustable bicycle handlebars that house brake, speed controls, dimmer, and signal switches; four 95-amp batteries, two 24-volt motors; 3 speeds standard in low range (6 mph and 12 mph), high range (12 mph and 24 mph); dynamic over mechanical brakes, plastic windshield, fiberglass canopy. Overall width, 57"; height, 64"; length, 63". Chauffeur-driven model available. (About $2,600 for basic model, FOB Idaho. Contact Trans-Electric Engineering Co., P.O. Box 701, Meridian, Ida. 83642, [208] 888–6954.)

FREEDOM VAN: Have your own van adapted for driving from your chair or order a van from Gresham. Adaptations include large wheel wells and locks to hold your chair; extended steering column with extended hand controls and shift lever; remote panel with extension on toggles; left-hand remote panel including ignition, lights, wipers, windows. (Total about $5,000, Gresham Driving Aids)

*Note:* Vans and accessories similar to the Freedom Van are manufactured by Mobility Systems.

VANS AND MOBILE HOMES MADE ESPECIALLY FOR WHEELCHAIR USERS: Manufactured by The Braun Corp., Mobility Systems, and O. & C. Conversions, Inc.

## WHEELCHAIR LOADING

### *To lift chair into back of car*

ANTHONY'S AUTO WHEELCHAIR LIFT: For standard or intermediate 2-door car; track and extension arm installable with 5 screws behind front seat; wire to car's 12-volt system; choice of easily operated switches. To operate, fold chair and remove right armrest and footrests; push switch to bring lift arm under chair seat, then push switch to lift chair to car opening; push car seat forward; press switch to bring chair into car. VA, Vocational Rehabilitation-approved. (About $1,240, Anthony's Enterprises, Inc., 3293 S. Seymour Rd., Swartz Creek, Mich. 48473, [313] 635–9698)

### *To lift chair into car without a device*

The first step is to hook or strap your chair securely so that it will remain in the folded position. Then either lift the front wheels or roll the chair on a portable ramp (see page 216 of Ramps, Lifts, and Elevators) with wheels locked in backward position, up to the car door threshold. Next, sitting in the right-hand car seat, reach over to the back seat and grasp the wheelchair's footrests with your right hand. With your left hand, grab the chair's vertical bar or armrest and pull the chair in. (Or move over to left car seat, reach behind back of the right seat, and pull the chair in via a strap that has been put around top of extended vertical rods.)

It also helps to put a block of wood into the front seat hinge opening to tilt the front seat forward. If the back floor of the car is not level, either fill in the depression between the threshold and the center hump with a piece of heavy plywood[2] or order:

AUTO FLOOR BOARD: Height-adjustable, plywood and steel "bridge"; place between threshold and back-of-car floor hump. (About $19, Nelson)

*To lift chair onto back bumper of car*

NO-LIFT TILT 'N' TOTE:  Virtually no effort required; roll chair up to rack, which tilts to ground, then automatically tilts up to lock into place. (About $260; with cover, additional $55; Wheelchair Carrier Company)

A similar model that does not tilt up to bumper when not in use costs about $190. (Wheelchair Carrier Company)

PARTIAL-LIFT CARRIER:  Similar to Tilt 'n' Tote but *you* must lift the rack into place rather than this happening automatically. (About $100, Cleo, Nelson)

*Automatic car/van top-loaders*

THE FREEDOM MACHINE:  Raises chair to top of auto, van, pick-up, or mini cars via 12-volt car battery; carrier shell; *no assistance required for loading or unloading.* (About $1,900 for aluminum, about $2,000 for fiberglass; write Wheelchair Carrier Sales Corp., P.O. Box 16202, Phoenix, Ariz. 85011—*do not confuse this company with Wheelchair Carrier Company.*)

## MANUFACTURERS OF
## SPECIAL CONTROLS FOR SEVERE DISABILITIES

*Manufacturers of single-lever, joystick, and light-contact push-button systems*

Lehr Products, Inc., 340 S. Pine St., York, Pa. 17403
Lift Aids of Texas, Inc., 2381 Pecan Ct., Fort Worth, Tex. 76117
Mobility Engineering and Development, Inc., 7131 Hayvenhurst Ave., Van Nuys, Cal. 91406
Target Industries, Inc., 1264 Union St., West Springfield, Va. 01089

*Manufacturers of hand controls*

Brake Center, Inc., 3716 Queens Blvd., Long Island City, N.Y. 11101
Car Controls, Inc., 51–11 43rd Ave., Woodside, N.Y. 11377
Drive-Master Corp., 16 Andrews Dr., West Paterson, N.J. 07424
Gresham Driving Aids, P.O. Box 405, 30800 Wixom, Wixom, Mich. 48096
Hand Driving Equipment, 266 East Park, Elmhurst, Ill. 60126
Kroepke Mfg. Co., City Island 64, New York 10464
Wells-Engberg Co., 2505 Rural St., Rockford, Ill. 61111

*Manufacturers of foot controls*

Cameron Enns Co., 13637 S. Madsen Ave., Kingsburg, Cal. 93631
Die-A-Matic, Inc., 4004 Fifth Rd. N., Arlington, Va. 22203

# 20

# Fatigue-free Gardening

Some days the lark is on the wing, God's in His heaven, all's right with the world, and you love yourself and your garden because all your weeding is done. Other days, your back is killing you, you know you'll never get it all done because it *can't* all be done, and why did you ever take on so much garden anyway?

What makes the difference between these two attitudes? It depends on the kind of garden you have, how comfortable it is to work in it, how bad the weed situation is, and whether you have the right type of tools.

## SOME GENERAL TIPS

*To make your garden more comfortable to work in*

Consider growing plants in tubs, pots, raised boxes, raised beds (edged with masonry or railroad ties and then filled in—perhaps with movable pots), trellises, vertical planters (see page 149), window boxes, hanging baskets, and water gardens.

You should also be able to work from a sitting position when you want to, carry things while sitting, and be able to move from place to place without getting up. (See ideas on page 147.)

### To prevent fatigue or backstrain when standing

Use tools that are long enough for your height, bend from the hips (rather than hunching over), and keep one foot ahead of the other.

### If you are in a wheelchair

You need long-handled tools that are lightweight (see page 147); you need easy ways of irrigating without having to move hoses and sprinklers (see page 149); you need a way of hauling trash, etc., without strain (see page 148). You should also have curved paths rather than paths that turn sharply. The paths should be made of wide flat boards, bricks, concrete, slates set closely together on sand, even hard-packed gravel—any material other than grass or loose gravel.

You can also raise your garden. Have an 8-foot metal or redwood (redwood will not rot) circular window box, pierced for drainage and supported on 8 strong metal legs, placed on wooden or concrete bases in the ground. Make sure the legs are the proper height for you to work from your wheelchair. The circular design will enable you to simply turn your wheelchair slightly to reach other parts of the garden when your chair is positioned in the center of the raised garden.

### For gardeners with impaired vision

Run a guide rope from the house to the garden. This will help you find your way back and forth without assistance from another person. Also run strings between the various types of plants for help in identifying them.

### To weed your beds more easily

It helps to be able to get in among the weeds. Put wide boards or flat stones together at intervals within the beds.

### Eliminate weeding altogether

Cut down on weeds by adding mulches—after the ground has thoroughly warmed up and the spring rains have stopped. Black plastic (which comes in sheets) works best weighted down with stones or bark; poke holes in it for insertion of seeds and plants. Next best is compost, which will leach nutrients into the soil and help keep it moist. Compost, like all mulches except redwood bark, should be spread at least 3″–5″ thick. Hay and straw —even newspapers—are also effective weed stoppers. Redwood bark is also great; you can use it year after year, it will not rot.

The other mulches have drawbacks. Pine bark robs the soil of nitrogen, which you then have to replenish once or twice a season. Peat is good only in sheltered areas; full sunlight dries it out quickly so that a hard crust forms that is difficult for the rain or sprinkler to penetrate. Peanut shells and cacao beans are expensive and tend to dry out quickly and blow away in the wind.

## TOOLS

Your tools must be lightweight but strong enough to withstand years of hard use while never bending or rusting. A wide variety is available.

### *Cultivating, transplanting, and weeding*

TROWEL:   Rust-proof, bend-proof, guaranteed against breakage for 5 years; made of one-piece heavy aluminum; trigger for extra grip; weighs 6¼ oz. (About $8, Nichols Garden Nursery)

TRANSPLANTER:   (like a narrower trowel) Same features as above, lighter, weighing 4½ oz. (About $8, Nichols Garden Nursery)

FORK:   Same features as above, weighs 7¼ oz. (About $8, Nichols Garden Nursery)

STEP-WEEDER:   Nonstoop weed remover, 43"-long; push steel tines into roots, lift weed out by removing foot, push handle forward to eject weed from tines. (About $27, Brookstone)

FIRM GRIP WEED PULLER:   With one hand, squeeze trigger hand grip of this 34" weeder and other end grabs and pulls weed. (About $25, Walter F. Nicke)

WEEDER ROOTER:   Has 15" hardwood handle; at one end a pick with steel teeth, a flat-ended pick at the other end; weighs 1 lb. Can be used for breaking ground, chopping out weeds, digging small holes for bulbs, etc. (About $11, Walter F. Nicke)

LONG-HANDLED TROWEL:   Sheffield steel shank riveted to hardwood handle; overall length, 17"; made in England. (About $10, Walter F. Nicke)

GARD-A-RAKE:   Self-cleaning; pull one side of rake to collect debris, push it to unclog; turn over with double-flared tines down and use it in garden; 15" wide, 54" handle. (About $11, Walter F. Nicke)

### *Flower cutters*

(See also Scissors, page 154.)

FLOWER GATHERER:   Wide-bladed shears, 6" long with serrated jaws; cuts and holds flowers, strips rose thorns. (About $8; extra blades, 2 for $1; Walter F. Nicke) (O-H)

CUT-AND-HOLD FLOWER GATHERER:   Long handled; Sheffield steel blades; overall length 31"; weighs 14 oz.; one-handed bicycle grip; made in England. Great for picking and holding flowers, light pruning, reaching into bottle gardens through a 1" opening. (About $26, Walter F. Nicke) (O-H)

FREEHAND SNIPS: Padded handles designed to leave fingers free for tying, etc., while working in garden or arranging flowers; notched blades of Sheffield steel; made in England. (About $12, Walter F. Nicke)

### Pruners and shearers

COMPOUND LEVERAGE RATCHET PRUNER: Apply pressure with one hand, relax—the ratchet automatically takes new position with more leverage. Requires far less pressure than ordinary pruner. Teflon-coated steel blade; nylon handles; lightweight and measures 7¼"; comes with holster to fit a belt. (About $16, Brookstone) (O-H)

HEAVY-DUTY PRUNER: Lever action for less effort; 22" long; cadmium-plated head (will cut up to 1⅛" diameter branch); 2 hands needed to operate; extra blades available; made in England. (About $25; spare blade costs about $6; Walter F. Nicke)

STAND-UP BORDER SHEAR: Has 8"-long carbon steel blades; Teflon-coated; tubular steel handles; vinyl-contoured hand grips; 32" long; weighs 3½ lbs.; made in England. (About $33, Walter F. Nicke)

SLIMLINE HEDGESHEAR: Notched, 8½" Sheffield steel blades; Teflon-coated; made in England. (About $13, Walter F. Nicke)

### For harvesting

FRUIT PICKER: Cushioned tines attached to wire basket; tines pluck fruit, basket catches it; attaches to any pole. (About $12, Burpee) (O-H)

PICKER POCKET: Nylon bag that fits between thumb and forefinger, then hangs over wrist to hold small fruit, etc.
Small—1¼-qt.; about $7
Large—3-qt.; about $8
Giant—10-qt.; about $11
All from Garden Way. (O-H)

HARVESTING BAG: Heavy-duty, cotton duck bag on metal frame; adjustable shoulder and back straps; holds up to a bushel; opens at bottom to unload without removing bag. (About $22, Burpee) (O-H)

SUSSEX TRUG: Long, oval hardwood basket; handle fits over elbow to carry tools or picked flowers, etc. Small, 19" x 4", about $24; large, 27½" x 5¾", $30. (Brookstone) (O-H)

### Compost

COMPOST MAKER: Powder to sprinkle on a 3"–6" layer of leaves or clippings, then add 2" or so of good soil, water every 10 days, keep repeating; no forking necessary. (About $10 for three 16 oz. bottles, Brookstone)

COMPOST SHREDDER: Shreds small amounts of compost. Toss in garden and kitchen wastes, crank handle to shred pieces of less than ½" in size. Consists of a hopper with 12" x 8" opening on tubular steel legs; steel cutter blade resharpens easily. Whole unit measures 49″ high. (About $100, Brookstone)

## Seeders

SEEDMASTER: Trowel-type scoop to hold seeds; thumb-turned wheel in handle to feed seeds forward for precise planting. (About $7, Nichols Garden Nursery)

ONE-PUSH SEEDER: Small hopper that sits on ground and holds seeds; push plunger to insert seeds at correct depth; 8¾″ high. (About $12, Brookstone) (O-H)

STANDING SEEDER: Has 34″ steel shaft with wheel container for seeds; push wheel along as you walk upright. (About $14, Park's) (O-H)

## Light-weight, long-handled tools

To make a long-handled tool, remove the existing handle and insert a broomstick into the tool socket.

All of the following are stainless steel tools with lightweight aluminum, vinyl-covered angled handles.

WEEDING FORK: Fork 5″ long x 3″ wide; overall length, 56″. (About $25)

GARDEN BED EDGER: Open handle for 2-handed grip; overall length, 39″. (About $30)

SWOE: A 3-edged device to cut weeds below the soil, 5½″ blade; overall length, 56″. (About $22)

DUTCH HOE: Measures 4⅞″; triangular cutout in center; front edge beveled for cutting weeds below the soil. (About $25)

GARDEN RAKE: Rake is 11″ long, tines are 3½″; overall length, 56″. (About $30)

(Set of all 5 of the above tools about $115, from Brookstone)

## Miscellaneous helpful gadgets

KNEE PADS: Soft rubber; leather straps. (About $15, Brookstone)

FLOWER CADDY HANDLE: A 2′ wooden enameled handle clamps together three #3 cans (you provide cans) to carry flowers in water. (About $4 each, Walter F. Nicke)

## GARDENING IN COMFORT

For instructions to make a portable planting station, see page 243.

## To sit while working

A very simple solution is to put locking castors or wheels on a plain wooden chair or stool with the legs cut down to the right length for sitting. Add small bags to carry things (or use while wearing an apron with pockets).

You can also buy a child's coaster wagon or "little red wagon" to sit on or one of the following devices.

BURPEE'S GARDEN STOOL: Lightweight plastic, strong enough to sit or stand on; slip your hand into slot in top for carrying; removable insert tray for supplies or transplants. Black, 9½" x 11½" x 10" high. (About $18, Burpee)

MECHANIC'S ROLL-ABOUT: Castored (good for hard-paved surfaces); contoured seat; platform beneath seat for tools, etc.; 14" x 16" x 10" high. (About $28, Brookstone)

THE "NORMAN": Small rolling seat (see page 204 of Wheelchairs).

### Instead of a wheelbarrow

GARDEN WAY CART: Cart on 2 bicycle wheels; can't tip sideways, great for use with one hand; many models available. (From about $55 for a make-it-yourself kit—you add the plywood—to about $170, Garden Way) (O-H)

### To haul things while in a wheelchair

You can attach a couple of plastic trash bags to your chair as an easy solution, or buy:

HAUL-ON-WHEELS (AND SIMILAR DEVICES): See page 14 of How to Do a Lot Less around the House. Also see ideas for carrying things while in a wheelchair on page 210 of Wheelchairs.

## WATERING

### Hose accessories

HOSE HOLDER: Wrought iron, 42" high; adjustable-angle holder to hold hose off ground and aim it at whatever needs watering, so you can do something else. Doubles as a basket holder when picking flowers, vegetables, etc. (About $25, Brookstone)

WATER MISER: Shuts itself off; bend it and water flows, drop it and water shuts off. (About $6, Walter F. Nicke) (O-H)

QUICK-TITE HOSE COUPLER: Snap-on, snap-off connection between faucet and hose. (About $4, Walter F. Nicke) (O-H)

CONTROLLED SOAKER: Cuts force of water for gently soaking around shrubs, etc. (About $5, Walter F. Nicke)

FAN SPRAY: Brass nozzle on rustproof spike for watering narrow sections of lawn. (About $4, 2 for about $8, Walter F. Nicke)

THE NOZZ: Fan-shaped head; delicate spray for seedlings. (About $5, Walter F. Nicke)

## *Irrigation systems*

IRRIGRO TRICKLE KIT: For watering beds, 100′ porous tubing, 8′ header tubing; hose and tank connections; feeder tubes and tees; connector cones and O-rings. Run tubing between 2 rows, water trickles out through tiny pores in tubing. Enough tubing to water 100 sq. ft. of land. (About $19, Park's)

SPOT IRRIGATION SYSTEM: For watering trees or shrubs; 60′ of ½″ diameter hose; 28 "drippers," 3 tees, 2 elbows, 4 hose-and-clamps, 1 hose adapter, filter washer, 1 flow control. Equipment allows you to change the shape of your hose to direct it around obstructions. Run hose along an area around a tree or shrub, cut hose with knife, and install a "dripper" near each area to be watered. (About $29, Brookstone)

# VERTICAL, RAISED, AND PORTABLE GARDENS

One of the most satisfactory types of garden is the miniature Japanese "landscape" in which you create a small scene with sand, pebbles, small rocks, and miniature plants. Terrariums or bottle gardens are also fun, as are bonsai and water gardens.

Another interesting way to garden is in large pots or tubs that you can put on:

EASY-ROLL PLANT CADDY: Made of styrene to carry heavy plants in pots up to 11″ in diameter; 2½″ lip to hold water; nonmar castors. (About $7, Walter Drake)

Hanging baskets are also an easy way to garden indoors or out, particularly if they are dangling on a . . .

PLANTER PULLEY: Raises and lowers hanging plants; self-locking pulley, metal swivel hook, wooden handle for excess cord, stout nylon cord; holds up to 20 lbs. (About $5, Walter F. Nicke)

VERTICAL OR WALL PLANTERS: You can make a vertical planter by bending chicken wire into a circle, lining it with plastic or sphagnum moss, filling it with dirt, then sinking the bottom of it into the ground. Or hang a lined semicircle of chicken or other wire on a wall.

REDWOOD WALL PLANTER: Moistureproof backing; recessed mounting rails; tray to catch drips; 32″ high x 19½″ wide x 5¼″ deep. (About $28, Park's)

PATIO PYRAMID: Free-standing vertical planter, smaller at top than bottom; 2′ square at base x 4′ high, holds 4½ cubic feet of soil; 46″ of planting space. (About $60, Park's)

## INDOOR GARDENING

(See also ideas under Vertical, Raised, and Portable Gardens, above.)

### Gardening under fluorescent or plant lights

This is a very satisfactory way to garden. Each October, some Sears stores have a sale on fluorescent light fixtures (inquire at your local store early in September) and they often come to about half the price you would have to pay at a plant store. Because fluorescent bulbs give cool light, they are never too hot and your plants should thrive under them. There is no real need to invest in more expensive plant lights, as long as you experiment until you have the lights close enough to your plants or seedlings to give them enough light.

### Water aids

WATER WAND:   Squeeze the bulb and water shoots up into high curved tube for watering hanging baskets. (About $5, hardware stores)

PLASTIC HOSE TO CONNECT TO FAUCET:   Measures 50'. (About $12, Burpee)

## EXTRA TIPS TO SAVE WORK

### To avoid planting new bulbs every year

Your bulbs will multiply by themselves if you snap off their heads as soon as they've finished flowering, and then work a small handful of bone meal or wood ash into the soil around their bases.

### To help prevent pests in the garden without spraying

Explore the possibilities of the ancient art of companion planting: placing certain plants near each other creates beneficial effects. To learn more about it, send for:

> *Companion Planning Chart*, Organic Gardening Readers Service, Rodale Press, Emmaus, Pa. 18049 (enclose a stamped, self-addressed envelope). It's free!
>
> *Companion Plants and How to Use Them* by H. Philbrick and R. Gregg, Nichols Garden Nursery ($5.95)

### For a complete bibliography

Write to the Library of Congress, Washington, D.C., for their publication *Gardening for Handicapped and Elderly Persons.*

# 21

# Arts, Crafts, and the Workshop

If you enjoy working in any of the arts and would like to market the results of your creative effort, contact the United Cerebral Palsy Associations of New York. Their International Marketing program was created to promote products made by disabled people. Write to International Marketing Program, United Cerebral Palsy Associations of New York City, Inc., 122 East 23rd St., New York, N.Y. 10010.

## MUSIC

### Piano or organ playing

If the full range of the keyboard of an ordinary piano or organ is difficult to cover, consider:

CHILD-SIZED STANDING OR TABLE ORGANS: Several Emenee models. (From about $30 to $80, Ohio Art, P.O. Box 111, Bryan, Ohio, 43506, [419] 636–3141)

### Sheet music and books

BRAILLE MUSIC: Available from American Printing House for the Blind, 1839 Frankfort Ave., Louisville, Ky. 40206, as well as Howe Press,

Perkins School for the Blind, 175 North Beacon St., Watertown, Mass. 02172.

FOR THE ONE-HANDED:    A book, *One-Handed Piano Method for Beginners*, National Easter Seal Society (30 pages), 1952.

## PAINTING

There is a wonderful organization, called Handicapped Artists of America (8 Shady Lane, Salisbury, Mass. 09150), which functions as sales agents for severely handicapped artists, works to get scholarships for them, and often sells their designs for Christmas cards. The Sister Kenny Institute in Minneapolis, Minn., conducts an art show for disabled artists each October.

There are a number of devices that a handicapped artist would find helpful. One is the Mouthstick with Quick Change described on page 118. Other devices and tips can be found in the chapters Writing and Typing and Getting a Better Grip on Things.

## PHOTOGRAPHY

Volunteer Service Photographers, Inc., is an organization that offers invaluable advice and tips to photographers with handicaps. You can contact them at 111 West 57th St., New York, N.Y. 10019, or by phoning (212) 246–3965.

One of the most important tips is to buy equipment that is comfortable to use. The Sonar SX-70, made by Polaroid, is an extremely easy-to-use camera because of the following features: easy-loading cartridge; tripod socket hole for insertion of a "minipod" (or smaller tripod for use on a table over your bed or wheelchair); easy-to-use shutter release button and viewfinder.

## RADIO

In Touch is a radio information service for the disabled. It broadcasts closed-circuit programs over the subcarrier channel of WKCR-FM from 6 A.M. to 2 A.M. A special receiver, distributed to the blind and physically handicapped, is required. The service features call-in shows, health programs, independent living courses, readings of daily newspapers, magazines, best sellers, stock market reports, and television programs. Contact

In Touch Networks, Inc., 322 West 48th St., New York, N.Y. 10036, (212) 586–5588.

## THEATER

### *Helpful groups*

The Performing Arts Theater of the Handicapped is an organization dedicated to training disabled people for careers in the theater, film, and television industries. Write to Tim Taylor, The Performing Arts Theater of the Handicapped, 7214 Fountain Ave., #205, Los Angeles, Cal. 90046, (213) 876–7849.

Also serving the West Coast area is a group that trains deaf *professional* screenwriters, actors, and technical people for TV. Contact Sol Rubin, 6253 Hollywood Blvd., Suite 1010, Hollywood, Cal. 90028.

The National Theatre of the Deaf serves the eastern part of the country and runs a training school for professional actors throughout the month of June each year. (Apply by March 1st.)

They also concurrently run a National Deaf Playwrights Conference, to which playwrights submit work (by March 1st), then work during the June session with a master writer and see their plays produced and performed by the actors who attend the training school.

To apply for either program, contact either Director of Professional Actors' School or Director of National Deaf Playwrights Conference at O'Neill Center, 305 Great Neck Road, Waterford, Conn. 06385. (Both programs are free for deaf people; tuition is charged to hearing people.)

The National Theatre of the Deaf also offers information to amateurs (write to the address above), and they sponsor a Theatre in Sign trio, consisting of a director and two actors, who give performances and assist other deaf actors.

### *Job-hunting*

The National Theatre of the Deaf also has an actor's advocate, Elizabeth House, who runs a job-hunting resource center for all disabled actors, writers, and technical people, not just professionals and not just the deaf. She publishes *The Advocate's News*, a quarterly newsletter that lists jobs and other news, and *The Deaf Player's Guide*, an annual guidebook of deaf talent (which will soon be expanded to include hearing people as well). *The Deaf Player's Guide* is mailed to casting directors in New York City and Los Angeles. For information on any of the above, write to Elizabeth House at the O'Neill Center (see address above).

## GENERAL CRAFT EQUIPMENT

(See also Magnifiers on page 115.)

### Scissors

FOR WEAK FINGERS:   Short-bladed pincers operated by gripping scissors in palm and placing thumb against one blade; uses 50 percent of energy normally required. (About $10, G. E. Miller)

ALWAYS-OPEN:   Scissors remain open; require only extremely light pressure to close between fingers and thumb or fingers and palm of either hand; specify large, medium, or blunt-ended. (About $10, Nelson)

QUICK-CLIP:   Spring open; built-up grip, plastic handles; gentle palm pressure required. (About $14, Cleo)

ELECTRIC:   Guide with palm, electricity does the work. (About $20, Cleo)

DOUBLE-FINGER-RING:   Two rings on each side of scissors so another person can insert his or her finger into rings outside those in which disabled person has placed fingers; adds additional guidance to scissors; short, blunted blades; specify right or left hand. (About $8, Cleo)

HOUSEHOLD SNIPS:   Vinyl-coated spring handles; short, strong pointed blades for precise maneuvering; strong enough to cut a penny in half. (About $12, The Vermont Country Store)

LEFT-HAND SCISSORS:   Bent-handle style; long blades; overall length 7½″. (About $14, Cleo)

### Storage equipment

UNDERSHELF UTILITY BASKET:   Openwork plastic, handles slide over top of any shelf up to 1″ thick and hold basket underneath; blue, white, yellow; 19¾″ x 6″ (about $7, Lillian Vernon); 12″ x 3″ (about $9), 16″ x 3″ (about $10), 20″ x 3″ (about $11), all from The Pottery Barn.

(See also Drawer Kit for drawer that goes under workbench—Work Areas, page 156.)

PEGBOARD SHELF:   Nine inches long. (About $5, Miles Kimball)

THE SPEEDY STITCHER:   Built-up, handled, 4½″ awl for mending shoes, tents, suitcases, etc.; 2 needles, threaded bobbin. (About $6; extra thread and needles and/or leather carrying case, each under $6; L. L. Bean)

## CARPENTRY AND THE WORKSHOP

### A few general tips

TO DRIVE A NAIL MORE EASILY:   Put the nail through a small piece of paper to help hold it erect; secure nail to wall or board with florist clay and hammer it partway in; remove paper, wipe off putty, and finish hammering.

FOR EASIER SANDING:  Tack or staple sandpaper to a board about 15″ x 25″; place the board on a wet cloth to keep it from sliding; rub the item to be sanded against the sandpaper-mounted board.

TO BETTER USE A SCREWDRIVER:  Drill a small hole in the wood (or use an awl); rub the screw threads across a moistened bar of soap to enable the screw to bite the wood more easily, then work the screw with your fingers to grab the wood; next, lower your chin to the top of the screwdriver to hold it erect, then turn the screwdriver with one hand while exerting chin pressure.

(These 3 general tips courtesy Julius Lombardi's *Handy, Helpful Hints for the Handicapped*, National Easter Seal Society.)

## Storage equipment for carpentry tools and the workshop

MAGNETIC TOOLHOLDERS:  For heaviest tools, such as big Stillson wrenches, sledgehammers, etc.; specify 12″ (about $15) or 18″ (about $19), Brookstone.

MECHANIC'S ROLL-ABOUT:  Castored, contoured steel seat; platform beneath seat for tools; 14″ x 16″ x 10″ high. (About $29, Brookstone)

TURNTABLE BEARING:  To make your own heavy-duty lazy Susan; easily attached to wood or metal; large (12″ diameter, ⅜″ thick), about $9; small (6″ square, 5/16″ thick), about $4; Brookstone.

MAGNETIC PARTS TRAY:  Holds many small metal objects in place; 6¾″ x 4¾″ x ⅝″ high. (About $12, Brookstone)

STORAGE ORGANIZER:  Five swing bins, each 10″ wide x 2¾″ deep x 14″ high; 2 dividers; rotates 180 degrees; includes hardware needed for hanging. (About $8, Spiegel) Similar Spiegel model with 10 bins costs about $13.

For additional tool-storage ideas, see page 9.

## Some helpful tools

ONE-HAND C CLAMP:  Position clamp around work; when handles are squeezed, it "sizes" and locks itself in place; 8″ model has jaw opening of 1¼″ (about $12), 12″ model has jaw opening 2½″ (about $15), Brookstone.

RATCHET BALL SCREWDRIVER:  A 2″ diameter ratchet ball doubles the turning power of an ordinary screwdriver; heavy-duty shaft; assorted bits. (About $22, The Vermont Country Store)

CORDLESS SOLDERING IRON:  Automatically feeds correct amount of solder (contained in internal spool) to work; for electronic or electrical work; heats in 5–10 seconds; built-in work light; full recharge in 12–16 hours, 2 tips, different sizes. (About $52, American Foundation for the Blind)

## WORK AREAS FOR CRAFTS AND CARPENTRY

WORKBENCH: Made of beechwood; 3½"-high ledge, tool recess, right and left vises; bolt-type construction; 55" x 30" x 29" high. (About $230, G. E. Miller)

A similar Miller model but with recessed storage compartment and 4 slotted drawers below bench costs about $320.

WORKBENCH DRAWER KIT: Measures 10" wide x 5¼" x 16" long; made of heavy-duty plastic; steel rails, nuts, bolts, drawer stop all included. (About $17, Brookstone)

THE UNIVERSAL WORKPLACE: Height adjustable 24"–39"; convenient to use whether you're standing or sitting in wheelchair; 24" x 28" top, tiltable up to 90 degrees; compartmented drawer; large magnifier, arm attachment, adaptations for deaf, blind, or partially sighted people all optional. (About $370 for basic unit with drawer, G. E. Miller)

## POTTERY

### Equipment

TABLE-MODEL KILN: Front-loading; maximum firing temperature, 2,000° F; 110 volts; 10" x 9" x 10" firing chamber. (About $270; about $320 with pyrometer; G. E. Miller)

FINE ART METAL ENAMELING KILN: Has 6¼" firing chamber, maximum firing temperature 1,500° F; 110–115 volts. (About $60; rack, fork replacement available, about $10 each; kiln available in larger sizes; G. E. Miller)

KILN STAND: Sturdy, gray enameled stand; 20" x 20"; legs height-adjustable 23"–32". (About $60 without castors, about $80 with, G. E. Miller)

TABLE-MODEL ELECTRIC POTTER'S WHEEL: Two-speed (65 and 95 rpm); 17" long x 25" wide x 12" with 12" wheel head, 110 volts. (About $380, G. E. Miller)

Note: G. E. Miller carries clay carts, wedging tables, larger kilns, and other pottery equipment. Cleo and Abbey also carry pottery equipment.

## SEWING, KNITTING, AND CROCHETING

### Sewing tables

(See The Able Table, page 180, and Utility Cart, page 17.)

SEWING-TABLE DESK: Birch veneer; 4 drawers; 2 flaps that when open provide a 63½″-length work area; sewing machine storage area, partial rise for flatbed sewing. (About $250, Sears)

Sewing Cabinet: Slides under Sewing-Table Desk; 2 drawers, 6.4 sq. ft. work area. (About $180, Sears)

## Threading your needle

TO STABILIZE THE NEEDLE: Cut a potato in half, place potato on table or at eye level; insert needle, then thread it. (Idea courtesy of Julius Lombardi's *Handy, Helpful Hints for the Handicapped*, National Easter Seal Society)

AUTO NEEDLE THREADER: Free-standing. Drop a thread across the channel of threader machine; drop the eye end of the needle into the inverted funnel in the machine; push button and the thread feeds into the eye of the needle. (About $3, Fashion-Able)

WIRE LOOP NEEDLE THREADER: Push wire loop through eye of needle; place thread into wire loop; pull loop back out of eye of needle, leaving thread in the eye. (3 for about $2, American Foundation for the Blind)

SELF-THREADING NEEDLE: Eye of needle has slots; stretch thread across slot, then pull it into the eye. Specify Milward (package of 6, sizes 4–8) or Sharps (package of 10, sizes 3–7). (Each package about $2, American Foundation for the Blind)

## Clamps

CLAMP-ON HOOP: Clamps to table, chair, lapboard; swivels, tilts; height-adjustable use. (About $15 for 8″ hoop, about $16 for 10″, Fashion-Able)

NEEDLEWORK HAND-KLAMP: For holding needlework frame; tilts, swivels; clamps onto any table top. (About $23, Meg Designs, Box 127, Dept. H28, Stone Harbor, N.J. 08247)

(See also Speedy Stitcher on page 154 of this chapter.)

## Machines and accessories

BERNINA 830: Sewing machine for the disabled or those with low vision; easy removal and insertion of bobbin case; effortless one-motion threading; automatic bobbin-winder and thread-tension equipment; enlarged knobs, elbow- or knee-lever speed regulator and presser-foot lifter; many other standard features. (Write Bernina Sewing Machines of Switzerland, 534 West Chestnut, Hinsdale, Ill. 60521.)

MAGNIFIER: Attaches to side of machine; guides thread into needle. (About $5, American Foundation for the Blind)

DIMMER SWITCH: Mounted in a box; operable with arm, hand, or elbow as a substitute for foot pedal on traditional machine. (About $7, available at hardware or lighting stores)

### Knitting and crocheting

For better grasp of knitting needles and crochet hooks, slip a foam hair roller (cut to desired length) or a piece of foam tubing onto the ends.

### Miscellaneous

LOW-VISION MEASURING TAPE:   Small hole at every ½″, larger hole at every 1″; double holes at every 12″ up to 5′; standard large-print markings; fiberglass, nonstretch. (About $5, American Foundation for the Blind)

## WEAVING AND RUG-MAKING

### Weaving

BELT LOOM:   Hardwood table model for making belts and headbands. (About $30, G. E. Miller)

TABLE LOOM:   Hardwood, molded-plastic heddle; for weaving fabric up to 20″ wide. (About $50, The Vermont Country Store)

Note: Larger looms, spinning wheels, etc., available from G. E. Miller. Looms also available from Cleo.

### Rug-making

YARN-THREADER:   Operates in the same ways as the Wire Loop Needle Threader (see page 157), but it's larger for use with yarn (about $2, Fashion-Able); 2 threaders on 40″ neck chain (about $5, Fashion-Able).

RUG TOOLS AND ACCESSORIES:   (all from G. E. Miller)

Locker Needle, size 8 (about $3)
Latchet Rug Hook (about $3)
Tapestry Rug Needles #13 (about $5 for package of 12)
Tenter Hooks for warps 18″–30″ and 24″–43″ (about $18)
Rug Weaving Shuttle, 8″ (about $3)
Metal Beater (about $40)
Rug-Beater, 7-pronged (about $15)
Rug-Weaving Shuttle, 34″ long x 2″ wide (about $13)
Rug Prodder, for use on hessian (about $5)
Replacement spring for Rug Prodder (about $4)
Rug Wood Cutting Gauge (about $3)

# 22

# Sports and Games

Run your eye down the list of activities given here, and if you don't find anything that fulfills your idea of recreation, try Chapter 21, Arts, Crafts, and the Workshop.

## BOWLING

TELESCOPING BALL PUSHER:   Handle that helps you push ball down alley; adjusts 18"–30" in length; weighs 14 oz. (About $33, Help Yourself Aids, Nelson)

HANDLE-GRIP BALL:   Easy-to-grasp handle that retracts into ball when released; specify 10, 12, or 16 lb. ball. (About $70, G. E. Miller)

ROLL-A-BALL:   Slide made of tubing that acts as a guide to start ball rolling; no bending necessary; usable in front of wheelchair or from standing position; disassembles. (About $88, The Easter Seal Society for Crippled Children and Adults of Iowa, Inc., 612 S. Delaware, Mason City, Iowa 50401, [515] 423–2200)

WHEELCHAIR BALL HOLDER:   Attaches to side of chair via steel ring; no nuts or bolts. (About $23, Nelson)

## BICYCLING

HANCYCLES: Propelled by arm rather than leg motion; 3-wheeled, 3- or 5-speed bicycles with wheels 24″ or 26″ in diameter; 7 models (plus 2 for children). (From about $530 to $810; write or call Janssen, U.S.A., Tri-World Industries, Inc., 2885 S. Santa Fe Drive, Englewood, Colo. 80110, [303] 781–8589)

TO ELECTRIFY YOUR STANDARD (NOT HAND-OPERATED) BIKE: Drive unit without battery and charger, 5 models from about $160 to $250; with battery and charger, from about $35 to $100 additional. (Write or call Palmer Industries, Electric Products Division, P.O. Box 707, Endicott, N.Y. 13760, [607] 754–1954)

## EXERCISE EQUIPMENT

Write Abbey, Cleo, or G. E. Miller for details about home rowers, bicycles, and other stationary exercise equipment. Sears also carries many types of equipment, not specifically made for disabled people. But do compare and let your doctor help you decide which unit(s) would be best for you.

## FISHING

See Folding Seats under Spectator Sports on page 161 for more comfortable sitting in boats.

ONE-HANDED FISHING: A 14-oz. around-the-neck harness to act as your second hand; aluminum holding tube with lock to hold rod firmly; works for right or left hand. (About $25, Fashion-Able)

LEFT-HAND REEL: Crank on left; closed-face style for thumb-only casting; thumb-operated drag; prewound with monofilament line. (About $25, Fashion-Able)

ELECTRIC SPINNING REEL: Operable with one hand. (About $280; write or call Miya Epoch, 1635 Crenshaw Blvd., Torrance, Cal. 90501, [213] 320–1174)

ADJUSTABLE ROD KEEPER: Frees hands when used with Miya reels; takes load off shoulders and back; movable vertically and laterally. (About $160, Miya—see address under Electric Spinning Reel)

*Note:* Miya also makes electronic reels with memory banks for automatic transmission, winding, etc.

TO GET A BETTER GRASP ON YOUR ROD: (See page 32.)

# FLYING

RUDDER PEDAL HAND CONTROL: For some Piper Cherokees, Cessnas, and Grumann aircraft. (About $275, Nelson) To find out which models of each plane rudder pedal will fit, contact Wheelchair Pilots Association, 11018 102nd Ave., North, Largo, Fla. 33540, (813) 393–3131.

# HOCKEY

KIT: Twelve ice-hockey-style sticks; 6 red, 6 yellow blades; 3 pucks for floor and street hockey. (About $45, G. E. Miller)

# SPECTATOR SPORTS

*Folding seats*
PADDED: A 12″ x 12″ x 2″ vinyl-covered padded seat, 6″ x 12″ padded center-of-back support (no support for lower back); spring clamp for bleacher, bench, or boat seat. (About $20, Henniker's)
CANED: Has 16″ x 21″ seat; full back 18½″ high; folds to 5″; on runners for ground or boat deck. (About $85, Sportpages)

# SKIING

To learn about amputee skiing, and regular skiing with a disability, and the special outrigger equipment you need for it, contact PSI, 125 Columbia Ct., Chaska, Minn. 55318.

# WHEELCHAIR DANCING

For a 30-minute cassette of instructions for square dancing from a wheelchair, write Colorado Wheelers, 525 Meadowlark Dr., Lakewood, Colo. 80226.

# GAMES

*Active games*
For specially-adapted equipment for badminton, billiards, Ping-Pong, pool, shuffleboard, and tetherball, write to G. E. Miller for their catalog.

## Board games

TO BUILD GRASP ON COUNTERS FOR BOARD GAMES: Try building their height by gluing small pieces of thick cardboard, felt, foam rubber, or wood under them. As a last resort, try dipping your counters into Dip-It-Yourself Plastic Compound, described on page 31.

FOR EASIER ACCESS TO GAME BOARDS: Lay gameboards on a lazy Susan, or buy:

> *Revolving Games Stand:* Height adjustable 27"–36"; 22"-square turntable top; center post; made especially for people in wheelchairs. (About $120, Cleo)

BACKGAMMON: Low-vision. (About $10, American Foundation for the Blind; magnetic, about $11, Cleo)

BACKGAMMON-AND-CHECKER COMBINATION: Low-vision. (About $11, American Foundation for the Blind; magnetic, about $15, Cleo)

BARRIERS: Board game depicting a miniature city with wheelchaired "men" competing to overcome architectural barriers and get around 6 city blocks in the shortest time. (About $12, write Message Management Consultants, P.O. Box 20010, Indianapolis, Ind. 46220)

BINGO: Cards with metal slides instead of markers. (About $4 per card, Cleo)

CHECKERS: Low-vision. (About $8, American Foundation for the Blind; magnetic, about $14, Cleo)

CHESS:

> *Low-Vision:* (About $22, American Foundation for the Blind)
> *Magnetic:* (About $16, Cleo)
> *Oversized:* Scaled to a king 3½" high; weighted, felted pieces; folding board. (About $15, Cleo)

*Note:* There is a Braille correspondence chess organization. Contact Gintautas Burba, U.S. Braille Chess Association, 30 Snell St., Brockton, Mass. 02401.

CHINESE CHECKERS: Instead of marbles, tape several plastic toothpicks together (a different color for each side) or use golf tees. Or buy:

> *Peg Chinese Checkers:* Colored metal pegs to replace marbles. (About $36, J. A. Preston)
> *Low-Vision:* Round "men" instead of marbles. (About $14, American Foundation for the Blind)

LOW-VISION CRIBBAGE: Made of wood; raised holes for easier scoring; pegs marked for easy identification. (About $11, American Foundation for the Blind)

CROSSWORD PUZZLES:

> *Low-Vision:* Large type. (About $4, American Foundation for the Blind)

*Low-Vision: New York Times* large type. (About $6, American Foundation for the Blind)

DOMINOES:

*Low-Vision:* (About $9, American Foundation for the Blind)

*With Locking Features:* To prevent dominoes from shifting; double 6. (About $13, Howe Press, Perkins School for the Blind)

*A set with additional pieces:* Makes a game of double 9; 55 pieces. (About $24, Howe Press, Perkins School for the Blind)

*Oversized:* Measures 2¼" x 1⅛" x ½" thick. (About $17, Cleo)

MONOPOLY:    Standard board with transparent overlay in Braille, plus combination Braille and inkprint on all other components. (About $27, American Foundation for the Blind)

SCRABBLE:    Put the board on a lazy Susan or buy:

*Turntable Scrabble:* (About $25, Cleo)

*Magnetic Scrabble:* (About $17, Cleo)

*Low-Vision:* Depressed squares for holding letters; pegs for score-keeping. (About $16, American Foundation for the Blind)

## Playing cards and accessories

GIANT-FACED:    Standard-sized. (About $3, Help Yourself Aids)

JUMBO-SIZED:    Standard decks and pinochle, about $3; standard with jumbo Braille overlay, about $5, American Foundation for the Blind.

BRAILLE:    Standard-sized; plastic; standard decks and pinochle. (About $9, American Foundation for the Blind)

MAGNETIC:    With board, about $15; extra deck cards, specify red or green, about $5. (Cleo)

G. E. Miller sells a similar set with double-well cardholder. (About $20)

LOW-VISION:    Standard-sized, see also Giant-Faced, Jumbo-Sized, and Braille above; 2" numbers or letters instead of standard center symbols and pictures; suits in different colors and shapes. (About $5, American Foundation for the Blind)

CARD-SHUFFLER:    Heavy steel, holds 1–3 decks. Place half of the cards on each shelf, turn knob and cards will drop to the bottom, shuffled and ready to play. (About $20, Fashion-Able)

HOMEMADE HOLDER FOR CARD HAND:    Insert cards between the bristles of an upended floor scrubbing brush or into a flattened piece of floral clay (available at florist shops) or children's plastic modeling clay.

CARD "HAND" DISK:    Holds cards in your hand in fanned-out position. (4 for about $9, Help Yourself Aids)

CIRCULAR HOLDER:    Holds fanned-out cards in holder, no hands necessary; clamp for table edge. (About $6, Help Yourself Aids)

A wood-grained, free-standing model needs no clamp. (About $8, Help Yourself Aids)

FOUR-TIER HOLDER:   Use to line up your "hand" of cards. (About $12, Help Yourself Aids)

SOLITAIRE MASTER BOARD:   Molded plastic; 4 upper slots for suits, 7 center slots, lower rest slot for remaining cards; for use with standard-sized Low-Vision cards above. (About $9, American Foundation for the Blind)

TO PICK UP CARDS WITH ONE OR MORE FINGERS:   Attach a small magnet to a rubber finger cover (or several magnets to several fingers of a glove) and use Magnetic Cards.

## SPORTS ORGANIZATIONS

There is an organization for virtually every kind of sport. A valuable source of reference is *Sports and Games for the Handicapped*, Reference Circular No. 79–1. This free circular is compiled by the National Library Service for the Blind and Physically Handicapped of the Library of Congress. Here you'll find lists of organizations for the following sports: baseball, basketball, biking, bowling, cycling, flying, golf, physical fitness, riding, skiing, softball, swimming, tennis, track and field. Also included are associations for national and international competitions, information centers and clearinghouses, and periodicals on sports and recreation.

# PART SIX

# FURNITURE
# AND HARDWARE

# 23

# Multiuse
# Furniture and Devices

When you go to the supermarket to buy milk, lettuce, bread, and a hunk of cheese and you leave the store twelve dollars poorer, it makes you think. It makes you think that all your money is going to your stomach. And it also makes you think that you don't want to spend a penny on anything except what you really want or absolutely have to have.

So you certainly don't want to spend more than you have to on any of the devices in this book. There are two ways to cut costs. One is to consult Chapter 28 to find out how you can be reimbursed for expensive equipment or how to get it free. The other way is to buy gadgets that will do more than one job.

Many are the uses of humble things, like dowels, belts, and backscratchers—things you may already have around the house. They can perform in some areas as well as any expensive invention. More about this later on. First, consider the following inventions that can each do the work of several different gadgets.

## Carts, tables, chairs, and trays

UTILITY CART: (See page 17.) Probably the most versatile unit you could own is this combination transporter and work area, usable as: laundry and carrying cart; sit-to-work place for meal preparation, etc.; food-transporting and serving cart; dining table; baby dressing table and transportation; desk; drawing or writing table; typing or sewing table.

THE ABLE TABLE:   (See page 180.) Portable, foldaway; adjustable to any height, any angle; usable on or beside a bed or wheelchair as: desk; overbed or on-bed tray, reading stand, or desk; wheelchair tray, table, or reading stand (on chair or standing beside it); easel; dining table; free-standing book or magazine stand; end table or occasional table for guests.

MULTIUSE CHAIRS:   There are so many recliners, commode-armchair-glider combinations, and other combination chairs sold by Lumex, Skandi-Form, and Winco that it would probably pay to send for free catalogs from all 3 companies before deciding.

### For one-hand or no-hands transporting

CASTORED DISHPAN:   (See page 5.) Transport a strapped-in baby (pull along with cane); kick things from room to room; use on shelf to store lightweight things such as sweaters or paper products; pull toward you; use as a mop pail; kick or pull along with cane.

PERSONAL MOBILITY AID:   (See page 22.) Tray (or wire basket, if you wish) on wheels for transporting a meal, etc. To be pushed with one hand.

STACKING BASKETS:   (See page 17.) Use instead of lower shelves under counter top to store things and pull them toward you; store things in corners and push or pull them around easily.

### To carry things

HAVE-A-TRAY:   (See page 185.) Attach to walkers, wheelchairs, and crutches to carry food, beverages, and other things.

LIFT-OFF, SWING-AWAY, OR TOTER TRAY WITH STORAGE COMPARTMENT: (See page 210.) Use to write, read, carry things, prepare food, do hobbies while in your wheelchair.

PICKER POCKET:   (See page 146.) Hang small things from your wrist, leaving hands free.

HARVESTING BAG:   (See page 146.) Hang over your shoulder.

Note: Be sure not to overload any carrying bag to throw you off balance or strain your muscles.

Now for some of those humble, around-the-house things mentioned earlier. Use a straightened-out wire coat hanger, dowel with closet hook attached, or a Chinese back scratcher as dressing stick, tap turner, reacher, door closer, to pull things toward you (like shoes out from under the bed), and to reach clothes down from hangers. Wire coat hangers are also good for narrowing wheelchairs (see page 212).

Notched dowels are good for opening car doors (see page 137), removing and returning clothes to the rod, and turning taps on and off (if notched to fit tap lever).

Use shoehorns as reachers and sheet tuckers when making the bed (or use a sturdy wooden spatula as a sheet tucker).

Buckle old leather belts (usually about 25¢ from thrift shops), tape the buckle so there will be no rough places, and attach to door and drawer handles for pulling open with wrist or forearm; to headboard or side rail of bed to pull yourself up or down or get in or out; to bannisters for support in going up and down stairs; to garbage pail handles to keep animals out of them (see page 15).

Use Zipper Pulls (see page 47) for pulling zippers, or whenever it would be easier for you to pull with your finger rather than your whole hand.

If you think about how many different tasks you can do with each item you make or buy, you'll find that you can save energy, time, and money.

# 24

# *All about Beds*

If you've given up an activity because you thought it couldn't be done from your bed, read further. For whatever business or craft you want to pursue, there may be a device to help you do it while in bed.

For example, are you in business as a stock analyst, real estate broker, typist, or another field in which you utilize files or other reference material and/or a typewriter and a phone? It might be worth your while to look into the Turntable Desk on page 180, which can bring your materials into reach with a flick of a finger or mouthstick. Or adapt the idea by using a lazy Susan or two on one of the overbed tables on page 180. For any work or hobby, a lazy Susan on a table will bring supplies into reach.

If you love to cook, consider putting a work surface on your overbed table or tray. Then ask someone to place work tables on each side of your bed: one for a small refrigerator like the one on page 21; the other for a mini-electric skillet or a single-burner stove (see page 21).

Before discussing further details about being *in* bed, what about beds themselves? What kind should you get? What kind of mattress is best for you? Should you consider a hospital bed? The best person to answer these questions is your doctor. To help you formulate the questions to ask him, here are a few ideas.

## WHAT KIND OF BED?

A bed can consist of a mattress with springs under it and a bedboard in between, or a mattress with a flat wooden or metal panel under it instead of springs. The panel eliminates the need for a bedboard.

Use castors on your bed only if all 4 have secure locks. For maximum stability, remove the castors and use gliders with caps. This also lowers the bed from 3 to 5 inches.

If you decide to use a hospital bed, it is often more practical to rent rather than buy. Some surgical supply stores have rental-purchase plans under which the rental already paid is applied to the purchase price, should you later decide to buy the bed.

### Hospital beds

SEARS HAND-CRANKED:   Three-position; 36″ x 86″ long; 4 plastic rollers; 18″ from floor. (About $200 without mattress; about $270 with innerspring, water-repellent mattress, Sears)

A similar model is height-adjustable, 18″–27″. (About $300 without mattress; about $370 with innerspring or foam mattress)

J. A. PRESTON HAND-CRANKED:   Same as Sears nonadjustable bed above, but 2″ shorter, on 4 castors (2 with locks); 17″ from floor. (About $300 without mattress; about $450 with foam, water-repellent mattress) Preston model is height-adjustable 18″–25″. (About $450 without mattress, about $600 with mattress) The Preston models must be ordered through surgical supply.

### Electric hospital beds

SIX-WAY CONTROL:   For raising and lowering head and knee sections as well as height; 4 castors (2 with brakes); 36″ x 87″. (About $625 without mattress; about $650 with foam or innerspring mattress; Sears)

A similar model from Abbey is 36″ x 80″ or 84″. (About $925 without mattress; about $1,070 with foam mattress)

REMOTE CONTROL:   Operates 6 ways via sip-and-puff or other remote means. To be used with MED Micro Dec environmental control system, the price of which varies according to the components selected. (MED)

### Electric nonhospital beds

EASE-O-MATIC:   Remote control elevates head or legs; for use with your own headboard; 39″ x 80″ x 17″ high; coil mattress, does not look like a hospital bed. (About $600 with mattress, Sears)

DOUBLE:   Same as the Ease-O-Matic but measures 54″ x 80″ x 17″ high. (About $700 with mattress, Sears)

*Note:* A similar bed is offered by Craftmatic, 1077 Rydal Road, Rydal, Pa. 19046. Dial toll-free (800) 523–3643, or from Pennsylvania (800) 822–3975.

## WHAT KIND OF MATTRESS?

For anyone who tends to develop bedsores, sponge rubber mattresses with a firm density (or special flotation mattresses) are best. For people with normal sensation, a cotton felt or innerspring mattress is fine.[1]

### Waterproof sheeting

For mattresses that do *not* come with stain-resistant covers, buy:

FLANNEL-COVERED RUBBER: Cotton flannel top and bottom; rubber in between; by the yard, 35″ wide (about $8 per yard, Vermont Country Store); precut pads, 36″ x 36″ (about $10, Fashion-Able).

PLASTIC: Machine-washable; 36″ x 47″ (about $6), 36″ x 66″ (about $7); Fashion-Able.

## BEDBOARDS AND FOOTBOARDS

### Bedboards

Price a piece of ¾″ plywood the size of your bedframe. If this is cheaper than the bedboards listed below, either bolt it to the frame or drill holes in each corner and tie it. For a hospital bed, use 4 separate pieces, leaving space between to allow for height adjustment. Or buy:

TWIN SIZE: Measures 5′ x 30″ x ½″ folding into four 15″ sections. (About $15, Nelson)

DOUBLE-BED SIZE: Is 48″ wide. (About $25, Cleo)

DOUBLE-BED, WEBBING-ATTACHED SLAT-TYPE: Made of plywood slats. (About $18, G. E. Miller)

HOSPITAL-BED SIZE: Measures 30″ x 80″. (About $28, Cleo)

### Footboards

A sandbag or heavy blanket—rolled up—can sometimes make an effective substitute footboard. If you use the Foot/Body Cradle on page 180 and a Foot Support, the 2 together can act as a footboard.

FOOT SUPPORT: Length of cotton or nylon to go across Foot/Body Cradle to help prevent foot drop; available for single and double beds. (About $15, G. E. Miller)

HOSPITAL BED FOOTBOARD: For hospital beds *only*; angle adjustable, removable for bed-making; optional foam-cushioned, antirotation supports to prevent foot drop. (Footboard only, about $95; footboard with blocks, about $120; blocks only, about $30 the pair; Cleo)

# PILLOWS

(See also the cushions listed under Bedsore Prevention on pages 174–176.)

### For neck support
CONTOURED HEAD REST: Foam oblong; central declivity for aching neck and shoulder muscles; 6″ x 14″ x 6″. (About $10, G. E. Miller)

CERVIPILLOW: Large polyester-fiber bolster; 18″ x 8″ diameter; flattened center for neck support. (About $15, G. E. Miller)

ROUND PILLOW OF VARYING FIRMNESS: Firm foam at sides for neck, softer center section; not washable, cover with standard pillowcase. (About $40, Abbey)

### For prone position
PRONE PILLOW: Molded soft foam to slightly raise shoulders and head while prone. (About $55, Abbey)

### For buttock support
RING PILLOWS: Hole in the middle, come in:
*Foam:* With 16″ diameter, washable Dacron cover (about $9); 18″ diameter, washable Dacron cover (about $12), both from Nelson.
*Inflatable:* Red rubber; inflating valve; ranges in size from 12″ to 18″. (About $15–$18, G. E. Miller)
*Square Inflatable:* Same as above but square, 15½″ x 15½″. (About $7, Nelson)

### For slope from buttocks to head
SLEEP WEDGE: Gradual slope to support head and torso; soft, firm foam; cover; 27″ x 27″ with 7½″ base (about $20), 10″ base (about $24), 12″ base (about $27), all from G. E. Miller.

# BACKRESTS AND BED BLOCKS

### Backrests
The following backrests will help make you more comfortable. Don't invest in a backrest that looks like an armchair without legs; it does not give adequate support for your back.

ADJUSTABLE BACKREST: Five-position; 16″ wide by 24″ high; folds; mahogany; elastics to hold pillow; weighs under 4 lbs. (About $16, Abbey)

MATTRESS RAISER: Raises head or foot end of your mattress; several positions; made of tubular aluminum; 31½″ wide for single bed; requires another person other than bedridden patient to adjust. (About $35, Cleo)

## Bed blocks

These are aluminum cones that elevate the legs of a bed. They come in:

6″ height, about $25 the pair, Cleo
8″ height, about $30 the pair, Cleo, Nelson
10″ height, about $35 the pair, Cleo, Nelson

# BEDSORE PREVENTION

Several devices help prevent pressure sores or bedsores. It might be helpful if you could find a therapist who has a "pressure evaluator" (a device that measures the pressure of one's buttocks against a surface and then advises the therapist as to whether you should use foam, air, water, gel, or whatever else might be best for you).

INSPECTION MIRRORS: Help you examine backs of legs, buttocks, and lower back for red spots that indicate excess pressure on skin; metal-coil, adjustable-angle handle or plastic loop handle enable you to hold mirror in flail hand; break-resistant; 3″ x 4″ or 4½″ v 4½″. (About $15, MED)

## Sheepskin and polyester pile

Which should you invest in: sheepskin or its less expensive, machine-washable stand-in, polyester pile?

Sheepskin is used in hospitals to prevent and relieve pressure sores. It is cut into pieces and inserted under the spine, buttocks, heels, etc., fleece-side up, so that the wool fibers can distribute weight and allow air to circulate.

Pile can be machine-washed. Sheepskin must be hand-washed in mild soap and lukewarm water, and must be air-dried or it will shrink. After washing sheepskin, rinse it thoroughly in lukewarm water, roll it in a towel, and rub a little mineral oil into the leather side of the skin while still wet to keep it pliable. Never dry sheepskin near direct heat or it will stiffen.

SHEEPSKIN: For 6–7 sq. ft., about $30, G. E. Miller; 8½ sq. ft., about $35, Cleo.

PILE (KODEL POLYESTER): Measures 15″ x 15″, about $5, Nelson; 24″ x

30", about $7, Abbey; 30" x 40", about $9, Abbey, 30" x 60", about $12, Abbey.

## Foam

PLAIN PADS:  In many sizes and thicknesses; available at most variety stores and shops that stock upholstery supplies.

OPEN CELL PADS:  Inverted egg crate design; nonslide, nontwist; for sore prevention use one pad, waved side up; for existing sores use 2 pads, both placed waved side up; for serious ulcers use 3 pads, all placed waved side up; 30" x 40" cushion, about $9, Abbey; 30" x 72" pad, about $22, Cleo; 36" x 74" bed pad, about $13, Abbey.

## Gel

SPENCO CUSHION:  Gel covered with hollow silicone shafts to properly distribute the weight of your body and relieve pressure points; 17" x 17" x 2"; specify multicolor velour or brown Naugahyde cover. (About $75, Nelson)

SPENCO CUSHION-AND-PAD SET:  Cleanable with detergent; 17" x 17" cushion with 13" x 16" back support; usable with or without slipcovered foam mattress-leveling pad; pad is 76" x 36" x 2" with central removable cutout for cushion—so you can sit on the cushion and be at same level as bed's surface. (About $100 for set, or cushion alone can be ordered, Rehab Equipment and Supply)

## Water

Try filling a waterproof camp mattress with water or, to avoid danger of motion sickness, look into buying:

OVERMATTRESS FLOTATION SYSTEM:  Vinyl water bed for use over hospital bed; minimal amount of water needed; 10–12 minutes to fill; stabilized, standard head pillow for less chance of motion sickness; comes with hose and thermometer to monitor water temperature; overflow-prevention indicators included. (About $65, Abbey)

FOAM-INSULATED FLOTATION SYSTEMS  May be recommended instead of the above since less massaging is required and one person can turn the patient more easily; solid form head section; leakproof; can be raised or lowered; for use on hospital bed; holds 20 gallons of water. (About $400, Abbey)

## Air-water

MATTRESS:  Inflatable air frame and liner plus 3 separate water chambers for preventing motion sickness; 32" x 75"; plastic-covered; head/foot sections may be elevated; holds 18 gallons of water. (About $250, Sears)

*Air*

EGG-CRATE DESIGN CUSHION OR MATTRESS: Air-filled; may be custom-ordered in cushion or mattress sizes; sections may be combined with inexpensive foam sections when full body flotation is not needed. (Write or call ROHO Research and Development, Inc., P.O. Box 866, East St. Louis, Ill. 62203, [618] 270–0450.)

*Alternating pressure units*

(See also Cushions in Chapter 26, Wheelchairs.)

AIR: Electric pump for gentle massage by air circulation throughout various chambers of a sealed pad. (About $125 for pad and pump, Sears; replacement pad, about $26, Sears)

WATER: Called Aquamatic; circulates hot or cold water through a sealed pad. (About $200 for pressure unit; 12″ x 15″ pad about $50; 17″ x 24″ pad about $55, Cleo)

## PROTECTING HEELS AND ELBOWS FROM CHAFING AND BEDSORES

Be sure to consult your doctor, as there are various ways to relieve pressure on these areas. One way is to roll up a large towel or blanket and place it under your ankles. Other suggestions are:

FOOT ELEVATORS: Foam-covered wraparound anklet; keeps the entire foot off the sheets. Insert a pillow under the knees to keep pressure off ankles. (About $25 the pair, J. T. Posey, G. E. Miller)

HEEL PROTECTORS: Similar to foot elevators, but lined with pile (J. T. Posey) or with foam (G. E. Miller); both types are ventilated and have washable liners. (About $15 the pair from either company)

ELBOW PROTECTORS: Foam or synthetic wool linings. (About $15 for a pair made of either material; G. E. Miller; Abbey—wool only)

*Note:* Do not wear heel or elbow protectors any longer than your doctor recommends. Also be sure to exercise these areas as soon as you remove protectors.

## EQUIPMENT FOR SAFETY IN BED

There are a few alternatives: side rails for regular or hospital beds, and safety vests and belts.

## Side rails for any bed

VERSARAIL:   Steel cross-braces; adjustable with pushbutton; use between spring and mattress; no tools required; pushbutton adjustable up or down. (Pair 42″ long, about $55; pair 64″ long, about $70; pair adjustable 50″–73½″, about $85; G. E. Miller)

HALF-LENGTH SIDERAILS:   Thirty-five inches for security without feeling shut in; can be lowered below mattress level. (About $55 the pair, G. E. Miller)

## Side rails for hospital beds only

SLIDING:   Brackets clamp onto bed legs at foot and head ends of hospital bed; no tools needed; adjustable from 81½″ to 88″ long. (About $110 the pair, G. E. Miller)

## Safety belt and vest

BELT:   Allows patient to roll from side to side and to sit up, but not fall out! Belt goes around mattress, then around patient's waist. Should be used with side rails for maximum safety. Specify ties, D ring, or snaps. Shoulder straps optional for added security. (About $16, J. T. Posey)

VEST:   Criss-cross in front; specify snap or buckle. Nylon, about $12; cotton, about $13; gauze, about $14; J. T. Posey.

# MOVING SAFELY IN BED

To use the following device to prevent the patient from sliding down, attach all 4 straps to the bedspring frame. To turn and hold the patient, attach the two straps on one side of the square to one side of the frame or the lower bar of a side rail. Then reach over the patient and pull the other 2, unattached straps to the same side of the bed and attach the straps—the patient will roll as you pull.

TURN-AND-HOLD PAD:   Pile square with strap at each corner; 24″ x 30″, about $18; 30″ x 40″, about $25; 30″ x 60″, about $33, all from J. T. Posey.

## To transfer a patient in bed

SPENCO ROLL-AID:   Transfer by tilting patient, slipping roller under his shoulders and hips, rolling into position, removing Roll-Aid; vinyl-covered frame, 15″ x 25″ x 1½″ contains 4 aluminum rollers; total weight, 7 lbs. (About $50, Rehab Equipment and Supply)

## TO SIT UP OR TURN OVER

If it's difficult to grasp side rails, build them up with foam, tape, or elastic bands. Also try attaching a leather, rope, or webbing loop to the rail and pull yourself up with your forearms. Another simple solution is to attach a cane or handle to one or both sides of the bed frame. Use the extra support to pull yourself up, turn over, or get in or out of bed. Check with your doctor about the proper positioning of any other pull-yourself-up device so you don't risk straining yourself.

If you tend to slide and/or have trouble turning over, attach leather, strong rope, or webbing loops to your headboard or footboard.

To sit up, have someone make a rope ladder by attaching some dowels, conveniently spaced, horizontally between 2 strong ropes. The ropes should be attached to the footboard or tied to the bedsprings.

If you'd rather buy an aid, a number of them are available.

POLECAT PICK-ME-UP: Movable spring-loaded, lightweight floor-to-ceiling aluminum pole for ceilings, 6½'–9½' high; has a horizontal bar attached at right angles; grasp bar, which revolves 360 degrees, assists you from a lying to a sitting to a standing position. (About $55, G. E. Miller)

### Trapezes

These can be angled out away from the wall to make them jut below wall-mounted fixtures, with or without floor stands, swivel or nonswivel, padded or not—the padded models provide a better grasp.

SWIVEL FOR ANY BED: Attaches to headboard, swivels 360 degrees, and locks at any point; nonangled, nonpadded. (About $140, G. E. Miller)

NONSWIVEL: Free-standing; angled, nonpadded. (About $145, Sears)

NONANGLED: Same as the Sears free-standing model, but nonangled. (About $90, Abbey, G. E. Miller, Lumex—order through surgical supply for the Lumex model)

SWIVEL FOR HOSPITAL BEDS ONLY: Attaches to headboard; lockable at any of 5 points; swivels 90 degrees; angled, padded. (About $100, Abbey, G. E. Miller)

NONSWIVEL FOR HOSPITAL BEDS: Attaches to headboard, but is *not* angled or padded; nonswivel. (About $85, Abbey, G. E. Miller, Lumex model—through surgical supply for Lumex model.)

## GETTING IN AND OUT OF BED

You have several options, some a lot newer and more exciting than others. The most innovative, called the Wilson Transporter, saved a woman from a nursing home. Her husband, who could no longer lift her, couldn't bear the idea of parting with her, so he invented a wonderful device that is a cross between a chair and a scooter. More about it later.

The Polecat and the trapezes already described as well as the hoists or lifts described in Chapter 27, Ramps, Lifts, and Elevators provide other alternatives.

Then there is the simple transfer board. Instructions for making one are in Make It Yourself, Chapter 30, but before doing this, check lumber prices; at the rate they are escalating, it may cost as much to make a board as to buy one of the models described below. You might actually save yourself work *and* money if you buy a board.

## *Transfer boards/transporter*

If your bed is higher than your wheelchair, build up the chair with a couple of cushions. If your chair is higher than the bed, use bed blocks (see page 174) to elevate the legs of the bed. But also consider buying a board.

WOODEN: Measures 27″ long x 7½″ wide x ¾″ thick; wooden, tapered at each end, plastic top for easy sliding. (About $25, Nelson)

> *Slotted wooden model:* Similar to above, but measures 8″ x 30″ with a slot at each end to grasp while transferring. (About $35, G. E. Miller)

PLASTIC: Measures 8″ x 27″; chipproof; crackproof. (About $35, Cleo)

LOCKING: For the wheelchair with removable arms; measures 7½″ x 22″; made of finished poplar; swivel hinge locks into front armrest of chair after arms have been removed. (About $33, Nelson)

THE WILSON TRANSPORTER: Takes you from bed to wheelchair to wherever you need to go. Requires assistance—you grab the handlebars while helper slides you onto the seat. Includes a hydraulic lift seat for heights 16″–31″, castors, and a footbrake. All models portable, fit into car trunk, and come equipped with commode seats. For people weighing up to 300 lbs. People under 200 lbs. should order the minitransporter.

> *Optional Accessories:* Security post to restrict forward movement; 6″-wide belt to go around lower back, then around security post; outrigger wheels for help in balancing.

About $670 for basic Wilson unit; all 3 accessories total about $150. (Contact the Shylar Corp., P.O. Box 1478, Colorado Springs, Colo. 80901, [303] 598–5134)

## TO KEEP WEIGHT OF BEDDING OFF FEET OR BODY

Roll up a thick blanket and put it against the footboard. Or order:

BLANKET SUPPORT: Aluminum tubular folding frame; keeps bedding off feet; bottom tucks under mattress. (About $30, Nelson, G. E. Miller)

A similar Cleo model is nonfolding, costs about $20.

FOOT/BODY CRADLE: Is 26″ high; frame keeps bedding completely off body, clamps onto mattress. (About $28, single-bed size; about $32, double-bed size; G. E. Miller)

## FOR A CHANGE OF SCENE WHILE PRONE

SELF-PROPELLED LITTER, STRETCHER, OR CARRIAGE: Looks like a bed without head or footboard; large 24″-diameter front wheels for propelling yourself from room to room, smaller back wheels; hand rims, safety brakes; height-adjustable 26¼″–32″; 60″ long x 26″ wide. (About $450, G. E. Miller)

Similar Preston model measures 72″ x 28″. (About $620, J. A. Preston; order through surgical supply)

Cleo model measures 72″ x 29″; height-adjustable 24″–30″. (About $650, Cleo)

## TABLES, TRAYS, AND DESKS

THE ABLE TABLE: Flexible enough to be a free-standing table or to stand on a bed or wheelchair; also a bed tray or desk, bookholder, easel, side table, portable desk, etc.; legs adjustable to any height and angle; has a folding or tilting top (180 degrees). (About $25, contact Able Table, P.O. Box 365, Santa Clara, Cal. 95052, [408] 296–3078)

### For over the bed

FREE-STANDING HOSPITAL-TYPE TABLES: Height-adjustable 39″–45″; tilting white plastic top, 18″ x 29″; bookstops, 2 glides, and 2 castors, or four 4″ castors. (About $110, G. E. Miller)

TRAY ON NONCASTORED STAND: Lighter weight than Hospital-type; 23″ x 17″ height-adjustable 24″–40″; beige, enamel-finished steel; tilts. (About $25, Sears)

TRAY ON CASTORED STAND: Measures 20″ x 16″; height-adjustable 29″–45½″; tilts both ways, but a small section remains level so supplies can't slip off. (About $90, Sears)

TURNTABLE DESK: Deserves a special introduction. Designed and manufactured by a quadriplegic, it is unique in that it is on castors and built to roll easily over your bed or wheelchair. It has single or double turntables (like huge lazy Susans) built into, and flush with, its surface. The turntables can be operated easily with a nonfunctional hand or a mouthstick.

Reference material, filing trays, etc., may be kept on one revolving surface, a typewriter or phone on the other. Two models are available: medium (74" x 44") or executive (48" x 48"). Each model has one extension table (more can be ordered) that attaches at right angles or diagonally at either end; detachable legs, height-adjustable 26"–34" or 32"–40"; extra motor attachment available for operation of turntables. (From about $600 for basic model plus one extension to $900, Extensions for Independence)

### For on the bed

FOLDING TRAY:    Measures 14" x 22"; fiberglass; 5 positions; rimmed on 3 sides; spill groove on open front; clips that slide and swivel to hold papers, napkins, books, and other supplies; tray tilts, locks flat; white or turquoise. (About $20, Abbey)

LAP DESK:    Tiltable white enamel center section for eating, writing, etc.; wicker-look side compartments on each end for books and equipment; 28" x 15" x 8½" high. (About $30, Sears)

BEAN BAG "SHUFFLE DESK":    Measures 12" x 16", pellet-filled cloth bag with flat vinyl surface and book ledge; lightweight, contours comfortably to lap. (About $15, Help Yourself Aids)

## READING, WRITING, AND PHONING FROM BED

The mail-order market is bursting at the seams with inexpensive gadgets to simplify reading, writing, phoning, typing, and other such tasks from bed. You will find these listed under the chapters Reading, Writing and Typing, and Phoning without Fuss.

## BATHING AND SHAMPOOING IN BED

### Bathing

PORTABLE ON-THE-BED BATHTUB:    Takes 60 seconds to inflate; roll over onto it while it is deflated, then have someone inflate and fill it; 18" x 4" x 4" when folded; weighs 6 lbs.; water pump, 50' hose, hose fittings, faucet adapters, inflate-deflate blower all included. (About $325, contact Bathing Aids to the Handicapped, 10–C Escondido Village, Escondido Road, Stanford, Cal. 94305, [415] 857–1053)

*Note:* Medicare might help defray the cost of the tub, and most visiting nurse associations will send someone twice a week free of charge to bathe you in bed.

## Shampooing

This is much easier than you'd think! All three of the following devices are based on the same basic structure: a comfortable neckrest attached to an inflatable ring or tray that forms a minipool for your hair, plus a drain-off or hose under which you place your own bucket (none of the devices comes with a bucket). The person shampooing your hair has to pour pitchers of water over your head and into the tray, whence it runs off into a bucket at the side of the bed.

SHAMPEZE: Flat-bottomed; inflatable vinyl ring; drain hose. (About $25, Waljan, 395 Atlantic Ave., East Rockaway, N.Y. 11518, or through surgical supply)

BEDFAST RINSER: Plastic tray with plastic run-off section rather than drain hose; hangs on wall when not in use. (About $27, Abbey, G. E. Miller)

PLASTIC RINSE TRAY: With neckrest, drain hose; 26″ x 18″ x 4″. (About $33, Abbey, MED)

*Note:* If wet shampooing is difficulty for you, try a dry shampoo made of 1 tablespoon salt, mixed with ½ cup cornmeal. Sprinkle on hair lightly, then brush out dirt. (Courtesy *Mary Ellen's Best of Helpful Hints.*) For other bathing ideas, see Sitz Bath for Bedside Use on page 63.

## TO CALL FOR HELP FROM BED

You've probably already thought of attaching a buzzer, any buzzer from a variety store, to your sheet and working out a code for each member of your household, plus a few special signals for most-needed supplies or help. Here are a few other ideas:

TAP OR CALL BELL: Three-inch diameter. (About $6, Cleo, G. E. Miller)

HAND-TOUCH CALL SYSTEM: Similar to call-button systems used to summon nurses in hospitals; clip-fastened microswitch with long lever; attaches to bed rail; 10′ wire cord, single-pronged jack. (Prices vary; order from surgical supply stores)

NURSE CALL SWITCH: Tent-shaped, ultra-sensitive touch plate that activates by turn of head; 10′ cord, standard phone plug included. (About $35, Abbey)

LITTLE COMPANION EMERGENCY PAGING SYSTEM: Cigarette-pack-sized CB transmitter that can signal a neighbor up to 4 or 5 houses away; receiver in neighbor's house beeps and flashes when you signal; not to be used in or near high-rise buildings. (Write Fred Sammons for brochure)

ONE-TOUCH PHONE DIALING: Single-touch dialer with memory bank to store 12 most-used numbers; if line is busy, will redial for you for 10 minutes. You must speak to person you reach, whereas the 2 devices listed next will play prerecorded messages for you. (Contact General Telephone and Electric)

THE SILENT COMPANION PAGING SYSTEM: Remote-control device for dialing a program of calls to designated people; delivers a prerecorded message; continues to call until help arrives; attaches to your phone, which continues to operate normally. (About $760, Ortho-Kinetics)

MICROALERT: Similar to Silent Companion. (About $760 for basic dialing unit, plus less expensive nondialing model; also more sophisticated units; write or call Microalert Systems International, 3029 San Fernando Blvd., Burbank, Cal. 91504, [213] 841–1878)

## CONTROLLING APPLIANCES FROM BED

REMOTE CONTROL SWITCH: Button set in veined, onyx-alabaster glass; requires only elbow or palm tap to turn on and off; 12' cord. (About $15, Cleo)

BLOW SWITCH: "Whistleswitch" plugs into any outlet; then blow or press the "Whistler" to turn appliance on or off; no cords or batteries, can operate via sound for any distance up to 50'; also useful from wheelchair to turn on lights before entering a dark room. (About $30, Cleo)

# 25

# *Walk and Stand Aids*

Once upon a time there was only one thing you could do on crutches or a walker: walk with them. Now there's a walker to help you conquer stairs, as well as walkers and canes you can sit on and walkers that will do the walking for you!

But don't read about these things and order them without consulting your health professional. The wrong walking aid can actually be dangerous for you. For example, some of the special features that sound so attractive may give your body more support than it should have and thus hinder muscular development.

## WALKERS

FOLDING ADJUSTABLE: Aluminum tubing legs, steel cross sections; to lock, unlock, and fold, push palm-release buttons under handles; height-adjustable, adult 32"–36" (base width 23"); youth 28"–32" (base width 21"); usable over toilet; plastic grips, rubber leg tips; folds to 3¾", weighs 5¾ lbs. (About $50, Abbey)

*EXTRA TALL: Height adjustable 36"–40". (About $75, Cleo)

*WHEELED: Various models. (About $60, Abbey, G. E. Miller, Cleo)

* Be sure to consult your doctor, nurse, or therapist about these before buying or renting, as they can be very dangerous if not used correctly.

WALKER WITH FOLD-DOWN SEAT: Weighs 5½ lbs.; seat, legs adjustable 31″–36″. (About $45, Nelson, Winco)

CHILD-SIZED WALKERS: (See list of manufacturers on page 75.)

## For arm support

Ask your doctor or therapist about using either a walker with one Arthritic Crutch Armrest, or a pair of separate Forearm Rest Attachments.

WALKER WITH ARTHRITIC CRUTCH ARMREST: Walker adjustable for rotation and angling; armrest height-adjustable up to 11″ from handrail. (About $130, J. A. Preston; order through surgical supply store)

FOREARM REST ATTACHMENTS: Extend 6″ above handgrips of any walker. (About $60 the pair, G. E. Miller)

## Stair-climbing

There are 2 types of walkers that will help you manage stairs: one requires another person's assistance; the other is self-operated. The self-operated type can be dangerous because you can very easily lose your balance. The following *may* be all right, *but not without professional advice.*

PATIENT ASSIST STAIR-WALKER: A 6-legged walker for appropriate spacing to fit most steps; lightweight, push-button; height-adjustable 32″–36″. (About $60, Abbey)

Cleo has a similar model, but it is 4-legged and can be used over a toilet; height-adjustable 33″–37″. (About $90, Cleo)

## For people with the use of one hand

HEMIAMBULATOR: Looks like conventional walker, but has a center handgrip for right or left hand; lock to prevent tipping or tilting; weighs 7 lbs.; height-adjustable 33″–37″. (About $55, G. E. Miller)

HEMI WALKERETTE: U-shaped tubing 15″ wide; 4 points of support at base; weighs 3 lbs.; height-adjustable 30″–38½″. (About $55, G. E. Miller)

## Walker accessories

HAVE-A-TRAY: Has 2 compartments for beverages, snacks, supplies; 11″ x 8″ x 3″; beige or gray plastic; specify whether for walker, crutch, or wheelchair. (About $15, Danmar)

CRUTCH ARMRESTS: Underarm supports with rubber pads like tops of standard crutches; clamp above walker handrail; adjustable 10½″–18½″ or 13½″–22½″—specify size. (About $55 the pair, Abbey)

POCKETED CARRYALL: Attach over top bar of walker with Velcro; one large, several small pockets; blue, brown, or gray. (About $22, Cleo)

UTILITY POUCH: Place on a hanger across length of walker top bar; washable blue duck. (About $20, Abbey, Cleo)

WIRE BASKET: Measures 17" x 7⅞" wide x 5" high, white, vinyl-coated steel wire on hooks. (About $17, Abbey, Cleo, G. E. Miller)

Or use a bicycle basket if you can get one cheaper.

SLING SEAT: Hooks to sides of walker; easily detachable; no interference with walking; washable blue, reinforced duck. (About $18, Abbey)

REPLACEMENT RUBBER TIPS FOR WALKER LEGS: Specify outside diameter of your walker leg. (About $8 the pair, Cleo)

SWIVEL LOCKS FOR ROLLING WALKERS: Prevent castors from swiveling and keep walker from traveling to the side as it moves. (About $12, Abbey)

# DEVICES THAT WALK FOR YOU OR KEEP YOU ON YOUR FEET

## *The walker that walks for you*

THE INDEPENDENCE WALKER: Battery-operated, motorized platform that can take you in a standing position all over your house, workshop, etc. Moves at a maximum speed of 1.6 mph and brings you to within 5 inches of any work surface, provided the floor you travel over is all on one level. Includes locking gate, sacral support, cushioned belt for stability while standing; no above-the-waist support; rear-wheel steering via tiller, front-wheel toggle brakes; rubber (nonmarking) tires; entire unit weighs 115 lbs.; 23¾" x 23¾" x 41⅝" high (46" to top of tiller); battery charger included. (About $1,000, Falcon Research and Development)

## *Standing aids*

STAND-AID: Helps you pull yourself up and remain standing or be pushed along by an attendant. Collapsible metal frame on wheels with platform and adjustable table work surface. To enter, pull yourself up with grab bars or Pow'r Lift described below. Unit has back support, heel, and knee stabilizers for additional support; castors, locking brakes; 4 models for people 3'–6'2" tall. (About $1,000, Stand-Aid)

STAND-AID WITH POW'R LIFT: Battery-powered to propel anyone under 400 lbs. to a standing position via switch; height-adjustable; can be disassembled. Designed for those who can't stand to get into a Stand-Aid or who don't have anyone to fasten its trunk support. *Do not use without professional advice, as propelling equipment can be very dangerous if used improperly.* (About $2,000, Stand-Aid)

STAND-IN TABLE: Includes a ramp for wheelchair access, then pull yourself up via parallel bars that extend from back of cabinet; 32" x 48", natural finish, wooden cabinet has work surface; height-adjustable 40"–60". Rigid back door of cabinet closes after you enter to become lower back support—also back rest and adjustable knee support. (About $1,700 if electrically operated; about $1,500 if hydraulically operated; Hausmann)

## CANE WALKERS

The following equipment is designed for the person who needs an ambulation aid more stable than a cane but lighter than a walker. It is also recommended for the one-handed person who needs walking help. Again, consult your doctor, nurse, or therapist before buying any of this equipment.

WALKANE: Looks like a slim walker with a center handle; 18″ wide x 12½″ deep; folds flat; push-button, height- and angle-adjustable 28″–32″; plastic handgrip. (About $32, Abbey)

SIDE-STEPPER CANE/WALKER: Has 2 levels of handgrips for ease in getting in or out of chairs; optional 2-handed usage; weighs 3½ lbs.; one-handed mechanism for easy folding/opening; adult 32″–36″, youth 28″–32″. (About $30, Abbey)

## CANES

Canes fall into 2 categories. The first is the straight or angled shaft we're all used to seeing, with U-shaped, T, or angled handle and variations on this theme. The second type rests on 3 smaller legs at its base (tripod) or four legs (quad). These splayed legs give additional support for walking and hold the cane upright when not in use.

Canes are made of wood, Plexiglas, or aluminum. Aluminum canes are most often recommended by health professionals. They frequently fold and are adjustable, while the wooden and Plexiglas models are rigid and nonfolding.

To carry your cane when not in use, loop leather or webbing twice around the handle, making the second loop large to insert your wrist.

Since many companies call the same cane type by different names, give a description *and* a little sketch of whichever cane your health professional advocates that you buy when ordering.

FOREARM CANE: Supports your weight on forearm when it's difficult for your hands to support your weight; handgrips rotate and adjust forward or backward. Velcro strap secures arm to 8″ armrest, but physical therapists advise against using this, as it would hamper you if you lost your balance. Height-adjustable 37″–47″. (About $70, Abbey, Cleo)

PYRAMID CANE: A 4-legged or "quad" cane; "legs" attached just below handle of cane for greater support, even for tall people; as cane's height increases, so does width of base; push-button; height-adjustable 23¾″–37¼″; weighs 3 lbs.; folds flat. (About $30, Abbey, Sears)

CANE SEAT: Three-legged; folds; 2 lbs.; aluminum with vinyl seat that lets down with flick of wrist; *requires very good balance.* (About $27, Abbey, G. E. Miller)

GADABOUT CHAIR-CANE: Folded, a cane; open, becomes an aluminum armchair with sling seat, full backrest; looks like a director's chair, weighs 3½ lbs.; opens easily, folds to 4″ x 4″ x 36″. (About $50, Walter F. Nicke)

## Hospital canes (standard ∪ handle)

NONADJUSTABLE ALUMINUM: Length is 36″. (About $9, Cleo, G. E. Miller)

ADJUSTABLE, TELESCOPING ALUMINUM: Measures 22″–38″. (About $20, Cleo)

ADJUSTABLE, NONTELESCOPING ALUMINUM: Measures 27″–36″ (about $17, Cleo, Nelson); 30½″–38½″ (about $28, J. A. Preston, order through your surgical supply store)

WOODEN: Length is 36″, ash, walnut finish, 1 lb. (about $11, Sears); 36″ or 42″, rock maple (about $9, J. A. Preston); 1″ diameter, men's "scorched" knotty chestnut (about $15, J. A. Preston)

PLEXIGLAS: May be shortened with hacksaw; all sizes about $40, Cleo.

⅞″ diameter—men's, 36″
⅞″ diameter—ladies', 34″
¾″ diameter—ladies', 34″

## Ortho canes

Aluminum, angled shaft with a straight handle that aligns weight of your body downward with cane shaft for better balance, less hand fatigue. Adjustable 27″–36″ and 33″–42″, both sizes about $12, Abbey.

## Pistol grip (straight cane, contour curved grip)

WOODEN: Length is 36″; in walnut or black (about $12, G. E. Miller: ask for "Derby"); 35″ maple, walnut finish, 1″ diameter; (about $15, Sears).

ALUMINUM: Adjustable, vinyl-covered nonslip handle. (About $15, Cleo)

## Spade handle (triangular snow-shovel-type handle)

WOODEN: Extra-sturdy maple; 36″. (About $15, G. E. Miller)

## T *handle*

WOODEN: Is 36″ long, ⅞″ diameter; walnut or black satin finish; pigskin band. (About $12, G. E. Miller)

## *Quad canes*

Made of aluminum and steel, mounted on 4 steel legs.

SPADE HANDLE: Adjustable 31″–38″ (about $35, Nelson); 27″–35″ (about $27, Cleo); 36″–42″ (about $28, Cleo)

ORTHO HANDLES: Set into angled shafts to concentrate body's weight at base; adjustable 28″–33″ (about $29, Cleo); 34″–39″ (about $29, Cleo)

QUAD CRUTCH: Quad cane and forearm crutch combination; angled shaft with cuff adjustable to any forearm length; base can be rotated and clamped at any position relative to the handle. Floor-to-handle adjustable: 24″–30″, 28″–34″, 33″–39″; (all about $45; J. A. Preston—order through surgical supply store.)

## *Tripod cane*

Made of aluminum and steel, with 3 steel legs.

FUNCTIONAL ADJUSTABLE GRIP: Contoured to fit hand; height-adjustable 29″–36″. (About $25, G. E. Miller)

U-SHAPED HAND GRIP: Shaft adjustable to straight or angled style; height-adjustable 35″–40″. (About $27, J. A. Preston—order through surgical supply store)

TO MAKE ANY CANE INTO A TRIPOD: Broad triangular base usable on any cane. (About $20, Cleo)

## CRUTCHES

All well-dressed crutches should have an underarm cushion, handgrips, and tips. Be sure to consult your health professional on what type and height of crutch to buy.

PLAIN WOODEN UNDERARM (OR "AXILLARY"): Adjustable handgrips; all about $14 from Cleo:

Height-adjustable: 42″–52″, 46″–58″

Youth: 37″–47″

Child: 25″–33″

Extra Tall: 50″–64″

ALUMINUM AXILLARY: Height adjustable 45″–55″, 50″–60″; youth 37″–46″; child 28″–37″. (All about $22, Cleo)

FOREARM: For forearm but not underarm support; single-shaft aluminum; height-adjustable 28″–38″; adjustable handgrips. (About $45, Sears)

Similar J. A. Preston model with swivel-action cuff that frees hands without removing them from crutch is height-adjustable 27″–34½″. (About $50, order through surgical supply store)

### Platform and trough crutches and attachments

These crutches provide other kinds of forearm support and are available from Abbey and J. A. Preston for between $50 and $60 per single crutch. Check with your health professional for advice. Abbey and J. A. Preston also make Platform Attachments that fit onto any one of their own two-shafted aluminum crutches for about $32 and $40, respectively, for a single attachment. (Don't order an Abbey attachment for a J. A. Preston crutch or vice versa; they are not interchangeable.) Cleo also makes a wooden platform attachment for fitting onto any of its wooden crutches for about $30.

### Ortho (angled single-shaft)

UNDERARM ALUMINUM: Height-adjustable 4′10″–5′8″, 5′5″–6′4″. (Both about $38, G. E. Miller)

FOREARM ALUMINUM: Height-adjustable floor to hand 20″–27″, 27″–36″, 32″–41″. (About $45 the pair, G. E. Miller)

## CANE AND CRUTCH ACCESSORIES

### To carry things

Wear an apron with pockets, or a knapsack, attach a lightweight bag to your belt or hang it on a hook on your crutch (be careful not to overload it and upset your balance), or buy.

CRUTCH BAG/PURSE: Fits over standard (axillary) crutch crosspiece; snap, straps; coral, beige, tan, light orange. (About $20, WINGS of VGRS)

ONE-HANDED TRAY: (See page 22.)

BRIEFCASE: Rivet a folding metal music stand to crutch shaft; attach foam-covered hook to crutch to hold handle of briefcase; attach 2 metal clips to bottom of stand to hold briefcase in place. (Idea from *Aids to Independent Living: Self-Help for the Handicapped* by E. Lowman and J. Klinger, copyright © 1969 McGraw Hill Book Co., New York. Reprinted by permission.)

### Aprons

THE WORK HORSE: Hangs from neck to upper thigh; four 9″ pockets, plus breast pocket; cotton duck; 10 oz., about $10; 15 oz., about $12. (Walter F. Nicke)

SHOP: Hangs from neck to knee; 2 waist pockets, 2 chest pockets (1 hinged to swing out and not dump contents as you bend); 8 oz. (About $14, Brookstone)

NAIL: Hangs from waist (no bib); 3 large pockets plus pencil pocket. (About $12, Walter F. Nicke)

## Other accessories

CANE/CRUTCH RACK: Three wooden horizontals, 60″ long; 6 steel hangers, each holding up to 3 pairs of crutches or 6 canes. (About $100, Abbey)

CANE/CRUTCH PARKER: Clamp to hold cane/crutch upright along table edges, chair arms, etc.; specify ¾″, ⅞″, or 1″ diameter. (About $5 the pair, Help Yourself Aids)

WHEELCHAIR CANE/CRUTCH HOLDER: Clamps to side of chair. (About $18, Abbey, Cleo)

SUCTION RUBBER CRUTCH TIPS: Diameter 2½″ (about $8 the pair), 2¹⁄₁₆″ (about $5 the pair), 1⅞″ (about $4 the pair), 1⁹⁄₁₆″ (about $3 the pair), Cleo.

SUCTION RUBBER CANE TIPS: Diameter ⁷⁄₁₆″ and ½″, about $5 per dozen; ⅝″, about $5 per dozen; ¾″, about $5 per dozen; ⅞″, about $4 per dozen. (Cleo)

UNDERARM CRUTCH CUSHIONS: (About $5 the pair, Nelson, Sears)

CRUTCH HANDGRIPS: (About $6 the pair, Nelson)

# 26

---

# *Wheelchairs*

Wheelchairs are on the market today that are only 22½″ wide, that weigh under 23 pounds, that fold to 10½″ wide, and that help you stand or elevate you to the right sit-to-work height. Some chairs even climb curbs, and others can be operated by almost any part of the body or by your breath!

Some of these chairs are expensive; others cost no more than an ordinary chair. If the one you want seems beyond your budget, don't forget to check the possibilities of Medicare, the Veterans Administration, and Vocational Rehabilitation for financial help. Also, consider renting a chair until you and your doctor decide on your precise needs.

There have also been dramatic breakthroughs in the wheelchair accessory area: a device, approved by both the VA and Vocational Rehabilitation in some states, that will load your chair into the back of your car; a wonderful scooter-type unit that helps you in and out of your chair, car or bed; power packs that can turn a manual chair into a powered one; lightweight, portable ramps that will help you over curbs and steps; and scales that will weigh you in your chair. These represent only a fraction of the devices now on the market—many will be described in this chapter.

Whatever your needs may be, if you are thinking of making a change in chairs, *please show pages 193–202 to your doctor or therapist*. They are directed to him or her to help you choose the chair best suited to your

# The Basic Formula In Selecting A Wheelchair

To help you establish an organized formula to work from, ABBEY MEDICAL has prepared several check lists to help systematize the proper choice of equipment. In the event further customizing may be required, your local Abbey medical equipment specialist is ready to help you. He can be of invaluable aid in helping you refine and extend your basic formula.

**Here are the basic areas to be concerned with:**

1. **Physical dimensions of the patient.**
2. **Diagnosis and prognosis.**
3. **Your program of rehabilitation.**
4. **Evaluation of work area.**
5. **Evaluation of home area.**

A-1

F—Straight
Across Hips

## 1. Physical Dimensions

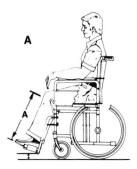

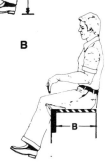

**A. Measure from bottom of foot to back of thigh area.**
This gives proper seat height and indicates if special seat height is required. **Caution:** If cushion is being used, take this into consideration. **RULE: Make sure that there is at least 2″ clearance between the bottom of the foot plate and the ground, footrest should then be adjusted up so as to eliminate pressure in the popliteal area.**

**B. Measure from the back of buttocks to the back of the calf.**
This indicates appropriate seat depth. **Caution:** If a back cushion or solid insert back is indicated, take this into account when measuring, allowing enough room so as not to cut off the circulation in the lower extremities. **RULE: Front edge of seat upholstery to back of calf should have a clearance of between 2″ to 4″.**

**C. Measure from seat to bottom of elbow with the shoulders in a normal position, generally horizontal to the floor.**
This gives the most comfortable arm height which also provides stabilization of the upper trunk and pressure relief when raising off the seat doing push-ups. **Caution:** Once again, if a cushion is being used, take this into consideration. **RULE: Add 1″ to "C" dimension for correct wheelchair arm height.**

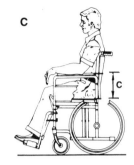

**D. Measure from seat to underarm (axilla).**
By subtracting 4″ you will have the proper wheelchair back height. This dimension will vary depending upon the individual's disability. As an example, a patient with quadriplegia may need an increased back height as well as an increased back angle, while another person with a very similar injury may be able to use a standard back height. Some paraplegic patients who are active in sports may use a 4″ back to allow for maximum mobility. **Caution:** If a cushion is to be provided, take this into consideration. **RULE: Back height should be approximately 1″ below the bottom of the scapula for people with good upper trunk balance, and 1″ or more above the bottom of the scapula for people with poor trunk balance.**

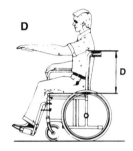

**E. Measure from seat to middle of the head.**
This gives total area of support for the back. It covers all areas of points of contact if full support is required. **Caution:** Again, remember the cushion.

**F. Measure straight across hips or widest part of the lap.**
This will give you the appropriate seat width and assist in determining the size; adult, junior, kid or tiny tot, etc. **Caution:** Although the rule is to add 2″ to this dimension, there are other factors to consider. These could include: **1)** Extremely narrow doorways and/or hallways in the home or place of employment. In this case, you may have to forego the additional 2″ allowed to relieve pressure on the trochanters and order the exact hip width (except in the case of the spinal cord injury patient in which you should forego a maximum of only 1″ to avoid pressure sores). Two other alternatives would be to order as prescribed (by adding 2″) and provide the patient with a Reduce-A-Width or have the family remove the lower part of the door jam and order wrap around armrests. **2)** Bulky clothing required in cold weather could require that you add more than 2″ to the hip measurement. Be aware, however, that doorways and hallways once again may be obstacles unless you have provided an alternative. **3)** Very active patients (e.g., paraplegics) may want a seat without arms to reduce the weight of the chair. **4)** Consider weight loss or potential of regaining weight. **RULE: Add 2″ to this dimension. However, make sure all factors are taken into consideration.**

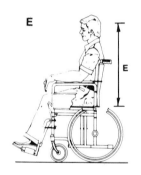

THE "MUST" TO ALL THESE MEASUREMENTS IS TO HAVE THE PATIENT IN A SITTING POSITION, EITHER IN A WHEELCHAIR OR IN A STRAIGHT BACK CHAIR. NEVER MEASURE WHILE PATIENT IS LYING DOWN IN BED.

## 2. Diagnosis and Prognosis
Why are these important in prescribing a wheelchair? Actually this further enables you to properly identify accessories and modifications. For example, if patient is a young, active paraplegic, you would want a good fitting wheelchair, durable frame with appropriate accessories (i.e., removable desk armrest, swing away legrests, heavy duty upholstery, etc.). However, if the patient has a progressive disease, you would want to fit the patient with a wheelchair that not only fits him now but also would be appropriate for him later. Once you cull the physical and environmental requirements, your Abbey medical equipment specialist can be of great aid in further customizing your patient's wheelchair needs.

## 3. Program of Rehabilitation
It goes without saying, that if you are teaching a side transfer, you do not want a wheelchair with non-removable armrests. There are other considerations if your program is designed toward the eventual total independence of your patient. This not only gives us an idea as to what type of chair, modifications and accessories are needed, but also if additional equipment would be applicable. Equipment such as patient lifter, transfer boards, raised toilet seat, grab bars and other aids for independence in activities of daily living.

# 4. Evaluation of Work Area

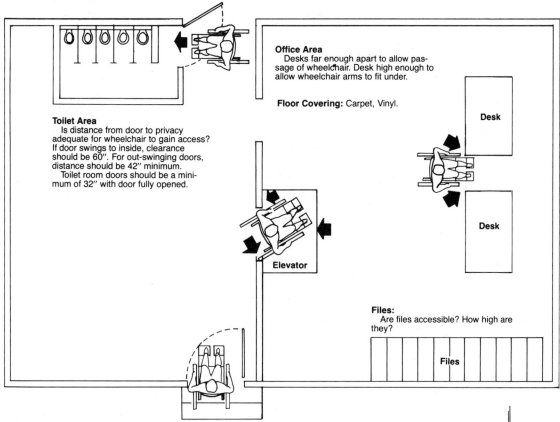

**Office Area**
Desks far enough apart to allow passage of wheelchair. Desk high enough to allow wheelchair arms to fit under.

**Floor Covering:** Carpet, Vinyl.

Desk

Desk

**Toilet Area**
Is distance from door to privacy adequate for wheelchair to gain access? If door swings to inside, clearance should be 60″. For out-swinging doors, distance should be 42″ minimum.
Toilet room doors should be a minimum of 32″ with door fully opened.

**Elevator**

**Files:**
Are files accessible? How high are they?

Files

## Toilet Area
Is distance from door to privacy adequate for wheelchair to gain access? If door swings to inside, clearance should be 60″. For out-swinging doors, distance should be 42″ minimum.
Toilet doors should be minimum of 32″ with doors fully opened.

## Office Area
Desks should be far enough apart to allow passage of wheelchair. Desk should be high enough to allow wheelchair arms to fit under desk.

## Doors
Open to inside or outside?

## Elevators
Deep enough to accept length of wheelchair?

## Toilets
Accessible? Doors wide enough? Enough room in stall for transfer?

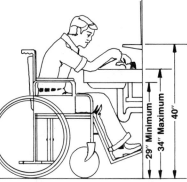

## Wash Basins
Accessible? Should have a clearance of 29″ from floor to underside of sink and should not be higher than 34″ to top of sink. Mirrors should not be higher than 40″ from floor.

## Steps
How many? Accessible by use of ramp? RULE: 1′ rise to 12′ length of ramp. Possible wheelchair elevator (AM 15-1056) or portable ramp (AM 18-1127).

## Parking Facilities
Stalls wide enough?

## 5. Evaluation of Home Area

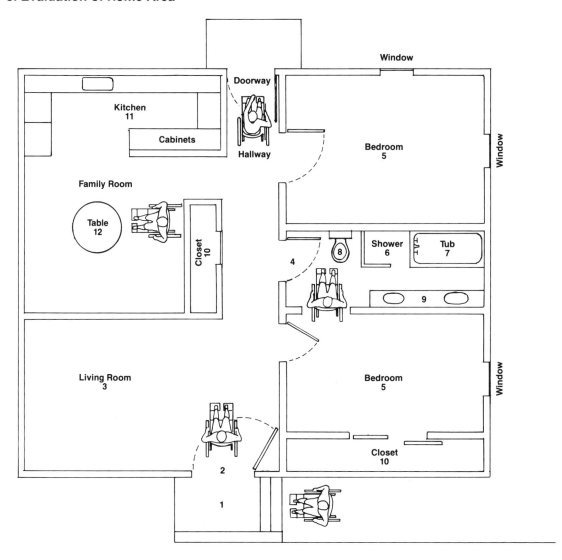

1. **Determine if ramp is needed.** Also determine if handrails are designed to bear weight. And, check the back exit, for there may be fewer steps involved. RULE: 1′ rise to 12′ length of ramp.

2. **Check width of doors.** Especially width of bathroom doors to make sure wheelchair will fit through. Also, check whether the doors open outward or inward.

3. **Bathroom doors.** As mentioned above, bathroom doors are a very big consideration, since they are the narrowest in the house. If door opens inward, check distances between door edge and toilet to make sure that wheelchair can be maneuvered in space. Doors could be removed and replaced with a curtain.

4. **Check distance between furniture.** Be sure wheelchair can pass through safely. Also, check height of sofa or easy chair, in case patient is capable of transferring from chair to sofa or chair. Height should ideally be the same.

5. **Check height of bed.** A very important consideration, since the transfer from the chair to the bed should be effected with a minimum amount of lifting. Also, check the space between objects such as the bed, dresser, etc. Again, check door widths. And last, but not least, make sure the clothes pole in the closet is at a reachable height. If you find the bed is too low, consider raising it with wooden blocks. If positioning is important, look into AM 10-1224 hospital beds.

**6. Stall shower.** In most instances, the stall shower can be more easily adapted to the bathing of the disabled patient than the standard bath tub. The use of hand rails, shower extension AM 20-0215 shower chair AM 18-2197 would enable many patients to become as self-sufficient as possible.

**7. Bath tub.**
This is one of the most difficult areas in which to bathe without assistance. The problem is that of entering and exiting the tub independently. However, there are a few pieces of equipment to consider: patient lift, AM 15-1068 ; water pressure bath lifts, AM 15-1049, AM 15-1084, bath transfer seats, AM 13-1002, to name a few. .

**8. Toilet.** The problems here consist of doors opening inward or outward, the area necessary for transfer from wheelchair to toilet or the actual room necessary for the wheelchair. The height of the commode and the lack of stabilizing bars to effect a safe transfer are also serious considerations. Be sure to check accessibility and height. **(a)** If the door opens inward, it may create an obstruction for the wheelchair. The door could be reversed to allow more room or could be removed and replaced with curtains. **(b)** Toilet seat arms, AM 13-1034. **(c)** Raised toilet seats, AM 13-1656, AM 13-1027. **(d)** Over-toilet commode. If the situation in the toilet bathroom area is such that all related activities within are impossible (lack of room, etc.), then it may be necessary to resort to performing these activities in the privacy of a bedroom. Toileting could be accomplished by using AM 18-1500 ; bathing by use of the inflatable tub, AM 13-1308 or just plain old sponge bathing, using AM 13-1201 for the hair, for example. Be sure to check with your Abbey medical equipment specialist for the many items available in helping solve the problems of space and other special equipment.

**9. Wash basin.** Accessibility is the only real problem that the wash basin poses. If the basin is enclosed in the front by a cabinet, the wheelchair bound person will have difficulty in getting close enough to use the wash basin. Consider replacing the cabinet with a free-standing unit or remove the doors and replace with a curtain.

**10. Closets and hallway storage space.** As mentioned with bedroom closets (5), make sure clothes pole or rod is low enough to be reached. In the hall storage area, make sure that only the most frequently used supplies are kept on the lower shelves. Consider AM 20-0136, reacher, as an assist in reaching lightweight items on higher shelves.

**11. Kitchens.** Accessibility and usability height of counters pose the main problems. There are many small items which are applicable in this area. There are, however, other areas to be dealt with. The most important, being accessibility, as far as room to work freely in the kitchen is concerned. Next, is the counter top area (for this, consider a wheelchair cushion to raise the person to a height that is convenient to enable better access to the working area). Another factor to be considered is the sink area. Many people have completely removed the under shelving and kick plate, so that the footrest can extend under the sink and the patient can gain closer access to the sink. Finally, make sure all more commonly used items are on the lower shelves, within easy reach.

**12. Dining table height.** This is a social consideration as it is very important for the disabled person to participate in normal daily activities, and among these is the dining table. Make sure the underside of the table is high enough for the wheelchair so that your patient can get close enough to the table or recommend desk arms or a lap board.

**THESE HINTS ARE JUST A FEW WHICH SHOULD BE CONSIDERED AND AS MANY OF THE AREAS TO CHECK WERE LEFT OUT, WE FEEL THAT THIS WILL GIVE YOU SOMETHING TO THINK ABOUT WHEN YOU ARE PRESCRIBING THE BEST POSSIBLE WHEELCHAIR AND ACCESSORIES FOR YOUR PATIENT. ON THE NEXT PAGE IS A COPY OF THE HOME CHECK OUT GUIDE WHICH IS USED BY THE ABBEY MEDICAL EQUIPMENT SPECIALISTS WHEN PRE-SCRIBING WHEELCHAIRS OR OTHER RELATED ITEMS. IF YOU RUN INTO ANY SPECIAL PROBLEMS, OR IF YOU HAVE ANY QUESTIONS OR NEED GUIDANCE ON SPECIAL AREAS, PLEASE DO NOT HESITATE TO WRITE OR CALL THE ABBEY MEDICAL EQUIPMENT DEPARTMENT.**

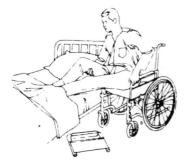

# WHEELCHAIRS & ACCESSORIES

## Home Check Out Guide

### Home Check Out Guide

Name_____ Date _____ PX _____

Address_____ Age _____

Hospital_____ Insurance_____

**Patient's Mobility:** Amb. Crutches, Cane, W/C._____
_____

**Type of Residence:**

One-Story _____ Two-Story_____
Apartment _____ Mobile Home_____
Rent _____ Own_____

**Is there need for outside assistance?**_____

**Access From Parking To Entrance:**

# of Front Steps_____ Total Height _____ Rails L or R _____
# of Back Steps_____ Total Height _____ Rails L or R _____

**Comments:** _____
_____
_____

**Living Room:**

Door Widths _____ _____ _____     Threshold _____
Suitable Chair_____     Floor Covering _____
Obstacles _____     Enough Room for W/C _____
Thermostat _____     Throw Rugs _____
                               (Should Be Removed)
**Comments:** _____
_____
_____

**Bathroom:**

Door Width_____     Toilet Approach _____
Tub/Shower Approach_____     Sink Access _____
**Patient needs or has:** Grab bars, tub seat, raised toilet seat, etc. _____

**Comments:** _____
_____
_____

**Bedroom:**

Type of Bed _____ Height _____ Area Around _____
Door Widths_____ **Reach:** lights, clothes, commode,
bed board _____

**Comments:** _____
_____
_____

**Kitchen:**

Door Width _____ Size_____ ___ Obstructions_____
Patient use of 1, 2 hands.
**Assistive Devices:** Grab bars, easily reached goods, stove, refrigerator,
sink, pans and appliance. _____

**Comments:** _____
_____
_____

**Check laundry room, workshop and hobbies patient may do:** _____
_____
_____

**Summary & Recommendations:**
_____
_____
_____
_____
_____

Date Completed: _____ Signed _____

## Process of Selecting Appropriate Wheelchair

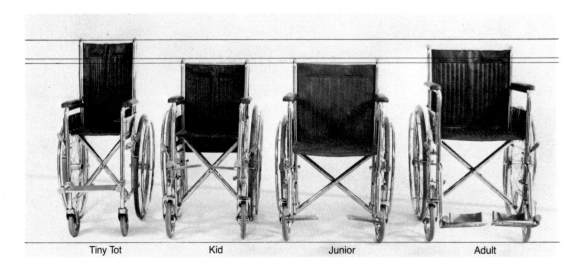

Tiny Tot          Kid          Junior          Adult

Once all the dimensions (physical and environmental) have been determined, you are now ready to begin the process of selecting the appropriate chair. The following is a list of basic wheelchairs and their respective dimensions:

| General Dimensions | | Tall* Adult | Adult | Narrow Adult | Junior | Kid | Kid Grow. | Tiny Tot | Adult Hemi Chair | Hemi Chair Junior | Pre-Schooler |
|---|---|---|---|---|---|---|---|---|---|---|---|
| Seat Width | | 18" | 18" | 16" | 16" | 16" | 14" | 12" | 18" | 16" | 12" |
| Seat Depth | | 17" | 16" | 16" | 16" | 13" | 11" | 12" | 16" | 16" | 10" |
| Back Height | | 18" | 16½" | 16½" | 16½" | 16½" | 14" | 17½" | 16½" | 16½" | 16½" |
| Seat Height | | 19¾" | 19½" | 19½" | 17½" | 17¼" | 19⅝" | 19⅝" | 17½" | 17½" | 18" |
| Arm Height | | 10⅜" | 10⅛" | 10⅛" | 9¾" | 9¾" | 7⅜" | 6⅛" | 10" | 10" | 6" |
| Footrest Adjustment | Min.: | 16½" | 16½" | 16½" | 14" | 9⅞" | 6¾" | 12" | 14" | 14" | 4½" |
| | Max.: | 22" | 22" | 22" | 18" | 13⅞" | 10¾" | 15¾" | 19½" | 18½" | 8½" |
| Overall Length w/o Footrest Assembly | | 31⅝" | 30⅝" | 30⅝" | 30⅝" | 30½" | 30½" | 26⅝" | 29½" | 30½" | 28" |
| Overall Height | | 38" | 36" | 36" | 33" | 32" | 32" | 36½" | 33¼" | 33" | 34" |
| Weight w/o Footrest Assembly | | 33# | 41# | 40# | 39# | 38# | 37# | 37# | 38# | 39# | 32# |

*Lightweight frame.

Now that you have determined the chair size which most closely fits the patient, you can now determine what modifications to the frame are necessary. This can be done by referring to the physical dimension chart and following the guideline.

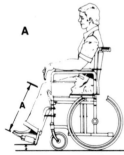

**A**

**A. Footrest length.** If measurement is between the minimum and maximum adjustments, there is no need to modify this assembly. (Remember to take your cushion into consideration). You should calculate your dimensions based upon the fact that the cushion will compress approximately to half its original thickness.

If (A) measurement is longer than maximum listed, you can do one of several things:
(1) You can suggest a cushion and use the guideline above, or
(2) Have special extended footrests installed by the manufacturer. This is done by extending the entire hanger away from the chair. Not just the footrest extension, or
(3) Special frame construction with raised seat. On this modification, check back to the diagram on table and desk heights, to make sure your patient's legs will fit under the table.

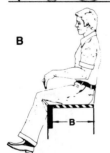

**B**

**B. Seat depth.** If your patient's measurement is between 2" to 4" greater than the chart dimension, then there is no reason to change the chair's frame configuration.

If patient's dimension is greater than the 4", you will have to provide more seating platform to accommodate, by one of several methods:
(1) Have a special solid insert seat made up (this is an upholstered cushion with a ⅝" plywood base, 1" foam rubber), or
(2) Modifying the frame by extending the seat depth, or
(3) On detachable arm models, the seat upholstery can be extended approximately 1" with a slight up charge. (This cannot be done on a standard arm model.), or
(4) Also, on detachable arm chairs, an extension can be inserted into the seat rail tube which will enable you to increase the seat depth up to 3" total.

If your patient's measurement is less than the chart dimension, seat depth could be decreased by:
(1) Shortening seat upholstery so that it is 2" behind the calf, or
(2) Use a back cushion to move hip out.

**C. Arm height.** Once again, if your patient's dimensions are within the range of the chart, then no modifications are necessary.

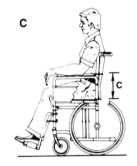

C

If patient's dimension is 2″ lower than chart arm height and you are prescribing a standard non-detachable arm model, you can do one of several things:

**(1)** Use a cushion to raise the patient, or

**(2)** Lower the arm by construction. On the standard arm model, you can only lower it one inch. On detachable arm chairs, in the top of the line, you can lower them as low as necessary. (Note: construction requires approximately 4–6 weeks manufacturing time).

If patient's dimension is greater than the chart arm height, then you can have the armrests raised to accommodate by modifying the frame (which is special construction and requires 4–6 weeks manufacturing time), or

If you are ordering a detachable arm model, you should consider the adjustable height arms or have them raised by construction.

**D. Back height.** Depending upon the diagnosis, the chart dimension should fall 1″ below the bottom of the scapula. Or if the diagnosis is such that your patient has little or no upper trunk balance, then the top of the chair back should be 1″ above the bottom of the scapula.

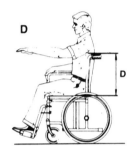

D

If the top of the chair back is too high for the patient, you can do one of two things:

**(1)** Add a cushion to raise the patient, or

**(2)** Lower the back height by construction.

If back height is too low, again you have several choices:

**(1)** Raise the back height by frame modification, or

**(2)** Consider a reclining back chair (semi-reclining or full-reclining). Caution: The overall length will increase on these two models. The semi-reclining by 2½″ and the full-reclining by 3″. Please take this into consideration.

**E. Total back height.** This will be used primarily by the high (C1–C4) quadriplegic patient who has poor trunk control and will need as much support as possible.

In this case, your consideration should be along the lines of a reclining back chair as you will have the total overall height to accommodate most people and you will also have the benefit of the adjustable angle back, which relocates the center of gravity, thereby stabilizing your patient.

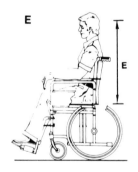

E

**F. Seat width.** Based upon the rule, allow 1″ on each side to provide enough room on the side so as not to create pressure on the trochanters. If your patient's measurements are within those on the chart, you can determine the chair size.

If a patient's measurements are less than those on the chart, you have two alternatives:

**(1)** The width can be decreased by installing narrower upholstery. If this is done, please take into consideration that there will also be an increase in seat height, with a corresponding decrease in back height and arm height, or

**(2)** The second alternative is to construct the chair with the narrower seat width, but maintain standard seat heights, back heights and arm heights. This is done by the manufacturer.

If the seat width dimensions of your patient are greater than those on the chart, again, you can do several things:

**(1)** Have larger upholstery installed, but keep in mind that you should not increase the upholstery over 1″. Also keep in mind that this can only be done on the standard arm chair. Remember too, that by installing the extra wide upholstery, you will lower the seat height by 1″ and increase the arm and back height by 1″. Note: There are some models available that will not have the seat height affected by the installation of wide upholstery. Be sure to check this out with your Abbey medical equipment specialist, or

F

**(2)** You can provide your patient with greater width seats by construction. Actually, this is preferable as the manufacturer has models available with various seat widths greater than 18″ and the chairs are designed with heavy duty features which include heavy duty axles, heavy duty seat and back upholstery, reinforced cross braces. There are two important things to be aware of with this type of chair:

**(a)** As the seat width is increased, it is necessary to increase the seat height in proportion to the width. As an example, on a chair with a seat width of 21″, your seat height would also be 21″. Therefore, if you wish to have a standard seat height of 19½″, you must have a special seat height modification to lower it once again. This is all done by frame construction, so there will be no change in other dimensions such as back and arm heights.

**(b)** Any width over 18″ and constructed with heavy duty features, has to be constructed with detachable arms or offset, non-detachable arms. Not available on standard arm models.

The following measurement chart will assist you in determining the actual size wheelchair required. Simply insert your dimensions from the measurement section into the appropriate boxes; A, B, C, D, E & F. Then add or subtract the dimensions indicated. You are now ready to proceed to the next step.

| Physical Measurements | Normal Clearance | | | Chair Size Measurements: (Compare Against General Dimensions Chart.) | Chair Size from Chart | Seat Cushion: (Cushion Will Compress to ½ Its Thickness.) | Back Cushion: (Depends Upon User, Depression of Cushion Approximately ½ Its Own Thickness.) | | Chair Size with Cushion. |
|---|---|---|---|---|---|---|---|---|---|
| **A** | + | 2″ | = | | | + | N/A | = | |
| **B** | − | 2″ to 4″ | = | | | N/A | + | = | |
| **C** | + | 1″ | = | | | + | N/A | = | |
| **D** | − | 4″ | = | | | + | N/A | = | |
| **E** | | | | | | + | N/A | = | |
| **F** | + | 2″ | = | | | N/A | N/A | = | |

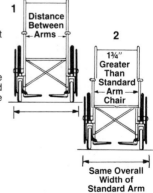

F. Seat Width

## Wheelchair Accessories

Once you have determined the correct size chair and the frame modifications, your next step is to determine the accessories and the particular models which will conform to the patient's needs and environment.

Starting with arms, these are the basic features to consider:

**1. Standard Non-Detachable Arms.** Usually used when a person can effect a standing, front transfer and when overall width of the frame is a consideration.

**2. Full length Offset Non-Detachable Arms.** These arms are offset to the outside of the frame, so as to provide more room between the front uprights and skirt guards. Person should be able to effect a standing transfer. Although there is more room between the uprights, the overall width is not affected.

1
Distance Between Arms

2
1¾″ Greater Than Standard Arm Chair

Same Overall Width of Standard Arm Chair

**3. Desk Arm Non-Detachable.** Same as number 2, but with a cut out at the front of the arm which allows close access to a table or desk.

**4. Full Length Offset Detachable Arms.** As indicated, these arms are removable and are recommended for the patient who can only effect a side transfer or when aid has to lift patient from chair and into bed. Arm is then out of the way and aid has full access to the patient. Caution: Overall width of this chair is increased by approximately 1¾". Make sure the chair will fit through any narrow doorways the patient may have in his home environment.

**5. Desk Offset Detachable Arms.** Same as number 4, except for cut out which allows close approach to tables and desks.

**6. Detachable Full Length Offset with Adjustable Height Arms.** Same as number 4, with the adjustable height feature. Used when standard armrest is not high or low enough for patient. Gives varying lapboard height to quadriplegic patient. Also enables patient to get near table or desk (in its lower position).

**7. Detachable Desk Arms with Height Adjustment.** Same as number 6, but with cut out for close approach to desk or table.

**8. Wrap-Around Detachable Full Length Arms.** When the overall width of the chair is critical and your patient definitely needs detachable arms, consider this feature. In order to locate the large wheels closer to the frame and decrease the overall width, the arm sockets which support the back of the arm tubes are located around to the back of the chair frame.

**9. Wrap-Around Detachable Desk Arms.** Same as number 8, but with desk cut out.

**10. Wrap-Around Detachable Full Length Arms with Height Adjustment.** Same as number 8, but with the added feature of height adjustment with the features as described in number 6.

**11. Wrap-Around Detachable Desk Arms with Height Adjustment.** Same as number 10, plus desk cut out.

3

4

5

6

**1) Semi Reclining**

The next area of consideration would be the wheelchair back. There are actually only three frame configurations available basically (though there are some special frame modifications).

**1. Semi-Reclining Back.** This offers 30° recline and full height back, up to 24", plus 10" removable headrest extension.

**2. Full-Reclining Back.** This reclines from 90° vertical position, 24" back height, plus 10" headrest extension, to give full support in back area. This type of back is also used for quadriplegics, so they won't have to transfer to a bed when they become tired—though it is not to be used in place of a bed.

**3. Sectional Height Back.** The removable back section enables the active paraplegic patient to convert from a standard height back to a lower back, which in turn enables the patient to be unobstructed when participating in sports activities.

**2) Fully Reclining**

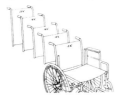

**3) Sectional Height**

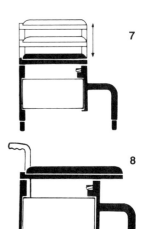

7

8

needs. These pages, reprinted from the *Abbey Medical Equipment Catalogue* with permission, describe all the considerations that should be weighed in selecting the best possible chair.

## WHICH CHAIR TO CHOOSE?

To choose an all-purpose chair, your best bet is to consult your doctor or therapist. He or she may suggest that you send for catalogs from several of the manufacturers listed below, or may have a specific chair already in mind for you.

Before choosing, you may want to look over the accessory options that also appear in this chapter, and the sections Special Chairs and Equipment for Special Needs and Wheelchair Alternatives, in case there is a chair that combines all your day-to-day needs with adaptations for situations such as travel, sports, getting through narrow places, and so on.

### Manufacturers and suppliers

MANUAL CHAIRS: Abbey Medical; C. R. Bard, Inc.; Everest and Jennings, Inc.; Fairfield Medical, Inc.; Falkenberg, Inc.; Freedom Chair Corp.; Gendron, Inc.; Invacare Co.; G. E. Miller; Ortho-Kinetics, Inc.; Sears, Roebuck and Co.; Stainless Medical Products, Inc.; Theradyne Corp.

MOTORIZED CHAIRS: Abbey Medical; American Stair-Glide Corp.; Everest and Jennings, Inc.; Fairfield Medical, Inc.; Falcon Research and Development; Gendron, Inc.; MED; G. E. Miller, Inc.; Sears, Roebuck and Co.; Steven Motor Chair Co.; Theradyne Corp.

## SPECIAL CHAIRS AND EQUIPMENT FOR SPECIAL NEEDS

### Folding

SPECIAL-NEED FOLDING: Folds to 10½″ x 19½″ high x 33″; weighs 36 lbs. (About $600, G. E. Miller)

SEARS FOLDING MODEL: Folds to 10½″ wide by 26¼″ x 30″; 33 lbs. (About $340)

ANOTHER SEARS MODEL: Folds to 13″ wide x 26¼″ high x 33″; weighs 51 lbs.; includes heavy-duty pneumatic tires. (About $400)

RECLINING FOLDING: Reclines up to 30 degrees; folds to 11″ wide; 24″ guide wheels with fluted handrims; removable and height-adjustable arms; 25″ overall width; 65 lbs. (About $520, Sears)

ANOTHER SEARS RECLINING/FOLDING MODEL: Folds to 11½″ wide; has independently adjustable backrest and hook-on legrests; 57 lbs. (About $370)

### Lightweight chairs

QUADRA-FOLD SPORTS CHAIR:   Weighs 22–25 lbs.; snap-off rear wheels for small-space storage; 16 different seat positions; able to turn on a dime. (About $1,300, Abbey)

QUADRA-LIGHT SPORTS CHAIR:   Similar to Quadra-Fold, but weighs 18–22 lbs. (About $1,100, Abbey)

QUADRA-SNOW SPORTS CHAIR:   Fits on any set of ski bindings; 22 lbs. (About $1,100, Abbey)

QUADRA-RACER SPORTS CHAIR:   Similar to first 2 sports chairs, but weighs 16 lbs. (About $1,100, Abbey)

*Note:* Other models of lightweight sports chairs are available through Abbey.

CONVERTIBLE:   Usable with either front or rear wheel drive; folds to 10½″ wide; 26″ overall width; 40 lbs. (About $250 plus shipping from Toledo, Ohio, Sears)

THE "NORMAN" CHAIR:   Great for travel or for gardening, if you can sit unaided (chair has no back) and use one leg for propulsion; convenient for negotiating aisles, doorways, and garden paths, and for stowing under seats, folds; weighs 18 lbs.; 25″ x 15″ x 17″. (Write Falkenberg, Inc.)

TALL PERSON:   Seat 1″ deeper, back 1½″ higher than traditional adult dimensions; detachable arm or detachable desk arm; swinging, detachable footrest; 56 lbs. (About $900, G. E. Miller)

G. E. Miller also makes a Narrow Adult model that costs about $900.

### Chairs for travelers

Any of the manual chairs described here (especially the lightweight, folding models) are convenient for traveling—there are also some smaller motorized models, described later, that travel well. You might also seek the advice of Safety Travel Chairs, Inc., 147 Eady Ct., Elyria, Ohio 44035, (216) 365-7593.

### Motorized chairs and equipment

MAINSTREAM ELEVATING WHEELCHAIR:   Battery-operated; seat may be elevated to 18″. Standard wheelchair except that it doesn't have detachable arms or swing-away, elevating footrests; has a bucket seat; a light touch on the buttons underneath seat elevates the chair; for indoor or outdoor use; battery included; weighs 75 lbs. (Several models available for about $2,000 and up, Mobility Systems)

WHEELCHAIRS TO HELP YOU STAND:   Three companies make chairs to help propel you to your feet; Abbey, American Stair-Glide, and Ortho-Kinetics. First, check with your doctor, nurse, or therapist to see whether you should consider buying such a chair—they may lift you too quickly.

## Power packs and equipment to motorize chairs

INSTA GAITER:   Modular power system for conventional folding or prescription chair; easily installed and disassembled; 24-volt battery-operated system; chair moves 3.5 mph. (About $1,200, Abbey)

STANDARD POWER KIT:   Mounts on any size, make, or style chair; moves chair at 4 mph. (About $1,550, Abbey)

TO MAKE A CHAIR INTO A POWERED RECLINER:   For Everest and Jennings chairs only; various electrical switching systems are available from $990 up. (Abbey)

BATTERY RANGE INDICATOR:   Tells you how much charge is left in your battery and how long to recharge to get maximum life. (About $45) Contact Donley Battery Co., 7521 E. Slauson Ave., Los Angeles, Cal. 90040, (800) 423–3934.

## Indoor/outdoor

There are 2 basic kinds of wheeled vehicles usable indoors or out: heavy-duty wheelchairs with pneumatic tires and sufficient power to go up ramps and inclines; and the lightweight "scoots," which have 3 wheels and bicycle-handlebar steering. (See also Mainstream Elevating Wheelchair, above.)

HEAVY-DUTY WHEELCHAIRS:   In addition to the chairs listed below, Abbey, International Medical Equipment Corp., and Saab-Scania carry such innovative models that it would probably be worth sending for all 3 catalogs if you have special needs and want to see the broad range of possibilities on the market today. Abbey's chairs run from about $1,500 to $3,000. International Medical's are more complex and prices start at about $5,000, while Saab's chairs are the most complex of all, with prices from about $8,000 on up.

>   *Folding:* A 24-volt system, battery charger included; desk length, detachable arms; semipneumatic tires; runs at speeds up to 3.5 mph; specify right- or left-hand joystick (steering mechanism). (About $1,690 plus charges from Minneapolis, Minn.; Sears) Gel-cel battery keeps the chair going for one day without recharging; sealed; removable; meets federal air travel requirements. (About $80 plus shipping, Sears)

>   *Semireclining:* Enables you to remain comfortably seated for long periods; leg supports raise, back semireclines; extra headrest unit, optional chin control; weighs 66½ lbs. without battery. (About

$2,450, Abbey) (Battery costs about $62; battery with recharge indicator costs about $65.)

*Slim Line:* Has 22½" overall width, lightweight; travels at speeds up to 4 mph; 2-speed microswitch; optional desk arms; sliding control box; elevating legrest; right- and left-hand control. (About $1,850, Abbey)

*Chairs with Special Controls:* Three companies—MED; Romich, Beery, and Bayer, Inc.; and Saab-Scania of America, Inc.—manufacture powered chairs operable by chin, joystick, head, arm, sip-and-puff, and other means, as well as multiuse remote control systems. Contact any or all of them for information. New York University Rehabilitation Center is also currently testing a voice-controlled wheelchair. For information contact The Institute of Rehabilitation Medicine, Occupational Therapy Dept., 400 East 34th St., New York, N.Y. 10016, or call (212) 340–6010.

*Curb-Climber: If your doctor says this vehicle is safe for you,* the Saab company will, without charge, train a technician at their service school to help you use it and to service it for you. Able to climb 30° inclines, climb 6" curbs, go in ice or snow, and fit through 28" spaces; usable indoor or out. *Do not consider a curb-climber without professional medical approval, as it could be very dangerous.* (About $8,500, Saab-Scania) International Medical Equipment Corp. sells a curb-climber that also climbs hills and 6" curbs, measures 27" wide, and sells for about $6,550.

"scoots": Of all those on the market, the Sears Portascoot seems to be the most reasonably priced. The Amigo model comes with the widest range of versatile accessories, including a "Boots" for carrying packages, and a unit that grows with a child. Then there are Braun's Tri-Wheeler, the Portascoot from Brewer, G. E. Miller and J. A. Preston's Motorized Handicap Chair, and Palmer's Happy Wanderer—all similarly priced. *Before buying, check with your doctor or therapist.* Also, if you can, try to contact people who have used the one(s) you are considering before making a final decision.

## WHEELCHAIR ALTERNATIVES

### Outdoor

MAKE-IT-YOURSELF: If you are a mechanic (or know one), it might be possible to buy a used riding lawn mower and adapt it. Remove the mower carriage and engine and install a battery-powered motor, easier-to-use shift control, and perhaps a more comfortable seat. (Idea reprinted by permission from *Accent on Living,* copyright © Winter, 1979, original idea by Suzanne Cook.)

ALL-TERRAIN BUGGIES: Open buggies that look like snowmobiles; have 4- and 6-wheel drive to go cross-country, over sand and snow, and even into water. Write or call Scrambler, Inc., 627 Wells Ct., Lexington, Ky., (606) 299–2646, and/or Summers A.T.V. Sales, Sherman, Ill., (217) 566–2453 for information on the Scrambler and Argo, respectively.

## Indoor

Lumex and Winco both carry such a diversity of chair-tables, wheeled recliners, easy chairs that convert to commodes, gliders, and rockers that it would pay to send for both catalogs to show your doctor, nurse, or therapist before deciding. Any chair you plan to use for relaxation should have arms and a firmly upholstered seat that is well padded toward the front for proper circulation, as well as a firm back properly contoured to your spine.

WHEELABOUT CHAIR: Push with feet to make it roll; 21″ wide; sling back, firmly padded seat; 5″ castors. (About $150 plus shipping, Sears)

## WHEELCHAIR REPAIR

A very good contact for repairs is your local bicycle dealer. The tools and techniques used to repair bicycle wheels also work for the wheels of wheelchairs.

A bicycle dealer may have trouble getting parts, but if he is a clever mechanic, he may be able to make wheelchair parts for you or modify bicycle parts to fit your chair. If all else fails, he can buy parts at retail prices from wheelchair distributors or suppliers (if they won't sell parts to him at wholesale prices). Even if you have to pay the bicycle dealer more because he was forced to buy parts retail, it may prove to be more convenient—you won't have to wait weeks while your chair is shipped back and forth to a distant repair shop.

## Other alternatives

Abbey and Sears have outlets all over the country, so if you buy from them, the cost of shipping your chair back for repair will probably be lower than if you bought a chair from far away. Some local surgical supply stores do a bit of repair work on the premises—be sure to check this before purchasing equipment from them.

## WHEELCHAIR ACCESSORIES

Before discussing accessories, a word about availability. The accessories listed below are available from Abbey, Cleo, and other dealers, but not all of them fit all makes and models of chairs. Most of them can be attached at home to your chair, but only if they are the right size for your particular model. So before ordering any accessory, check with your dealer or supplier; describe the make and model of your chair and the accessory in question—then leave it to the dealer to order the unit from the right manufacturer.

### To prevent feet from slipping off foot plates

HEEL LOOPS, TOE LOOPS, HEEL LOOPS/ANKLE STRAPS: Hold your foot in place on the footrest.

FOOT PLATE ANGLE ADJUSTMENT: Knob and lock to create comfortable foot plate angle.

NO. 2 FOOT PLATES: Add 2½″ to depth of foot plate.

### To add extra leg support

H STRAP: Attach to swinging, detachable footrests.

FABRIC LEGREST PANEL: Hooks on for calf support with footrests.

### Head support

HEADREST EXTENSION: Hook-on model to extend back height 13″ (about $30, Abbey, Cleo); or another type that screws to chair back to add 15″ (about $20, Cleo). Both types removable.

HEAD WINGS: Foam-padded for comfortable side head support. (About $38 the pair, Cleo)

### The back of your chair

ZIPPERED: To exit (or enter) chair from rear; especially useful in the bathroom; not for reclining chairs. (About $38, Abbey, Cleo)

DETACHABLE BACK: Similar to above, but swivel lock instead of zipper. (About $38, Cleo)

### Wheels and castors

Generally come in 20″ or 24″ sizes, are factory installed, and are available with regular or pneumatic tires. Pneumatic tires are best for outdoor use. Sears sells replacement 24″ tires for about $17 each, 2 for about $29. For better grasp of wheels, consider:

SNAP-ON HAND-RIM COVERS: Provide friction surface on handrims; gray rubber. (About $20, Cleo)

PROJECTION HAND RIMS:  Several models with knobs. (About $50–$70, Abbey)

Castors come in 5″ or 8″, the 8″ being better for rolling over carpets and doorways. These are factory-installed with regular or pneumatic tires.

CLAMP-ON LOCKS:  Clamp on to lock 8″ castor in place for stability in transferring. (About $35 the pair, Cleo)

## Devices to stabilize, balance, or increase leverage

AMPUTEE ADAPTER:  Sets rear wheels back to compensate for weight loss. (About $35, Abbey, Cleo)

ANTI-TIPPING DEVICE:  A bent rod with a rubber foot that hits the ground and stops the chair as it tilts; with wheels or tips; spring-locked lever to rotate device out of the way when not needed. (About $33, Abbey, Cleo)

GRADE-AID:  Assists ascent, prevents rollback on inclines; brakes and mounting plates included. (About $25, Cleo)

BRAKE EXTENSION:  Fits over standard brake levers to extend height, increase leverage. (About $17 each, Cleo)

## Arm and hand devices and position adjustors

ONE-ARM DRIVE ATTACHMENT:  Locates both propelling handrims on the same side of chair to convert standard chair to one-arm drive; specify whether for removable or fixed arms, occupant's right or left side. (About $235, Abbey)

ARM SUPPORT:  Plastic, washable fleece cover for standard or desk-style arms; Velcro strap; 4″ x 19″. (About $23, Nelson)

ARM POSITIONERS:  Also known as ball-bearing feeders, mobile arm supports, or balanced forearm orthoses; steel arm with aluminum trough; padded elbow; clamps to most chairs to support weight of arm on ball bearings and to increase range function for those with shoulder and elbow weakness. (About $100 each, Cleo)

"RANCHO" ARM SLINGS:  Height- and angle-adjustable to support arm in comfortable and correct position. (About $60, Abbey, Cleo)

WHEELCHAIR CUFF:  Leather to wear on hand for added traction and protection on wheels for quadriplegics and others; specify small, medium, or large. (About $12, Nelson)

BODY POSITIONER:  Multiadjustable pads that adjust in height and angle; made of foam-padded Naugahyde; stabilize upper body, hip, or thigh area. (About $150 the pair, Abbey)

KNEE SEPARATORS:

*Bar:* Adjustable 5″–9″; curved ends to hold knees apart. (About $12, Nelson)

*Curved Plastic:* Foam-padded; supports ⅓ of each limb while holding knees apart; specify small (for 12″–14″ thigh), medium (for 15″–17″ thigh), large (for 18″–20″ thigh). (Each about $12, Cleo)

## To carry things on your chair

LUGGAGE RACK:   Clamps on to fit between rear wheels; strap included. (About $33, Cleo)

CANE AND CRUTCH HOLDER:   Clamps on to either side of chair. (About $15, Abbey, Cleo)

OXYGEN TANK CARRIER:   Holds tank behind chair back. (About $45, Abbey)

ADJUSTABLE I-V HANGER:   Carries 2 bottles on chair; no support stand needed. (About $80, Cleo)

ASHTRAY/COASTER:   Snaps onto chair leg. (About $5, Nelson)

LAMPS:   Use a Velcro strap to fasten a small-based, high-intensity lamp to the chair arm. Or put lamp into a Chair Caddie (see below).

FOR THE BACK OF YOUR CHAIR:

*Pouch:* Measures 14″ x 15″ x 2″; made of Naugahyde. (About $18, Nelson)

*Swing-Away Pouch:* Screw mount; swivels from back to side of chair. (About $45, MED)

*French String Bag:* Drapes over chair handles; made of cotton fishnet; holds up to 5 lbs.; stretches to 20″ x 24″. (About $5, Lillian Vernon)

FOR THE SIDE OF YOUR CHAIR:

*Single-Pocket Pouch:* Measures 16″ x 16″; made of Naugahyde; with straps and zipper. (About $12, Nelson)

*Chair Caddie:* Folds; 2-compartment plastic box to hook onto chair. (About $13, G. E. Miller)

## Trays

LIFT-OFF, SWING-AWAY:   Easily attachable to arm upright; 11″ diameter. (About $22, Nelson)

SWING-AWAY TOTER TRAY:   Measures 14½″ x 15½″; rimmed; storage compartment 2″ deep below tray surface; on swing-away, lift-off bracket; for motorized or regular chairs. (About $60, MED)

SWING-AWAY STUDENT "DESK":   Has 10″ x 12″ tablet arm; lift-off bracket attaches to chair arm, flips down out of the way. (About $50, MED)

LAPBOARD:   See instructions for making one yourself on page 242.

*Masonite:* Unfinished; Velcro straps; 24″ x 19″. (About $18, Help Yourself Aids)

*Plastic:* Measures 21″ x 24″; wood-grain finish; Velcro straps. (About $19, Sears)

*Rimmed Maple Plywood:* Measures 19″ x 23½″; Velcro straps. (About $22, Nelson)

FORMICA: Measures 19″ x 23″; wood grain finish; belt goes under armrests and hooks to sides of tray; large D rings for quadriplegics. (About $33, Help Yourself Aids)

BUTCHER BLOCK: (About $35, Abbey)

TRANSPARENT: Is 23″ square: ¼″-thick polycarbonate with T bars; rubber O rings with straps. (About $85, Help Yourself Aids)

MOLDED PLASTIC RIMMED: Heavy-duty; 23″ x 21″. (About $36, Nelson)

TO SIT ON YOUR LAP: Attaches with hoop around your waist; Masonite; 1″ rim; tan, rust, orange, coral. (About $27, WINGS of VGRS)

## Safety belts/vests

STRAP: Threads around chair back uprights and between a person's back and chair upholstery; Velcro and D ring; specify regular (up to 32″—about $9) or long (up to 38″—about $20). (Help Yourself Aids)

BAR KIT: Bar that straps across waist; several models. (About $40–$50, Abbey)

VESTS: (See page 177.)

## Cushions

RING: Inflatable and noninflatable. (See page 173.)

INFLATABLE: Different shapes. (See page 173.)

EXTRA-THICK: A 3″-thick urethane foam pad; washable plaid cover; 16″ x 17″. (About $13, Miles Kimball)

CUTOUT CUSHIONS:

*Ischial:* Four-inch latex. (About $46, Cleo)

*Sacral:* Two-inch latex (about $39, Cleo); 4″ latex (about $41, Cleo)

*Coccyx:* Vinyl-upholstered over pressed wood; 16½″ x 16½″ x 2″. (About $22, Cleo)

WEDGE: Place high side in back to help you rise; or use high side in front to prevent sliding; 16″ x 18″ vinyl; 3″ deep at high end (about $20); 4″ deep (about $21); 5″ deep (about $22); Help Yourself Aids.

ECONOMY WEDGE: Same as the above but this one is 16″ square; 4½″ deep at one end, tapering to ¾″. (About $13, Help Yourself Aids)

WATER-FILLED

*Flotation:* Vinyl-covered 1″ foam; usable with or without water; 16″ x 16″ x 1¼″ when filled. (About $15, Sears)

*Aqua Seat:* Leakproof; 1-year guarantee; 8 lbs.; 17″ x 17″. (About $65, Abbey)

GEL: (See page 175.)

BALLOON OR "DRY FLOTATION": Inverted egg crate design any section of which can be collapsed separately; washable; should be used with adjustable footrests for better weight distribution throughout thigh area. (About $200, Abbey)

PNEUMATIC: Heavy rubber; pocketed for alternating weight distribution; quilted cover; air vent holes throughout. (About $50, Abbey)

POSTURE BACK SUPPORT: For proper support while in wheelchair, regular chair, car, etc.; molds to spinal contours. (About $30, Sears)

CUSHION-STOP: Fastens to chair seat and back to keep cushion from sticking out of back of chair. (About $8, Nelson)

### To narrow your chair

Pull your 2 front or rear posts together 2"–3" with a strong leather belt or straightened wire coat hanger. You can also have the spaces that connect the handrims to the wheels removed and shortened. Or look into buying whichever one of the following fits your chair.

REDUCE-A-WIDTH: Crank to pull up chair sides; narrows chair up to 4"; fits Everest and Jennings chairs—perhaps others as well. (About $63, Abbey, Cleo)

NARROMATIC: Crank to narrow chair up to 2½"; fits Invacare Rolls chairs—perhaps others also. (About $73, Cleo)

### To weigh yourself in your chair

Make a platform from a 3' x 4' piece of plyboard. Center a flat-topped scale on the board and draw an outline. Remove the scale and draw the dial. Cut a window in the board the size of the dial. Reinforce the underside of the board crosswise with four 2" x 1" slats. Place the board over the scale, ride up, balance, weigh, and deduct the weight of the board and the chair.[1]

WHEELCHAIR WEIGHING PLATFORM: Folds; fits over any bathroom scale; easily removed. (About $50, Nelson)

### Miscellaneous accessories

ROLLER BUMPERS: Nonmarking, gray rubber bumpers to protect walls. (About $12 the pair, Cleo)

SOLID FOLDING SEAT: Padded, folding, firm seat to replace sling or hammock seat (about $35, Sears); with upholstery to match chair (about $40, Abbey, Cleo).

COMMODE ATTACHMENT: Converts most standard chairs into a commode chair without modifications; includes seat, seat cover, and pan. If converting your existing chair, special back upholstery is required so you can remove the pan through the back without interfering with the back upholstery. (About $100, Abbey, Cleo)

DAVIS SUSPENSION FORK: Shock-absorbing device to absorb vibration and deflect front wheels back and up on impact with bumps, threshold, etc. (About $72, MSE Corp., P.O. Box 11742, Palo Alto, Cal. 94306, [702] 825–7650)

## TO PREVENT PRESSURE SORES

Try to keep your clothing from wrinkling under you. A daily bath also helps promote circulation. Or consider relieving pressure by placing your footrests slightly forward and tilted upward at the front.[2] Also consider using one of the cushions described on page 211 of this chapter or try sheepskin or pile (see page 174 of Beds) used fleece-side up.

## OTHER HELPFUL CHAPTERS IN THIS BOOK

A number of other chapters in this book might be of interest to wheelchair users. You will find devices for your chair and for your car/van in Control of Your Car. The chapter All about Beds describes devices to help you in and out of your chair and into bed. In Walk and Stand Aids, you will find special devices to help you stand and a platform that walks for you. Self-rising armchairs are listed in the chapter How to Do a Lot Less around the House, and the chapter Ramps, Lifts, and Elevators describes many devices for transporting wheelchairs.

## ORGANIZATIONS FOR PEOPLE IN WHEELCHAIRS

Disabled American Veterans, 1425 E. McMillan St., Cincinnati, Ohio 45206. Publication: *DAV* magazine.

Indoor Sports Club, Inc., 1255 Val Vista, Pomona, Cal. 91766. Publication: *National Hookup* magazine.

National Association of the Physically Handicapped, Inc., 2 Meetinghouse Road, Merrimack, N.H. 03054.

National Committee on Architectural Barriers for Rehabilitation of the Handicapped, Social and Rehabilitation Services, Washington, D.C. 20210.

National Congress of Organizations of the Physically Handicapped, 7611 Oakland Ave., Minneapolis, Minn. 55423.

National Easter Seal Society for Crippled Children and Adults, 2023 W. Ogden Ave., Chicago, Ill. 60612.

National Paraplegia Foundation, 333 N. Michigan Ave., Chicago, Ill. 60601. Publication: *Paraplegia Life* magazine.

National Shut-In Society, Inc., 11 West 42nd St., New York, N.Y. 10036. Publication: *The Open Window* magazine.

Paralyzed Veterans of America, 3636 16th St., N.W., Washington, D.C. 20010. Publication: *Paraplegia News* magazine.

Rehabilitation Services Administration, U.S. Dept. of Health, Education and Welfare, Washington, D.C. 20402.

Sister Kenny Institute, Chicago Ave. at 27th St., Minneapolis, Minn. 55407.

Visiting Nurse Association (check your local telephone directory).

Vocational Guidance and Rehabilitation Services, 2230 East 55th St., Cleveland, Ohio 44103.

# 27

# Ramps, Lifts, and Elevators

Mechanical lifting devices fall into 3 basic categories: ramps to get you over curbs and steps; lifts to get you from bed to wheelchair, to car or van, to easy chair, bathtub, or swimming pool; elevators and stair lifts to help you—or you in your wheelchair—up the stairs.

## RAMPS

If you are planning to install a ramp leading up to your front door, it is important to have a flat area 3 feet deep in front of the door if the door opens in, or an area 5 feet deep if it opens out. Good ramps should have handrails, be 30″–36″ wide for wheelchair use; be painted with sand paint for better traction if made of wood—or covered with roofing material or Adhesive Scotch Tread. When the weather forecast predicts snow, lay a piece of heavy-duty plastic along the ramp, then pull it up to remove the snow after the storm subsides.

### What size do you need?

For wheelchair use, the following height of rise in relation to ramp length is recommended:

| *Unassisted Wheelchair Use* | | *Assisted Wheelchair Use* | |
|---|---|---|---|
| Rise | Ramp Length | Rise | Ramp Length |
| 4½" or less | 3' | 6" | 3' |
| 9" | 6' | 12" | 6' |
| 13½" | 9' | 18" | 9' |
| 18" | 12' | 24" | 12' |

### Fixed and self-installable ramps

DURATECH MODULAR: Steel-framed, slip-resistant plywood; set in place, then bolted to top step or platform. If not enough room for a straight ramp, these ramps can be placed in right- or left-angle configurations if you provide a midsection platform. When used with $50 Splice Supports, 2 or more ramps can be linked together. Comes in a variety of sizes (all from Abbey): 5' (about $225); 6' (about $238); 7' (about $250); 8' (about $265); 9' (about $300); 10' (about $325). Each ramp also needs a Terminal Plate; specify shallow or acute angle; about $15 each.

*Optional Handrails:* Measure 7', about $60; 8', about $65; 9', about $70, all from Abbey.

ADD-ON: Three-foot, heavy-gauge, rustproof mesh aluminum; 3' add-on sections with connecting bars and legs, each weighing 12½ lbs.; nonskid, with built-in ramp anchor, safety wheel guides; 3' base, about $120; 6' base with one 3' add-on, about $250; 9' base with two 3' add-ons, about $375; 12' base with three 3' add-ons, about $500; all from Nelson.

### Portable

FOLDING WHEELCHAIR RAMP: Set of tracks, connected by carrying handle, to fit over curb or single step; size when pushed together, 3" x 14" x 36" long; size when open, 36" long x 28" wide; 8½ lbs.; nonrusting, nonslip aluminum. (Heavy-duty for people up to 200 lbs., about $72; extra-heavy-duty for people over 200 lbs. or for electric wheelchairs, about $82; Nelson)

PORTABLE METAL TRACKS FOR OVER CURBS AND STEPS OR TO ENTER CARS/ VANS: Measures 6" x 30", 12 lbs., about $90 the pair; 5½" x 60", 35 lbs., about $160 the pair; 5" x 60", 25 lbs., about $195 the pair; 5" x 90", 40 lbs., about $250 the pair. (Handi-Ramp.)

## LIFTS

There are a number of lifts to choose from, but here's something to keep in mind. Medicare will often pay for a multiuse lift with bath adapter, but it does not cover separate bath lifts. So the lift with a bath adapter, even though it's more expensive, may be covered, but the less expensive bath lift probably will not be.

### Patient lifts

(Also consider The Wilson Transporter on page 179.)

In addition to the patient lifts below, other models are sold by Abbey, Invacare, Nelson, Sears, and Ted Hoyer.

All of the following lifts are portable (but do not fold for travel, with the exception of Travel Lift), and are designed to get you from bed to wheelchair, commode, bath, and (over flat surfaces) to the car. You may choose the type of sling you want—either nylon or canvas (about $36 from Abbey) or open mesh nylon for bathing (usually a few dollars more). All slings are available with commode openings at no extra charge. Lift-off slings, slings with straps (about $7 more) and with commode seats are also available, as well as head support or head support with commode seat. (Both about $36, Abbey)

STANDARD LIFT: Adjustable U, ball-bearing base; opens to 34", closes to 24"; holds 400 lbs. (About $530, Abbey)

HYDRAULIC: Minimum-effort lifter; adjustable V, ball-bearing base; 40" wide open, 22" closed; holds 400 lbs. (About $500, Abbey)

LIFT AID WITH BATH ADAPTER: Open C base, ball-bearings; lifting mast for passage through narrow doorways; base and lifter separate into 2 parts; wraparound seat recommended; holds 300 lbs. (About $500 without bath adapter, Abbey)

*Bath Adapter:* Has 4 clamp knobs that attach and detach; saddle section for over tub. (About $300, Abbey)

HOYER SCALE: Chrome, attaches to any Hoyer Patient Lifter; 320-lb. capacity; specify metric or regular. (About $250, Abbey)

### Bath lift

SELF-OPERATED: Powered by water pressure alone (no electricity or cranking); with control in Up position, seat swings out over tub, bather transfers to molded fiberglass seat with back, puts control in Down position, and the seat glides as low as 3" into tub; diverter spout included to replace tub spout or to connect to shower head; installable without plumber; portable; 26" high x 18" wide; holds 200 lbs.; one-year guarantee. (About $400, optional safety strap about $20 extra, Fashion-Able)

### Toilet lifts

These lifts operate on the same principle as self-rising easy chairs that push you gently to your feet. They have padded arms, back support, and push-button electrical controls. Three companies make them: Burke, The Independence Chair Company, and Ortho-Kinetics. They cost about $700.

### Travel lift

FOLDING:  Folds to 6″ to fit easily into average car trunk along with folding wheelchairs; weighs 42 lbs.; base adjustable in width from 23″ to 29″, 4″ castors (3″ or 5″ also available); holds 300 lbs.; hydraulic or mechanical jack. (About $530, G. E. Miller)

### Car top lifts

(See also Wheelchair Loading on page 141.)

FOR REGULAR-SIZED CARS:  To transfer from wheelchair to car seat; hydraulic; fits tops 53″–62″. (About $550, Abbey)

FOR SMALL CARS:  For tops 45″–53″. (About $550, Abbey)

Van lifts are sold by Cheney and Golden Boy. (Portable ramps—see page 216—may also be used to enter vans or cars.)

### Porch lift

Operable without assistance for lifting wheelchair on nonskid platform to heights of 4½′, 6′, 7′, and 8′ (you must specify); 110-volt; adaptable for many interior uses; push-button controls. (About $2,950, Abbey)

Other porch lifts sold by Abbey, American Stair-Glide, Fairfield, Medical, R. J. Mobility Systems, and Wheel-O-Vator.

### Swimming pool lifts

HOYER:  Similar in design but not interchangeable with other Hoyer lifts; chrome; holds 400 lbs. (About $520, G. E. Miller)

NOLAN:  Operates in same manner as Self-Operated Bath Lift but this lift lowers you into pool instead of tub. (Contact J. E. Nolan and Co., Inc., Box 43201, Louisville, Ky. 40243, [502] 425–0883.)

Other swimming pool lifts sold by Cheney, Industrial Research and Engineering, R. J. Mobility Systems, and Ted Hoyer.

## STAIR LIFTS AND ELEVATORS

Ask your local Vocational Rehabilitation office for help in planning for a stair lift or elevator. Both are tax-deductible when prescribed by a doctor.

CHENEY THRIFT LIFT:  Seat that carries a person upstairs; install on any straight stairway; call-and-send controls; padded seat; folding footrests. (About $1,800, Abbey)

STAIRWAY ELEVATOR:  Similar to above with 12″ track that screws to top and bottom landings; no special wiring; plugs into 110 outlet; rotating seat. (About $2,100, Abbey)

WHEELCHAIR ELEVATING DEVICE: For any straight stairway 35″ or more; requires 10″ minimum space from wall when folded; 28″-wide platform lifts 350 to 400 lbs., depending on model ordered. (Write or call Earl's Stairway Lift Corp., 2513 Center St., Cedar Falls, Iowa 50613, [319] 277–4777.)

WHEELCHAIR ELEVATOR: Standard car size 3′ x 4′; needs clear space of 3′9″ wide x 4′3″ long; often installable in closet space, stairwell, corner, or side of room. (Earl's, address above)

WHEELCHAIR ELEVATOR FOR CURVES, CORNERS, AND SPIRALS: Carries person in a seat or in a wheelchair up most straight, curved, or winding staircases; with or without intermediate landings; 10″ wide when folded; installable with few or no staircase alterations—therefore less expensive than shaft elevator. Usable indoors or out. (Write or call Garaventa [Canada] Ltd., 7505 134A St., Surrey, British Columbia, Canada V3W 7B3, [604] 594–0422.)

Other elevators and stair lifts are carried by the following.

*Elevators:* Earl's Stairway Lift, Fairfield Medical, Inclinator

*Stairway Lifts:* Abbey, American Stair-Glide, The Cheney Co., Earl's Stairway Lift, The Flinchbaugh Co., Fred Scott and Sons, Inclinator

# PART SEVEN

# ECONOMICS

# 28

# *How to Get Government Money, Home Care, Tax Breaks, and Other Help*

This chapter introduces you to some of the public and private organizations that can help you with financial and other problems. But before deciding which of these leads to follow up, check with the health professionals you know and any friends who have applied for help. The aid available from many organizations varies from area to area according to the knowledge (or lack of it) of the people running the offices.

When requesting help from an organization, be specific. Spell out precisely what you need. If you don't, you may be bombarded with pamphlets directing you to many different sources, and these sources in turn will send further literature directing you to yet more sources. Very often it is more effective to make a phone call and stick with the agency you're calling, even if they switch you from person to person. You'll eventually get someone who can answer your question. It may cost a little more than a letter, but you save a great deal of frustration.

## FOR GENERAL HELP—FINANCIAL AND PHYSICAL

### *If you need care after leaving the hospital*

Go to the discharge planning office in the hospital. They will help arrange home care, including visiting nurses and therapists. Some hospitals now have home care visiting units to provide X-rays, radiation, medication, and other treatment.

### Visiting nurses and therapists

A visiting health professional can show you things to do, and do things for you, to change your life. Just the sight of one of them coming to your home can give you a lift. If you can't find them listed in the phone book under "Visiting Nurses" or "Visiting Home Health Care" or "District Nurses," call your State Department of Health.

### Volunteer groups

Many towns have Meals on Wheels, a volunteer group that delivers hot meals to homebound people. Look in your phone book for their number and address.

There is also an organization called FISH (Friends for Immediate and Sympathetic Help) that maintains a 24-hour-a-day volunteer service to drive you to the hospital, to your doctor, etc. Check your phone book. Also call your nearest hospital, the Red Cross, or the Junior League for information about other volunteer groups in your town; for example, many towns have shopping volunteers.

### Division of Vocational Rehabilitation

Called by different names in different states (check under "State Government" in the phone book), this organization is primarily concerned with helping you become employable after rehabilitation. But they do more than this. They will often provide guidance and/or financial aid in such areas as home remodeling and home health care, driver training if it will lead to employment, interpreter services for deaf people, reader services for the blind, self-help and technological devices, and much more.

You are eligible for aid if you have a disability that severely limits your capacity to work outside the home, or if you are a homemaker and unable to perform as such (homemaking is now by law a vocation).

Contact your local office for information or write The State Education Dept., Office of Vocational Rehabilitation, U.S. Dept. of Education, 330 C St., S.W., Washington, D.C. 20202.

## GOVERNMENT HELP IN GENERAL

For an overview of all that is available to you through the federal government, write or call Clearing House on the Handicapped, Office of Information and Resources for the Handicapped, U.S. Dept. of Education, 330 C St., S.W., Room 3106, Washington, D.C. 20202, (202) 245–0080.

## Medicare

Medicare, as you probably know, is for everyone over 65 years of age, and for disabled people under 65 who have been receiving Social Security or railroad disability annuities for 2 or more consecutive years. It may also be available to an individual or anyone in his or her family who requires dialysis or a kidney transplant due to kidney failure.

Medicare will pay up to 80 percent of the rental or purchase price of certain "durable medical equipment," after you have paid the first $60 of medical expense each year. "Durable medical equipment" is defined as equipment that can withstand repeated use, is primarily used for a medical purpose, and is generally not useful in the absence of illness or injury.

What this means is that you need a doctor to fight for you if Medicare says they will not allow something that has been prescribed for you. If your doctor will take the time to argue the case for you on the basis that the prescribed item is essential to your health and/or independence, very often Medicare will reverse their original refusal.

But do be careful if faced with a decision between several models of a specific device. Medicare *will* pay for a multiuse Patient Lift Aid with Bath Adapter (such as the one on page 217 of Ramps, Lifts, and Elevators); it will *not* pay for a separate Bath Lift, even though a Bath Lift is cheaper! So when you or your doctor or therapist are in doubt, call your local Social Security office to ask the allowable charge for major items before purchasing or renting—after which your doctor can still try to persuade them further if necessary

Medicare comes in two forms: Part A, which pays for hospital stays and posthospital care and is free; Part B, which is voluntary, costs $9.60 per month (as of April 1981), and helps pay doctor and other medical bills.

## Medicaid

And then there is Medicaid, not to be confused with Medicare. Medicaid pays your medical bills directly to your doctor, hospital, surgical supplier, etc., if you are on welfare; receiving Supplemental Security Income; blind; disabled or otherwise medically needy; or confined to a hospital where the expenses exceed a certain percentage of your income. Look in the phone book under your town or county Department of Social Services, or write Medical Services Administration, Social and Rehabilitation Service, U.S. Dept. of Education, 330 C Street, S.W., Washington, D.C 20202.

## Supplemental Security Income

If you are blind or disabled, your monthly income is below a certain level, and you have few valuables, such as stocks, bonds, or jewelry, you may be eligible for payments on the basis of need or of having been unable to earn regular Social Security benefits. (Even if you do have Social Security checks, or veteran's or other annuities, you may still be eligible, but these will reduce the amount of Supplemental Security Income you will receive.) For information on what records you must furnish in order to apply, call your Social Security office.

TO PREVENT THEFT OF SOCIAL SECURITY OR SUPPLEMENTAL SECURITY INCOME CHECKS: Ask your Social Security Office to deposit your checks directly into your checking or savings account.

### Additional help from the Department of Social Services

Besides Medicaid, other benefits may be available to you if you have minimal income or are now receiving or applying for Medicaid or Supplemental Security Income. Those benefits are aid in getting job training or health care; nutrition and shopping aid; visiting servics; housekeeping aid and better housing facilities. Check the phone book under town or county. Or get the booklet *Social Services for the Aged, Blind and Disabled* at your library or from the department.

## THE ORGANIZATION RELATED TO YOUR DISABILITY

These fine, specialized organizations provide a variety of services. Contact your local chapter, or write to the headquarters at the address given in the list entitled Organizations for Specific Disabilities at the end of this chapter.

### Veterans Administration

If you are a veteran who incurred a disability while in the service, you are entitled to housing benefits (see Housing section of this chapter). You may also be entitled to a pension, medical help, and services (through local VA centers and hospitals), and there are self-help devices that, if approved by a VA physician in your area, may be available to you free of charge. Check with your local VA office.

### Dental care

There are clinics for dental care for the disabled and some work may be done for you in the hospital. For information, write Academy of Dentistry for the Handicapped, 1240 E. Main St., Springfield, Ohio 45503, or American Dental Association, 211 E. Chicago Ave., Chicago, Ill. 60611.

### National Council for Homemaker–Home Health Aide Services, Inc.

This organization may be able to assist you in moving out of an institution back to your home. They will also help you get the home care you need. Located at 67 Irving Place, New York, N.Y. 10003.

### For part-time help

Have you considered asking a friend or local young housewife to clean your house, drive you or shop for you, make an extra portion of dinner for you, or otherwise help you for a few hours a day in return for cooking, dinner, babysitting, etc.? Or how about offering room and board to a student in return for household help? Call your local high school, university, or nearby medical school.

### For paid home health care

Professional home health care is tax deductible and sometimes funded by Medicare or Vocational Rehabilitation. Consult your Yellow Pages under "Health," "Home Health Care," or "Nurses" for agencies or write the main office of Homemakers Home and Health Care Services, Inc., c/o The Upjohn Co., Kalamazoo, Mich. 49001. They will furnish the address nearest you for hiring nurses, companions, and other home health aides.

Rep. Millicent Fenwick of New Jersey is at work on a bill, H.R. 2833, to pay a person to stay at home rather than go to a state health facility. Nursing home costs are so high that it would actually cost the government less to pay for care and equipment at home than it now pays to maintain an individual in a nursing home.

## FOR CHILDREN

### Crippled Children's Services

This is a joint federal/state project to help handicapped children up to age 21. For information, contact, local, county, or state health departments.

### National Easter Seal Society

The National Easter Seal Society for Crippled Children and Adults, 2023 W. Ogden Ave., Chicago, Ill. 60612 is an excellent source of all kinds of information.

### Organizations for specific disabilities

See list under the same name at the end of this chapter.

## FINANCIAL AID FOR SELF-HELP DEVICES

### Organizations

Find out whether Vocational Rehabilitation (see page 224 of this chapter), the Veterans Administration (if you are eligible—see page 226), Medicare (page 225) or Medicaid (page 225), or the organization related to your disability (see list at end of chapter) will pay for the device you need or provide it free of charge.

### To obtain a used device

Check the ads in your local newspaper, call your surgical supply house (they sometimes sell used devices), or advertise your needs in your local District Nursing Office or in a newspaper or rehabilitation magazine.

### Rental-purchase plans

If you are undecided about buying or expect to use the device for a limited time only, you may want to rent it until such a time as you decide to buy— at which time your previous rental payments can be applied to the purchase price. (Make sure that the store agrees to this arrangement ahead of time, as not all stores have rental-purchase plans.)

### Sharing

If the device is transportable and you expect to use it only occasionally, a friend might want to rent or buy it with you and share it. (However, if you decide to do this, agree ahead of time on how and by whom the device will be transported and/or repaired.)

### When you can't find the device you need

If you like making things yourself, refer to the chapter Make It Yourself to see if you find instructions for the needed device. (The chapter lists all the make-it-yourselfers described in this book, and lists all the items contained in booklets of instruction for which you can send.)

If you hate doing things with your hands, there are still other avenues to explore:

1. Ask your doctor, therapist, or nurse. One of them may have heard of a solution.
2. Write to the "Special Crew" of the Independence Factory. They have invented a great many devices already and are eager to help you come up with solutions to special problems. The Independence Factory is an all-volunteer, nonprofit organization dedicated to inventing and selling inexpensive devices to simplify everyday coping. Contact Fred Carroll, 514 Brelsford Ave., Trenton, Ohio 45067.
3. Contact the consulting rehabilitation engineer who may already have invented it (he's invented over 200 items to date!) If he hasn't invented it already, he'll be able to tell you how to make it or may even invent it for you! He's a very helpful gentleman indeed, and his name is Dr. Steven Kanor, 10 Lefurgy Ave., Hastings, N.Y. 10706.
4. Write to Accent on Information, Inc., Box 700, Bloomington, Ill.

61701 for a "Search Request Form." Fill it out, explaining your problem, and send it to them along with $6 for each request. They will then feed it into their computer and send you the computer printout of ideas or product information to solve your dilemma.

5. For answers to any question, other than purely medical ones, subscribe to the Information Service provided by contacting Information Officer, Disabled Living Foundation, 346 Kensington High Street, London W14 8NS, England.

6. For descriptions of 300 of the latest inventions in 4 Scandinavian countries (which house some of the most ingenious brains in the world), write Nordic Committee on Disability, Fack, S–161 25 Bromma, Sweden, and ask for a free copy of the committee's latest annual register of ongoing projects relating to disability.

# HOUSING

## General information

See the Bibliography (under Housing Design and Housekeeping; the list also includes material on creating barrier-free environments). Or write Housing and Urban Development, Office for Independent Living for the Disabled, 7th and D Sts., S.W., Washington, D.C. 20410.

## Adapted housing facilities in the United States

Continually updated files are kept by Rehabilitation Gazette, 4502 Maryland Ave., St. Louis, Mo. 63108.

## Loans and mortgage insurance

Apply for a Federal Housing Authority–insured loan from your local bank or:

FOR PURCHASING OR REPAIRING A RURAL HOME:    If you are in a low-income bracket, try applying for a loan to Farmers Home Administration, Dept. of Agriculture, Washington, D.C. 20250.

VA GRANTS:    For people disabled while in the service, the Veterans Administration gives once-in-a-lifetime grants up to $30,000 for building or remodeling a home.

VA MORTGAGE INSURANCE:    For service-disabled veterans, the VA offers once-in-a-lifetime insurance on mortgages for specially adapted housing—pays up to 70 percent of default on mortgage.

## Rent subsidies

To find out whether you are eligible, contact your local Public Housing

Authority, listed under "Housing," which in turn is under "State and Local Governments" in your phone book.

## TAX BENEFITS

If you are under 65 and totally and permanently disabled, you may be permitted to deduct part of your disability payment from your income tax. Check your local Internal Revenue Service office on this and find out what medical and dental expenses are deductible.

### *Items that are generally tax deductible*

> Motorized wheelchairs
> Special auto equipment
> Some telephone expenses
> Dentures
> Prostheses
> Eyeglasses
> Hearing aids and batteries
> Some health care insurance payments
> Cost of disabled dependent or spouse care
> Cost of and upkeep on seeing-eye and hearing dogs
> Cost of transportation to get medical care, including parking, tolls, and mileage—if you keep a log to prove these
> Payments to a special school if the main reason for attendance is disability
> Installation of special equipment for medical purposes, such as kitchen or bathroom improvements, ramps, lifts, etc. (If improvements increase property value, they are then deductible only insofar as they exceed the property value increase.)

In addition to these, there are special exemptions for blindness.

Be sure you keep receipts for payments made on all the foregoing, and to reduce medical and improvement costs, don't forget to consider the sources listed in this chapter under For General Help.

## STUDENT LOANS

Ask for help from the financial aid officer or guidance counselor at any college or vocational school, or write Bureau of Student Financial Aid, P.O. Box 84, Washington, D.C. 20044. You can also call Vocational Rehabilitation or your local Comprehensive Education Training Act (CETA) office to find out about programs in your area, as well as information on loans.

## YOUR RIGHTS

### *Your rights under the law*

Write to U.S. Dept. of Education, 330 C St., S.W., Washington, D.C. 20202 for the leaflet, *Your Rights as a Disabled Person.*

Or write President's Committee on Employment of the Handicapped, Washington, D.C. 20210 for the pamphlet, *Affirmative Action for Disabled People.*

There is also an excellent book describing legislation, government assistance, tax benefits, and all other aspects of your rights, as well as information on consumerism, travel, and much more. It is called *Access: The Guide to a Better Life for Disabled Americans* by Lilly Bruck, 1978, Random House.

### *If your rights have been violated*

Contact The Disability Rights Center, 1346 Connecticut Ave., N.W., Washington, D.C. 20036 for help. It's run by disabled people working with Ralph Nader. They publish, among other things, the booklet *Your Rights and How to Enforce Them.*

Or write National Center for Law and the Handicapped, Inc., 1235 N. Eddy St., South Bend, Ind. 46617, for legal assistance. They also publish a newsletter and magazine, both of which give information on what is happening to the rights of the disabled in the courts today.

If you are deaf, there is a special center to represent you and give you legal advice. Write National Center for Law and the Deaf, Gallaudet College, 7th St. and Florida Ave., N.E., Washington, D.C. 20002.

## CO-OP IDEAS

One community that houses a number of single people has a meal-sharing plan. Each person takes turns cooking dinner for several others. This way, no one has to cook for himself or herself every night, but can have the fun of wondering "What's for dinner?" And friends who so desire can dine together as much as they wish.

A lot of towns have "ring-a-day plans." People call shut-ins on a regular basis to check on them and then call a friend or neighbor if there is trouble or no answer. (Or several people could agree to call each other daily.) A brochure called *Suggestions for Operating a Ring-A-Day Telephone Reassurance Service* is available free of charge from Nassau County Office for the Aging, 33 Willis Ave., Mineola, N.Y. 11501.

To make shopping less tiring, why not get several friends together and approach store managers about keeping chairs, wheelchairs, or benches in the store for you. (Or consider buying the Gadabout Chair-Cane, described on page 188, together with a friend and share the use of it, each shopping with it on alternate days.)

## ORGANIZATIONS FOR SPECIFIC DISABILITIES

AMPUTEES

Amputees' Service Assoc., Suite 1504, 520 N. Michigan Ave., Chicago, Ill. 60611

The National Amputation Foundation, Inc., 12–45 150th St., Whitestone, N.Y. 11357

ARTHRITIS

The Arthritis Foundation, 3400 Peach Tree Rd. NE, Atlanta, Ga. 30326

BIRTH DEFECTS

The National Foundation/March of Dimes, P.O. Box 2000, White Plains, N.Y. 10605

BLINDNESS OR LOW VISION

See Sources of Additional Information in Chapter 13.

CARDIOVASCULAR DISEASE

The American Heart Association, 44 East 23rd St., New York, N.Y. 10010

Northeastern Association Post Stroke Clubs, Inc., 119 Arrow St. S., Schenectady, N.Y. 12304

CEREBRAL PALSY

United Cerebral Palsy Associations, Inc., 66 East 34th St., New York, N.Y. 10010

CYSTIC FIBROSIS

National Cystic Fibrosis Research Foundation, 521 Fifth Ave., New York, N.Y. 10017

DEAFNESS

See Sources of Additional Information in Chapter 12.

DIABETES

American Diabetes Association, Inc., 600 Fifth Ave., New York, N.Y. 10020

EPILEPSY

Epilepsy Foundation of America, 1828 L St., N.W., Washington, D.C. 20036

FRIEDREICH'S ATAXIA

Friedreich's Ataxia Group in America, Inc., Box 116, Oakland, Cal. 94611

HEMOPHILIA

National Hemophilia Foundation, 25 West 39th St., New York, N.Y. 10018

MULTIPLE SCLEROSIS

Association to Overcome Multiple Sclerosis, 79 Milk St., Boston, Mass. 02109

National Multiple Sclerosis Society, 205 East 42nd St., New York, N.Y. 10017

MUSCULAR DYSTROPHY

Muscular Dystrophy Associations of America, Inc., 810 Seventh Ave., New York, N.Y. 10019

MYASTHENIA GRAVIS

Myasthenia Gravis Foundation, Inc., 2 East 103rd St., New York, N.Y. 10029

OSTOMIES

The United Ostomy Association, 1111 Wilshire Blvd., Los Angeles, Cal. 90017

PARKINSON'S DISEASE

American Parkinson's Disease Association, 147 East 59th St., New York, N.Y. 10022

POLIO

National Easter Seal Society for Crippled Children and Adults, 2023 W. Ogden Ave., Chicago, Ill. 60612

SPINA BIFIDA

Spina Bifida Association, c/o The Texas Medical Center, 2333 Moursund, Houston, Tex. 77025

Spina Bifida Association of America, 104 Festone Ave., New Castle, Del. 19720

SPINAL INJURIES

National Paraplegia Foundation, 333 N. Michigan Ave., Chicago, Ill. 60601

Paralyzed Veterans of America, 7315 Wisconsin Ave., N.W., Washington, D.C. 20014

STROKE

See Cardiovascular Disease

# 29

# *Jobs and How to Find Them*

## ORGANIZATIONS THAT CAN HELP

Looking for a job is a little like searching for the perfect mate. You keep hoping one is out there somewhere, but the longer you look, the more you begin to wonder.

It doesn't have to be like this. Just as Brooklyn, N.Y., has its marriage brokers, there ought to be an organization that won't rest until it finds you a job.

Well, there is. It's run by each state and it's called:

### *Division of Vocational Rehabilitation*

(For further explanation of what they do and how to contact them, see page 224.) Not only will this organization train you for employment, they will stick with you until they have succeeded in finding the job that's right for you. They assign you a counselor who will help you in all aspects of finding a job, including home and auto adaptations and other equipment and services.

In addition to Vocational Rehabilitation, other avenues to explore are listed below.

## Local community rehabilitation agencies

For information about local agencies, ask your doctor, nurse, or therapist, or contact your local hospital and/or state department of health. Many counties have agencies not only to advise and/or train you for employment, but to provide sheltered workshops for those not yet ready to take outside jobs.

## Health agencies related to your disability

(See list at the end of Chapter 28, How to Get Government Money.) Often these agencies are able to help evaluate your needs and skills and help you train for a job.

## Local federal jobs

Call (800) 555-1212 and ask for the toll-free number for your nearest Federal Job Information Center.

## Rehabilitation centers at state universities

These centers often offer job counseling and training. Check with your state university.

## Federation of the Handicapped

Located at 211 West 14th St., New York, N.Y. 10011, this organization works without fee to develop plans to launch you into the job market. The federation often works closely with Vocational Rehabilitation.

## Just One Break, Inc. (JOB)

Founded to help disabled people find jobs, it is headquartered at 373 Park Ave. S., New York, N.Y. 10016 and has chapters in Queens, N.Y.; Boston, Mass.; Hackensack and West Orange, N.J.; Wilmington, Del.; and Toronto, Canada.

## Human Resources Center

This nationally known agency provides all kinds of vocational and educational training for severely disabled children and adults and publishes, among others, a booklet called *Vocational and Educational Opportunities for the Disabled.* Write Human Resources, I. U. Willets Rd., Albertson, N.Y. 11507.

## Goodwill Industries

This organization has local affiliates all over the country, providing vocational rehabilitation services and employment.

### Rehabilitation and Research Center

Contact this organization c/o Institute for the Crippled and Disabled, 340 East 24th St., New York, N.Y. 10010 for counseling and training.

### Clearinghouse for Employment

This group will help you find a job through United Cerebral Palsy Association affiliates and other potential employers. Contact them at United Cerebral Palsy Association, Inc., 66 East 34th St., New York, N.Y. 10016.

### Bureau of Apprenticeship and Training

You can get in touch with them through Manpower Administration, U.S. Dept. of Labor, Washington, D.C. 20210 for general career information as well as the address of the office nearest you. The local office will have lists of companies that offer apprenticeship training.

### The Electronics Industries Association

Provides training and career opportunities for disabled people in the electronics field. Write them c/o Electronics Industries Foundation, 2001 I St., N.W., Washington, D.C. 20006.

### Project for the Handicapped in Science

This group will help you find a job if you are a scientist. Contact them through American Association for Advancement of Science, 1776 Massachusetts Ave., Washington, D.C. 20036.

### Employment and Training Administration

This agency runs public employment programs and sheltered workshops. Write to them at U.S. Dept. of Labor, 600 D St., S.W., Washington, D.C. 20201

### Handicapped Employment and Economic Development, Inc.

Specializes in recruiting disabled people into corporations. The address is 115 East 57th St., New York, N.Y. 10022.

### Information on jobs for mentally retarded people

Write National Association for Retarded Citizens, 2709 Ave. East, Arlington, Tex. 76011.

## INCENTIVES FOR AN EMPLOYER TO HIRE YOU

Under a federal law called the Tax Reform Act of 1976, employers may now deduct from their taxes the *entire* cost of removing architectural barriers up to $25,000 per year. They may deduct up to this amount the first year, rather than having to spread the deduction over a 10- to 20-year period. Potential employers may not know this. It is up to you to point it out and to find out from the IRS the latest regulations for the percentages of your wages that an employer may deduct from his or her taxes under the Tax Reductions and Simplifications Act of 1977. By pointing out both of these advantages to a potential employer and perhaps offering to pay all or part of special equipment costs for items such as special typewriters and phone adapters, you may substantially increase your chances of being hired.

If an employer brings up any of the tired old saws about "insurance rates going up" if you were hired or tries to say that safety, attendance, and job performance could be a problem, quote the figures from a study made in 1973 by E. I. du Pont de Nemours and Co. The company at that time numbered 111,000 workers with 1,452 physically disabled employees. The study showed no increase in insurance costs; 79 percent of the disabled workers had an average or better attendance record than the employees in general; the job performance of 91 percent of the disabled people was average or better than the total work force; and the safety performance of 96 percent of the disabled rated average or better than the rest.[1]

## STARTING YOUR OWN SMALL BUSINESS

The first thing to do is decide what you like to do and how well you are able to do it. If you like and are good at more than one skill, you might be able to combine them, such as teaching as well as working with languages, music, crafts, etc. Or you could combine related activities like typing and research or an answering service and wake-up service.

If you can't decide what you want to do, but are anxious to start your own business, either get the *Dictionary of Occupational Titles* (published by the U.S. Department of Labor, Washington, D.C.) from your library for ideas, or look over the following general ideas list:

WORKING WITH YOUR HANDS: Artwork; leatherwork; refinishing or repair for local antique shop; general repair work; knitting, crocheting things to sell to local boutiques and department stores; sewing and alterations; ceramics; woodwork; pottery; cooking or catering; cabinetmaking; jewelry making; raising fruits, vegetables, flowering plants, etc.

WORKING WITH PEOPLE: Selling; tutoring; caring for children; running a boarding house; interior decoration; census taking; running a shop in your home if area is zoned for it

WORKING WITH FIGURES: Bookkeeping; tax work; making statistical surveys

PHONE WORK:    Phone surveys; election phoning; selling by phone; phoning daily to check on shut-in people; running an answering service or wake-up service; soliciting advertising; running a personnel agency, babysitting service, nurses' registry, or employment agency for the disabled; running a real estate agency

ART WORK:    Layout; designing; drafting

MISCELLANEOUS:    Typing or research for writers, college students, or the local paper; running a clipping service; raising and/or training animals or running a pet-sitting service

The possibilities are endless. But whatever you decide to do, get in touch with the Office of Public Information, Small Business Administration, Washington, D.C. 20416. They frequently extend loans to help start you, as well as offer a lot of helpful information.

You might also want to get the booklet *Home-Operated Business Opportunities* by sending $5.15 to Accent Special Publications, P.O. Box 700, Bloomington, Ill. 61701.

If you decide to make or produce a product or invention, the United Cerebral Palsy Associations of New York City sponsor an international marketing program to promote products made by the disabled. Write International Marketing Program, UCPA of New York City, Inc., 122 East 23rd St., New York, N.Y. 10010.

One final miscellaneous note—in case you're thinking about doing your business by mail, you can have stamps sent to you if you are unable to go to the post office. Just contact your local branch and ask that they be sent.

# 30

# *Make It Yourself*

Have you ever wondered why some people cringe and wave their hands when the word "screwdriver" is mentioned and others can't wait to run down to their workbenches? If you are not a make-it-yourselfer, consider this: It may be cheaper to get directions for making the item you want to ask someone to make it for you.

Besides the do-it-yourself ideas already in this book, you can send for 3 booklets of instructions.

## BOOKLETS OF INSTRUCTIONS FOR MAKING THINGS YOURSELF

### *How to Make It Cheap (Volumes I and II)*

These booklets show you how to make things at the lowest possible prices because the people at The Independence Factory care more about being helpful than making a profit. They also have an excellent short catalog of items made by their volunteers—things that are extraordinarily inexpensive because, of course, the factory has no labor costs. Write for both booklets (about $1.50 each) and the free catalog from The Independence Factory, P.O. Box 597, Middletown, Ohio 45042.

*How to Make It Cheap*—Volumes I and II—give instructions for making the following aids.

BEDS:
> *Volume I:* Riser legs
> *Volume II:* Trays, blocks

WHEELCHAIR:
> *Volume I:* Glass holder
> *Volume II:* Tray, blocks

WALKERS, CANES:
> *Volume I:* Cane
> *Volume II:* Conversion from regular to wheeled walker

EATING:
> *Volume I:* Adjustable Utensils

BATHING, TOILETING, AND GROOMING:
> *Volume I:* Commode seat riser, long-handled toe washer, sling towel, long-handled sponge, button aid, extension sponge cleaner-mop, extension toothbrush, extension nail-clippers
> *Volume II:* Enlarged-handled toothbrush, enlarged-handled comb, plastic funnel and tubing for toilet, commode safety rails, wash mitt

KITCHEN:
> *Volume I:* Floor sponge cleaner-mop, pop top and can punch, cutting board, tap turner
> *Volume II:* Oven scoop, mixing-bowl holder, enlarged handle for vegetable peeler, double-handled cooking pot

DRESSING:
> *Volume I:* Long-handled trouser aid, zipper pulls
> *Volume II:* Curved-handled dressing aid, boot jack, stocking aid

REACHERS:
> *Volume I:* Spring-closing utility stick

HOUSE:
> *Volume I:* Height-raiser for recliner chair, door opener, key T
> *Volume II:* Height-raisers for table, chair, sofa, and recliner chair legs, auxiliary light aid, auxiliary switch for electrical devices, wand dusting aid, permanent and portable half-steps, ramps

READING AND WRITING:
> *Volume I:* Penholder
> *Volume II:* Page turner

CAR:
> *Volume I:* Door-opening aid (for handle)
> *Volume II:* Ignition-starting aid, pushbutton car door aid

MISCELLANEOUS:
> *Volume I:* Extended cigarette holder

### Aids and adaptations

The great do-it-yourself instructions offered in the booklet *Aids and Adaptations* make it well worth your while to write to The Arthritis Society, 920 Yonge St., Suite 420, Toronto M4W 3J7, Canada (costs about $2.50). Included are instructions for the following.

BATHING:   Long-handled sponge; long-handled toe washer and drier, sling towel; wash mitt

DRESSING:   Sock sticks; stocking or sock aid; hinged shoe aid; long shoe horn; dressing stick; boot jack; button hook; overcoat aids

GROOMING:   Long-handled comb or brush; collapsible long-handled comb or brush; deodorant holder

EATING:   Handle padding

HOMEMAKING:   Jar opener; can opener; chopping board; food preparation board; tap turners; double-handled pot; pouring stand; kitchen carrier; cleaning aids; sheet tucker

RECREATION:   Book holder, card holder

PETS:   Bowl-holder with handle (lifts food and water bowls without bending); pet feeder

MISCELLANEOUS:   Pick-up stick; car door opener; wheelchair brake extension; key extension; telephone holders; watch winder—clock key; knob turner; ratchet screwdriver

BATHING AND TOILETING:   Bath stool, bench, and steps; raised toilet seat; raised toilet seat with handles or angled seat; raised toilet seat with sideward transfer; raised toilet seat with grab bar; commode; toilet paper holder

CHAIRS AND BEDS:   Chair or bed blocks; chair platform raise; raised cushions; chair-on-wheels; brakes for chair-on-wheels; wheelchair raise; table on wheels

AMBULATION AND TRANSFER:   Portable half-step; permanent half-steps; ramp; collapsible bus step for cane users; collapsible bus step with collapsible handle; car slide; sliding board; push-off handles

## BLUEPRINTS FOR MAKING
## A SMALL WHEELCHAIR FOR CHILDREN

To obtain free blueprints of a child's wheelchair and tricycle, write to R. J. Reynolds Tobacco Company, Winston-Salem, N.C. 27102.

The materials used to build the chair are readily available. You can get copper tubing from a hardware or plumbing supply store; to prevent the copper from darkening, it should be painted with an enamel of epoxy-based paint. The Naugahyde and foam rubber for the seat can be purchased from an upholstery shop and the wheels from bicycle shops. Tubing for the chair back is available in the lawn chair repair kits sold in variety and hardware stores. Carpet castors are available from hardware dealers. Galvanized sheet metal can be obtained from an air-conditioning or heating business, which will also do the necessary metal shaping. Brakes are a manufactured assembly available from authorized wheelchair dealers. The brakes used on the chairs built by R. J. Reynolds were obtained from an Everest and Jennings dealer. Brake assemblies made by other wheelchair dealers may also be appropriate; check an assembly's suitability before purchasing.

## OTHER MAKE-IT-YOURSELF PROJECTS

### Lapboard

PURPOSE:    A lapboard provides a table surface for a patient in a wheelchair or a chair with armrests.

FEATURES:    The board rests on the arms of the chair and extends over the sides and front. Cloth straps may be threaded through holes near the back of the board and tied around the chair to hold the board in place. Raised edging around the board prevents articles from slipping off.

MATERIALS:    For the board—½ in. good quality plywood. For edging— either ¾ in. quarter round, ¾ in. molding, or 1¼ in. wooden strips. Sandpaper. Varnish or shellac.

The size of the patient and chair and the amount of table surface needed determine the dimensions of the board. The inner edge of the board should rest close to the patient; therefore, the width and depth of the cutout may have to be adjusted for a very large or very small patient.

DIRECTIONS:    The holes for the cloth straps should be about 1″ in diameter. (Note: The wood will splinter if the holes are drilled too close to the edge.)

For edging, apply the quarter round or molding to the top of the board with the straight edge inside, or attach the wooden strips around the outside. Sand both surfaces of the board and then finish with varnish or shellac.

### Sliding board (transfer board)

MATERIALS:    ¾ in. lightweight pine board of desired length and width (plywood is unsatisfactory because of splintering). Coarse sandpaper for initial sanding, very fine sandpaper or steel wool for final sanding, varnish or shellac, paste floor wax.

DIRECTIONS:    Bevel the end edges of the board to one-half of the ¾ in. thickness. Bevel 10″ toward the center of the board, decreasing the amount of beveling as you move toward the center. Sand the board thoroughly; the beveled top and all edges need the most attention. Finish sanding with very fine sandpaper or steel wool. Shellac or varnish the board. When dry, sand with very fine sandpaper or steel wool. Repeat the process of shellacking or varnishing followed by sanding several times until a smooth surface is obtained. Again the beveled top and edges of the board need the most attention. Finish with a coat of paste floor wax.

## *Side rail that can be applied to a bed with a right-angle frame*

MATERIALS:

> 5′ of ¾″ or ½″ rigid conduit (regular electrical pipe)
> Two 3″ **C** clamps
> Four ¼″ round-headed stove bolts
> 4 lock washers
> 4 nuts or wing bolts

DIRECTIONS: Buy the material at an electrical shop and ask the electrician to bend the pipe so that the attached rail extends 11″ above the level of the mattress.

CAUTION: To apply this rail on a bed with the gatch feature, determine where the rail will be attached on the frame and adjust measurements accordingly. Drill holes for attaching **C** clamps. Bolt **C** clamps to either end of rail.

## *Side rail that can be bolted to a bed*

MATERIALS:

> 5½′ of ¾″ or ½″ rigid conduit (regular electrical pipe)
> Two ¼″ or ⅜″ round-headed stove bolts
> 2 washers
> 2 nuts

DIRECTIONS: Buy the material at an electrical shop and ask the electrician to bend the pipe so that the attached rail extends 11″ above the level of the mattress. Flatten attachment sites. Drill holes in the conduit and in the bed frame where the rail will be attached to the bed frame.

SUGGESTIONS: If you are attaching the rail to a wooden bed, use ¼″ or ⅜″ lag screws with washers. Use as many screws as necessary to make the rail secure.

## *Portable planting station*[1]

(See drawing on page 244.)

"This unique free-standing planting station can do double, even triple,

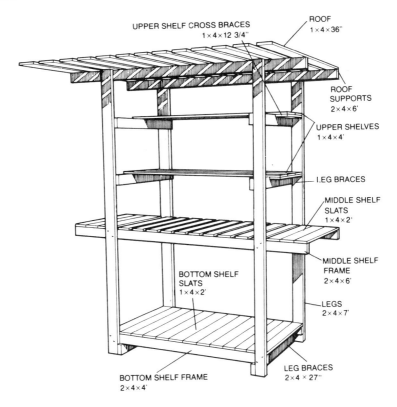

UPPER SHELF CROSS BRACES
1 × 4 × 12 3/4"

ROOF
1 × 4 × 36"

ROOF
SUPPORTS
2 × 4 × 6'

UPPER SHELVES
1 × 4 × 4'

LEG BRACES

MIDDLE SHELF
SLATS
1 × 4 × 2'

MIDDLE SHELF
FRAME
2 × 4 × 6'

LEGS
2 × 4 × 7'

BOTTOM SHELF
SLATS
1 × 4 × 2'

LEG BRACES
2 × 4 × 27"

BOTTOM SHELF FRAME
2 × 4 × 4'

PORTABLE PLANTING STATION   *A support to hold shade-loving plants, narrow shelves for display plants, a wide work surface for potting, even a storage shelf below—that's what this build-it-yourself garden table offers. It measures 4 x 2 feet wide with a generous 6-foot-long work table and stands 7 feet high.*

Reprinted with permission of *The Family Food Garden,* copyright © 1980, The Webb Co. Adapted from *The Redwood Book of Wood/Book of Could,* copyright © 1979, Simpson Timber Co., Seattle, Washington.

duty as an indoor/outdoor plant hanger, a garden workbench and storage shelf.

"It's designed to be constructed in sections and is fastened with removable bolts and wingnuts so that you can knock it down and position it inside or out, wherever the light conditions are best. We recommend using garden grade redwood for 2 x 4 components, and clear grade redwood for 1 x 4 components."

BASIC CONSTRUCTION METHOD:

1. Assemble leg module first. Nail together leg uprights and horizontal 2 x 4 members.

2. Build roof by nailing 1 x 4s to 2 x 4 roof supports. Space 1 x 4s approximately 1½"–2" apart.
3. Assemble middle shelf module by nailing 1 x 4 slats to 2 x 4 framing. Space slats in the middle approximately 1½" apart, closing the gap for end work spaces.
4. Assemble bottom shelf by nailing 1 x 4s to 2 x 4 framing. Nail slats together to provide a gap-free surface.
5. Join modules by drilling bolt holes at the junction of each module and attaching with bolts, wingnuts, and washers.

MATERIALS LIST:

|  | Quantity | Size | Length |
|---|---|---|---|
| Legs | 4 | 2 x 4 | 7' |
| Leg braces (construction heart) | 6 | 2 x 4 | 27' |
| Roof supports | 2 | 2 x 4 | 6' |
| Roof slats | 13 | 1 x 4 | 36" |
| (Space approx. 1½"–2" apart) | | | |
| Upper shelves | 8 | 1 x 4 | 4' |
| Upper shelf cross braces | 4 | 1 x 4 | 12¾" |
| Middle shelf frame | 2 | 2 x 4 | 6' |
| Middle shelf slats | 16 | 1 x 4 | 2' |
| | | | (spacing 1¼") |
| Bottom shelf frame | 2 | 2 x 4 | 4' |
| Bottom shelf slats | 14 | 1 x 4 | 2' |

twenty-four 3½" bolts with wingnuts and washers (2 bolts at each joint)

# MATERIALS FOR MAKING YOUR OWN INVENTIONS

## *Adhesives and pastes*

METAL PASTE: Patches holes, fills, repairs, preserves, rustproofs, waterproofs; spread to apply to metal, wood, plastic, or glass surface; can also be used for model-making; dries metallic gray. (Two 6-oz. cans, about $8, Brookstone)

SILICONE RUBBER COATING: Rust, water, and corrosion preventative for asphalt, paint, wood, masonry, tile, glass, canvas, other fabrics; seals metal; quart covers about 25 sq. ft.; dries in 2–6 hours; gray, may not be painted. (Quart for about $13, Brookstone)

EPOXY PUTTY: Molds like clay; shape to any form for watertight sealant, adhesive, putty, gasket filler, insulator; does not flow; cures in one hour at 75° Fahrenheit—rock-hard; can be machined, drilled, sanded, painted, used on metal, wood, brick, stone, concrete, plastic, glass, and tile. (1 lb. for about $8, Brookstone)

SPACE AGE ADHESIVE:  Bonds anything to anything, except certain types of rubber and plastic; dries clear; not available for shipment December through February. (14½-oz. plastic bottle, about $7, Brookstone)

## Tapes

ADHESIVE-BACKED MAGNET TAPE:  Creates magnetic catches for cabinet doors; holds small parts, tools; sticks to dashboard or refrigerator with second length stuck to notes, lists, etc.; 10' roll, ½" wide x $\frac{1}{16}$" thick. (About $8, Brookstone)

DOUBLE-SIDED FOAM TAPE:  Permanent, pressure-sensitive adhesive on both sides of $\frac{1}{32}$" foam, conforms to surface irregularities that make most double-sided tapes useless; for indoor or outdoor use; 54' roll, 1" wide; white. (About $9, Brookstone)

QUICKER STICKER TAPE DISPENSER:  Wheel that holds tape under the wrist, attached to adjustable band that goes *around* the wrist for one-handed application of tape. (About $3.30 from Quicker Sticker, 204 W. 50th St., Loveland, Colo. 80537) (O-H)

## Foam

INSTANT URETHANE FOAM:  Fills hollows, insulates pipes, patches leaks, seals holes; fills cracks, flotation chambers in boats; expands to 3 times its volume; dries to touch in 20 minutes; sticks to almost anything except polyethylene; 33-oz. can, 1 cu. ft. (About $20, Brookstone)

## Velcro, webbing, sheepskin, and other fabrics

VELCRO BY THE YARD:  Nylon tape; press together to close, peel apart to open; wonderful machine-washable substitute for zippers, snaps, buttons, etc.; white or beige. (About $3 per yd.; about $23 for 10 yds.; Fashion-Able)

WEBBING:  One-inch width, 100 percent cotton. (About $3 for 4-yd. strip; about $22 for 50 yds.; Fashion-Able)

SHEEPSKIN OR KODEL POLYESTER PILE:  (See page 174.)

OLD-FASHIONED COTTON FLANNEL:  White; 36" (also 47") wide cotton with flannel finish on both sides; *not* treated to be flame-retardant. (About $2.50 per yd., Vermont Country Store)

FLANNEL-COVERED RUBBER SHEETING:  (See page 172.)

PLASTIC SHEETING:  (See page 172.)

TURKISH TOWELING:  One hundred percent cotton, tough Navy toweling (not thick and fluffy); 1½" selvage every 36" for cutting and hemstitching your own towels; each 36″ x 18″ wide. (About $3.50 per yd., Vermont Country Store)

MONK'S CLOTH:    Looks handwoven; 100 percent cotton, durable fabric; tight or coarse weave; straw or natural. (About $8 per yd., Vermont Country Store)

## Miscellaneous

TURNTABLE BEARING:    Easily attached to wood or metal to make TV sets, seats, stands, shelves, etc., rotate; large bearing 12″ in diameter, ⅜″ thick; small bearing 6″ square, ⁵⁄₁₆″ thick; both run on metal steel races. (About $7 for large, about $4 for small, Brookstone)

ADJUSTABLE MULTIHANDLE:    To interchange files, hacksaw blades, drill bits, knives—any shank up to ⁷⁄₃₂″ thick, ¹⁹⁄₃₂″ wide; handle 4″ long, 1½″ diameter; varnished maple. (About $7, Brookstone)

HANDY MAGNET:    Attach to dowel or any unmagnetized reacher to make a magnetized "picker-upper" or to make anything magnetic; comes with handle. (About $3, American Foundation for the Blind)

HI-MARKS:    Tube of bright orange hardening (washable) substance to make raised letters, symbols, etc., on paper, cloth, wood, or metal. (About $4 per tube, American Foundation for the Blind)

PULL LOOPS:    Attach to anything to help you pull it with one finger (zippers, drawer handles, doorknobs, lids, etc.). (About $4 for package of 20, Fashion-Able)

OLD LEATHER BELTS:    To be found for pennies at any thrift shop and used to make strong loops for a number of tasks—pulling open drawers and doors, attaching to bannisters for pulling oneself upstairs, etc.

# Appendix:
# Sources of Equipment
# and Information

*Abbey Medical*, 3216 El Segundo Blvd., Hawthorne, Cal. 90250, (213) 973–3493
*Ability Building Center, Inc.*, 1500 First Ave., N.E., Rochester, Minn. 55901
*Able Table*, P.O. Box 365, Santa Clara, Cal. 95052, (408) 296–0378
*Adult Blind Engineering*, 4243 Warren Ave., Sacramento, Cal. 95882
*AliMed*, 138 Prince St., Boston, Mass. 02113
*American Foundation for the Blind*, 15 West 16th St., New York, N.Y. 10011
*American Home Products, Inc.*, P.O. Box 151617, Tampa, Fla. 33684
*American Hospital Supply Corp.*, 1450 Waukegan Rd., McGaw Park, Ill. 60085
*American Printing House for the Blind*, 1839 Frankfort Ave., Louisville, Ky. 40206
*American Stair-Glide*, 4001 East 138th St., Grandview, Mo. 64030
*American Telephone and Telegraph Co.*, 195 Broadway, New York, N.Y. 10007
*American Thermoform Corp.*, P.O. Box 125, 8640 E. Slauson Ave., Pico Rivera, Cal. 90660
*Amigo, Inc.*, 6693 Dixie Hwy, Bridgeport, Mich. 48722
*The Andis Company*, 1718 Layard Ave., Racine, Wis. 53404, (414) 634–3256
*Anik, Inc.*, P.O. Box 3232, San Rafael, Cal. 94904
*Anthony's Enterprises, Inc.*, 3293 S. Seymour Rd., Swartz Creek, Mich. 48473
*Apollo Lasers, Inc.*, 6357 Arizona Circle, Los Angeles, Cal. 90045
*Applied Communications Corp.*, P.O. Box 555, Belmont, Cal. 94002
*Aqua Survey and Instrument Co., Inc.*, 7041 Vine St., Cincinnati, Ohio 45216

*Argo, Summers ATV Sales*, Sherman, Ill. 62684, (217) 566–2453

*The Arthritis Society*, 920 Yonge St., Suite 420, Toronto M4W 3J7, Canada

*Bathing Aids to the Handicapped*, 10-C Escondido Village, Escondido Rd., Stanford, Cal. 94305, (415) 857–1053

*Bausch and Lomb Safety Products*, 655 St. Paul St., Rochester, N.Y. 14605

*L. L. Bean, Inc.*, 3380 Birch St., Freeport, Me. 04032

*The Bell System*, Special Needs, Dept. B, Box 99, Bowling Green Station, New York, N.Y. 10004

*Bernina Sewing Machines of Switzerland*, 534 W. Chestnut, Hinsdale, Ill. 60521

*The Braun Corp.*: 1014 S. Monticello, Winamac, Ind. 46996; 13710 49th St. N., Clearwater, Fla. 33520; 3651 Sausalito St., Los Alamitos, Cal. 90720

*E. F. Brewer*, P.O. Box 159, Menomonee Falls, Wis. 53051

*Brookstone Co.*, 475 Vose Farm Rd., Peterborough, N.H. 03458

*Burke, Inc.*, P.O. Box 1064, Mission, Kans. 66202

*Burpee Seed Co.*, 300 Park Ave., Warminster, Pa. 18991

*Cameron Enns Co.*, 13637 S. Madsen Ave., Kingsbury, Cal. 93631

*Camp International, Inc.*, Jackson, Mich. 40204 (Write for address of local supplier)

*Canine Companions for Independence*, P.O. Box 466, Santa Rosa, Cal. 95402, (707) 528–0830

*R. J. Chair Lift Co., Inc.*, 715 Fifth Ave., Maywood, Ill. 60153

*Chemical Bank*, Marketing Div., 20 Pine St., New York, N.Y. 10005

*The Cheney Co.*, 7611 North 73rd St., Milwaukee, Wis. 53223

*Chesebrough-Pond's Inc.*, Hospital Products Div., Greenwich, Conn. 06380

*Cleo Living Aids*, 3957 Mayfield Rd., Cleveland, Ohio 44121

*The Cleveland Illuminating Co.*, P.O. Box 5000, Cleveland, Ohio 44101

*Colonial Garden Kitchens*, 270 W. Merrick Rd., Valley Stream, N.Y. 11582

*Communication Outlook*, Artificial Language Laboratory, Computer Science Dept., Michigan State Univ., East Lansing, Mich. 48824

*Creative Services for the Blind*, 10600 Highland Lakes Blvd., N. Miami Beach, Fla. 33179

*Crestwood Co.*, 331 S. Third St., P.O. Box 04513, Milwaukee, Wis. 53204

*Danmar Products, Inc.*, 2390 Winewood, Ann Arbor, Mich. 48103, (313) 761–1990

*The Deerskin Trading Post*, Rte. 1 at 114, Danvers, Mass. 01923

*Developmental Learning Materials*, 7440 N. Natchez Ave., Niles, Ill. 60648

*Dialogue with the Blind, Inc.*, 3100 Oak Park Ave., Berwyn, Ill. 60402

*Donley Battery Co.*, 7521 E. Saluson Ave., Los Angeles, Cal. 90040, (800) 423–3934

*Drive-Master Corp.*, 16 Andrews Dr., W. Paterson, N.J. 07424

*Earl's Stairway Lift Corp.*, 2513 Center St., Hwy 218 N., Cedar Falls, Iowa 50613

*Easy Reading Aids*, C. Beil Designs, 5435 N. Artesian Ave., Chicago, Ill. 60625

*Easy Riser*, 87 Millstone Rd., Wilton, Conn. 06897

*EBSCO Curriculum Materials*, P.O. Box 11521, Birmingham, Ala. 35202, (800) 633–9623

*Edmund Scientific Co.*, Edscorp Bldg., Barrington, N.J. 08007

*Ednalite Corp.*, 200 N. Water St., Peekskill, N.Y. 10566

*EduTrainer, Inc.*, 415 N. Alfred St., Alexandria, Va. 22314

*Elkay Manufacturing Co.*, 2700 S. 17th Ave., Broadview, Ill. 60155

*Evans Specialty Co., Inc.*, 14 East 15th St., P.O. Box 4220, Richmond, Va. 23224

*Everest and Jennings*, 1803 Pontius Ave., Los Angeles, Cal. 90025 *or* 111 Snider-croft Rd., Concord, Ontario L4K 1B6, Canada

*Extensions for Independence*, P.O. Box 3754, Downey, Cal. 90242

*Facetglas, Inc.*, 10 Blackwell St., Rock Hill, S.C. 29730, (803) 328–0191

*Fairfield Medical, Inc.*, 10 Winters La., Baltimore, Md. 21228

*Falcon Research and Development, Inc.*, Whittaker Corp., 109 Inverness Dr. E., Englewood, Colo. 80112

*Falkenburg, Inc.*, 3612 S.W. Troy, Portland, Ore. 97219

*Fashion-Able*, Rocky Hill, N.J. 08553

*Ferry House*, 554 N. State Rd., Briarcliff Manor, N.Y. 10510

*The Flinchbaugh Co., Inc.*, 390 Eberts La., York, Pa. 17403

*Foster House*, 141 Foster Bldg., Peoria, Ill. 61632

*Fred Sammons, Inc.*, Box 32, Brookfield, Ill. 60513

*Fred Scott and Sons*, 1444 W. Rand Rd., Des Plaines, Ill. 60016

*Gambit Corp.*, 174 E. Bellevue Dr., Pasadena, Cal. 91105

*Garden Way*, 1300 Ethan Allen Ave., Winooski, Vt. 05404

*Gendron, Inc.*, Lugbill Rd., Archbold, Ohio 43502

*General Electric Co.*, Housewares Div., 2185 Boston Ave., Bridgeport, Conn. 06602

*General Telephone and Electronics Corp.*, 1 Stamford Forum, Stamford, Conn. 06904, (203) 357–2000

*George W. Park Seed Co., Inc.*, Greenwood, S.C. 29647

*Gillette Co.*, Personal Care Div., Merchandise Mart, Chicago, Ill. 60654

*Golden Boy Sales Corp.*, 2556 S. Fairview, Santa Ana, Cal. 92704

*Gorman Products*, 189 Lake St., Brooklyn, N.Y. 11223

*H. G. Grantham Co.*, 3401 Catherine St., Goldsboro, N.C. 27530

*Gresham Driving Aids, Inc.*, 30800 Wixom Rd., Wixom, Mich. 48096

*Greyhound Lines, Inc.*, Greyhound Tower, Phoenix, Ariz. 85077

*Hal-Hen* (Order through your hearing-aid dealer)

*Halls*, 505 Armour Rd., N. Kansas City, Mo. 64116

*Hamilton Beach Division, Scovill Manufacturing Co.*, Scovill Sq., Waterbury, Conn. 06720

*Handee for You, C. O. Smith*, 7674 Park Ave., Lowville, N.Y. 13367

*Handibend Manufacturing Co.*, R.D. 161, R.R. 2, Accord, N.Y. 12404

*Handicapped Artists of America*, 8 Shady Lane, Salisbury, Mass. 09150

*Handicappers of America*, R.R. 2, Box 58, Camby, Ind. 46113

*Handi-Dog, Inc.*, 5332 E. Rosewood Ave., Tucson, Ariz. 85711, (602) 326–3412

*Handi-Ramp, Inc.*, 1414 Armour Blvd., P.O. Box 475, Mundelein, Ill. 60060

*Hanover House*, Hanover, Pa. 17331

*Happy Wanderer, Palmer Industries*, P.O. Box 707, Endicott, N.Y. 13760

*Harriet Carter*, Dept. 32, Plymouth Meeting, Pa. 19462

*Hausmann Industries, Inc.*, 130 Union St., Northvale, N.J. 07647, (201) 767–0255

*HC Electronics, Inc.*, 250 Camino Alto, Mill Valley, Cal., 94941

*Hearing Dog Program, American Humane Assoc.*, 5351 S. Roslyn St., Englewood, Colo. 80110

*Helen Gallagher's*, 6523 N. Galena Rd., Peoria, Ill. 61632

*Helen Keller National Center*, 111 Middle Neck Rd., Sands Pt., N.Y. 11050, (516) 944–8900

*Help Yourself Aids*, Box 192, Hinsdale, Ill. 60521

*Henniker's*, 779 Bush St., Box 7584, San Francisco, Cal. 94120

*Home Care Health Products*, 6030 Wayzata Blvd., Minneapolis, Minn. 55416, (800) 328–5720

*House of Minnel*, Deerpath Rd., Batavia, Ill. 60510

*Howe Press, Perkins School for the Blind*, 175 N. Beacon St., Watertown, Mass. 02172

*Human Resources Center*, I.U. Willets Rd., Albertson, N.Y. 11507

*Inclinator Company of America*, 2200 Paxton St., Harrisburg, Pa. 17105

*The Independence Chair Co.*, Elm Grove, Wis. 53122

*The Independence Factory*, P.O. Box 597, Middletown, Ohio 45042

*Industrial Research and Engineering Co., Inc.*, 2409 N. Kerby, Portland, Ore. 97227

*Infanseat Co.*, 1709 15th Ave., Box 309, Eldora, Iowa 50627

*Institute of Rehabilitation Medicine*, 400 East 24th St., New York, N.Y. 10016

*International Business Machines*, Office Products Div., 400 Panson's Pond Dr., Franklin Lakes, N.J. 07417

*International Marketing Program, United Cerebral Palsy Associations of New York City, Inc.*, 122 East 23rd St., New York, N.Y. 10010

*International Medical Equipment Corp.*, 11000 E. Rush St., S. El Monte, Cal. 91733

*Invacare Corp.*, 1200 Taylor St., P.O. Box 550, Elyria, Ohio 44035 *or* 741 West 17th St., Long Beach, Cal. 90813

*JA Industries*, 440 Totten Pond Rd., Waltham, Mass. 02154

*J and J Enterprises*, Box 506, Merrick, N.Y. 11566

*Janssen, U.S.A., Tri-World Industries, Inc.*, 2885 S. Santa Fe. Dr., Englewood, Colo. 80110

*Joan Cook*, P.O. Box 21628, Fort Lauderdale, Fla. 33335

*Johnny Appleseeds*, 50 Dodge St., Beverly, Mass. 01915

*Johnson Electronics, Inc.*, P.O. Box 7, Casselberry, Fla. 32707

*Kindergard*, Dallas Tex. 75247

*King Size Company*, Brockton, Mass. 22402

*Knape and Vogt Manufacturing Co.*, Grand Rapids, Mich. 49505 *or* La Mirada, Cal. 90638

*Kurzweil Computer Products, Inc.*, 264 Third St., Cambridge, Mass. 02142

*Kwik Sew Pattern Co., Inc.*, 300 Sixth Ave. N., Minneapolis, Minn. 55401

*Lee Wards, Creative Crafts Center*, 1200 St. Charles Rd., Elgin, Ill. 60120

*Leinenweber*, Brunswick Bldg., 69 W. Washington St., Chicago, Ill. 60602

*Lillian Vernon*, 510 S. Fulton Ave., Mount Vernon, N.Y. 10550

*Lumex, Inc.*: 100 Spence St., Bay Shore, N.Y. 11706; 2860 Leonis Blvd., Los Angeles, Cal. 90058; *Bercotec, Inc.*, 3600 Boulevard Tri-Centenaire, Pointe-aux-Trembles H1B 5M8, Montreal, Quebec, Canada

*Maddak, Inc.*, 6 Commerce Rd., Pequannock, N.J. 07440

*Mauch Laboratories, Inc.*, 3035 Dryden Rd., Dayton, Ohio 45439

*The Maytag Co.*, Newton, Iowa 50209

*Mechstat, Inc.*, 830 N.E. Loop 410, San Antonio, Tex. 78209

MED, *Inc.* (Write or call for complete list of distributors or distributor in your area: AAMED, Inc., 1215 S. Harlem Ave., Forest Park, Ill. 60130, [312] 771–2000)

*Meg Designs*, Box 127, Dept. H28, Stone Harbor, N.J. 08247

*Mentor, Inc.*, 716 North Rd., Boynton Beach, Fla. 33435

*Message Management Consultants*, P.O. Box 20010, Indianapolis, Ind. 46220

*Microalert Systems International*, 3030 Empire Ave., Burbank, Cal. 91504

*Miles Kimball*, 41 W. Eighth Ave., Kimball Bldg., Oshkosh, Wis. 54901

G. E. *Miller, Inc.*, 484 S. Broadway, Yonkers, N.Y. 10705

*Miya Epoch*, 1635 Crenshaw Blvd., Torrance, Cal. 90501, (213) 320–1174

R. J. *Mobility Systems*, 715 S. Fifth Ave., Maywood, Ill. 60153, (312) 344–2705

*Montgomery Ward*, Albany, N.Y. 12201 (Check phone book for store nearest you.)

*MSE Corp.*, P.O. Box 11742, Palo Alto, Cal. 94306

*National Easter Seal Society*, 2023 West Ogden Ave., Chicago, Ill. 60612

*National Institute of Rehabilitation Engineering*, 97 Decker Rd., Butler, N.J. 07405

*National Odd Shoe Exchange*, 1415 Ocean Front, Santa Monica, Cal. 90401

*National Theatre of the Deaf*, 305 Great Neck Rd., Waterford, Conn. 06385, (203) 443–5375 (TTY: 443–7406)

*Nelson Medical Products*, 5690 Sarah Ave., Sarasota, Fla. 33581

*New Look Patient Apparel, Inc.*, 505 Pearl St., Buffalo, N.Y. 14202

*The New York Times*, 229 West 43rd St., New York, N.Y. 10036

*Nichols Garden Nursery, Inc.*, 1190 N. Pacific Hwy, Albany, Ore. 97321, (503) 928–9280

J. E. *Nolan and Co., Inc.*, P.O. Box 43201, Louisville, Ky. 40243

*Norm Thompson*, P.O. Box 3999, Portland, Ore. 97208

*North American Riding for the Handicapped* (See page 108 for names of regional directors.)

O. C. *Conversions, Inc.*, 9914 Oakland Dr., Kalamazoo, Mich. 49002, (616) 323–0160

*Ortho-Kinetics, Inc.*, P.O. Box 436, 1610 Pearl St., Waukesha, Wis. 53186, (800) 558–2151

*Palmer Industries*, P.O. Box 707, Endicott, N.Y. 13760, (607) 754–1954

*Para Quad, Inc.*, 3614 W. 2100 South, Salt Lake City, Utah 84120

*Park's Seeds* (See George W. Park Co.)

*Pelco Sales, Inc.*, 351 E. Alondra Blvd., Gardena, Cal. 90248

*J. C. Penney Co., Inc.,* 1301 Ave. of the Americas, New York, N.Y. 10019 (Check phone book for store nearest you.)

*Peterik Corp.,* 6572 S.E. Lake Rd., Milwaukie, Ore. 97222, (503) 659-8916

*PMI, Inc., Digivox,* P.O. Box 4634, Inglewood, Cal. 90309

*J. T. Posey Co.,* 5635 Peck Rd., Arcadia, Cal. 91006

*Possum, Inc.,* East Coast Div., P.O. Box 451, Midwood Sta., Brooklyn, N.Y. 11230

*The Pottery Barn.,* 2031 10th Ave., New York, N.Y. 10011

*Prentke Romich Co.,* R.D. 2, Box 191, Shreve, Ohio 44676

*Prestige Products Co.,* P.O. Box 20320, Ferndale, Mich. 48220

*J. A. Preston Corp.,* 71 Fifth Ave., New York, N.Y. 10003 (Order their products through surgical supply)

*PTL,* Box 364, Stillwater, Okla. 74074

*Rehabilitation Equipment and Supply,* 1823 W. Moss Ave., Peoria, Ill. 61606

*R. J. Reynolds Tobacco Co.,* Winston-Salem, N.C. 27102

*Rise-O-Matic Chair Co.,* 2294 Scranton Rd., Cleveland, Ohio 44113

*Romich, Beery, and Bayer, Inc.,* R.D. 2, Box 191, Shreve, Ohio 44676

*Roxter Corp.,* 10-11 40th Ave., Long Island City, N.Y. 11101

*SAAB-Scania of America, Inc.,* SAAB Dr., P.O. Box 697, Orange, Conn. 06477, (203) 795-5671

*Safe-T-Bath of NE,* 185 Millbury Ave., Millbury, Mass. 01527, (617) 865-2361

*Safety Travel Chairs, Inc.,* 147 Eady Ct., Elyria, Ohio 44035

*Salton, Inc.,* 1260 Zerega Ave., Bronx, N.Y. 10462

*The Saltus Corp.,* Pleasant St., S. Natick, Mass. 01760

*San Francisco Lighthouse for the Blind Store,* 75 Buchanan St., San Francisco, Cal. 94102

*SciTronics, Inc.,* 523 S. Clewell St., P.O. Box 5344, Bethlehem, Pa. 18015

*Scott Plastics Co.,* P.O. Box 2958, Sarasota, Fla. 33578

*Scrambler, Inc.,* 627 Wells Ct., Lexington, Ky. 40505

*Sears Roebuck and Co.,* Sears Tower, Chicago, Ill. 60684 (Check phone book for store nearest you.)

*The Seeing Eye, Inc.,* Morristown, N.J. 07960

*Seemore Industries,* 195 W. Gibbs St., Portland, Ore. 97201

*Self Start Manufacturers,* P.O. Box 232, Cambridge, Mass. 02141

*Sharp Electronics Corp.,* 10 Keystone Pl., Paramus, N.J. 07652

*The Shylar Corp.,* 140 E. Garden of the Gods Rd., Suite B, Colorado Springs, Colo. 80901, (301) 598-5134

*Skandi-Form, Inc., Rudd International Corp.,* 1066 31st St., N.W., Washington, D.C. 20007

*Sleepy Hollow Gifts,* P.O. Box 2327, Falls Church, Va. 22402

*Smith-Corona-Marchant, Div. of SCM Corp.,* Consumer Products Div., 65 Locust Ave., New Canaan, Conn. 06840

*Solar Products Co.,* Box 22004 Sappington Station, St. Louis, Mo. 63126

*Sonic Alert, Inc.,* 28 East Iroquois, Pontiac, Mich. 48053

*Space Quill Corp.,* Rte. 5, Box 166A, Martinsburgh, W.V. 25401

*Sped Publications*, 2010 Eagle View, Colorado Springs, Colo. 80909

*Spencer Gifts*, Spencer Bldg., Atlantic City, N.J. 08411

*Spiegel*, 1061 West 35th St., Chicago, Ill. 60609

*Sportpages*, 3373 Towerwood Dr., Dallas, Tex. 75234

*Stand-Aid, Inc.*, Box 386, 1009 Second Ave., Sheldon, Iowa 51201, (712) 324–2153

*Stanley Tools*, 480 Myrtle St., New Britain, Conn. 06050

*Starcrest of California*, 3159 Redhill Ave., Costa Mesa, Cal. 92626

*Simulation Learning Aids, Ltd.*, 65 Earl Ave., Lynbrook, N.Y. 11563

*Sunset House*, Sunset Bldg., Beverly Hills, Cal. 90215

*Sun-Tel Co.*, 3308 Midway Dr., San Diego, Cal. 92110

*Superior Optical Co.*, P.O. Box 15287, Santa Ana, Cal. 92705

*Swift Instruments, Inc.*, 952 Dorchester Ave., Boston, Mass. 02125 *or* P.O. Box 562, San Jose, Cal. 95106

*TASH, Inc.*, Sunnybrook Medical Centre, 2075 Bayview Ave., Toronto, Ontario M4N 3M5, Canada

*Telesensory Systems, Inc.*, 3408 Hillview Ave., Palo Alto, Cal. 94304

*Tensor Corp.*, 333 Stanley Ave., Brooklyn, N.Y. 11207

*Tomco Enterprises, Inc.*, 7701 Hoover Rd., Valley Ctr., Kans. 67147

*Touch Aids, C and E Kruger*, 1049 Redondo Way, Hemet, Cal. 92343

*TR, Inc.*, West 2563 Greer Rd., Palo Alto, Cal. 94303

*Trans-Electric Engineering*, P.O. Box 701, Meridan, Idaho 83642

*Truxes Adhesives and Chemicals Co.*, P.O. Box 633, Naperville, Ill. 60540

*Tufts New England Medical Center*, 171 Harrison Ave., Box 1014, Boston, Mass. 02111

*Turen, Inc.*, Box 270, Lebanon, N.H. 03766, (603) 448–2990

*Typewriting Institute for the Handicapped*, 3102 W. Augusta Ave., Phoenix, Ariz. 85021

*Unique Efficiency, Inc.*, 732 Valley Rd., Upper Montclair, N.J. 07043

*Universal-Rundle Corp.*, 217 N. Mill St., New Castle, Pa. 16103

*Velcro Corp.*, 681 Fifth Ave., New York, N.Y. 10022

*The Vermont Country Store, Inc.*, Weston, Vt. 05161

*Vibralite Products*, 1 Belleview Ave., Ossining, N.Y. 10562

*Visualtek*, 1610 26th St., Santa Monica, Cal. 90404

*Volunteer Service Photographers, Inc.*, 111 West 57th St., New York, N.Y. 10019, (212) 246–3965

*Votrax Div., Federal Screw Works*, 500 Stephenson Hwy, Troy, Mich. 48084

*Voxcom Div. of Tapecon, Inc.*, 100 Clover Green, Peachtree City, Ga. 30269

*Wal-Jan Surgical Products, Inc.*, 295 Atlantic Ave., E. Rockaway, N.Y. 11518

*Walter Drake and Sons*, Drake Bldg., Colorado Springs, Colo. 80901

*Walter F. Nicke*, Box 667G, Hudson, N.Y. 12534, (518) 828–3415

*Westek Corp.*, 7320 Convoy Ct., San Diego, Cal. 92111

*Wheelchair Carrier Co.*, P.O. Box 103, Waterville, Ohio 43566

*Wheelchair Carrier Sales Corp.*, P.O. Box 16202, Phoenix, Ariz. 80511

*Wheelchair Fashions, Inc.*, 142-A High and Congress, Portland, Me. 04101

*Wheel-O-Vator Div., Toce Brothers Manufacturing, Ltd.,* P.O. Box 489, Broussard, La. 70518

*Whitaker Surgical,* 230 E. Hartsdale Ave., Hartsdale, N.Y. 10530

*WINCO, Winfield Co., Inc.,* 3062 46th Ave. N., St. Petersburg, Fla. 33714

*WINGS of Vocational Guidance and Rehabilitation Services,* 2239 East 55th St., Cleveland, Ohio 44103

*The Wooden Spoon,* Rte. 6, Mahopac, N.Y. 10541

*Yeaple Corp.,* 1255 University Ave., Rochester, N.Y. 14607

*Yield House,* North Conway, N.H. 03860

*Zim Manufacturing Co.,* 2850 W. Fulton St., Chicago, Ill. 60612

# Notes

## Chapter 1

1. Idea from *Independent Living for the Handicapped and the Elderly* by Elizabeth Eckhardt May, Neva R. Waggoner, and Eleanor Boettke Hotte. Copyright © 1974 by Houghton Mifflin Company. Used by permission.
2. *Ibid.*
3. Ideas, except step four, are from *Aids to Independent Living: Self-Help for the Handicapped* by Lowman and Klinger, copyright © 1969, Blakiston Division, McGraw-Hill Book Company. Reprinted with permission. Step four reprinted with the permission of Julius D. Lombardi from *Handy, Helpful Hints for the Handicapped*, distributed by the National Easter Seal Society, Chicago.
4. Idea from *Mealtime Manual for People with Disabilities and the Aging* by Judith L. Klinger, O.T.R., M.A., and the Institute of Rehabilitation Medicine, NYU Medical Center, with the Campbell Soup Company, 1978.
5. *Ibid.*
6. Adapted from *Aids and Adaptations*, The Arthritis Society, Toronto. Reprinted by permission.
7. Lombardi, *Handy, Helpful Hints for the Handicapped.*

## Chapter 2

1. Idea from *Mealtime Manual for People with Disabilities and the Aging* by Judith L. Klinger, O.T.R., M.A., and the Institute of Rehabilitation Medicine, NYU Medical Center, with the Campbell Soup Company, 1978.

2. Idea from *Independent Living for the Handicapped and the Elderly* by Elizabeth Eckhardt May, Neva R. Waggoner, and Eleanor Boettke Hotte. Copyright © 1974 by Houghton Mifflin Company. Used by permission.
3. Klinger, *Mealtime Manual.*
4. Idea courtesy *Handy, Helpful Hints for the Handicapped* by Julius D. Lombardi, distributed by the National Easter Seal Society, Chicago. Reprinted by permission.
5. *Ibid.*

### Chapter 3

1. Idea from *You Can Do It from a Wheelchair* by Arlene E. Gilbert. Copyright © 1973. Reprinted with the permission of Arlington House Publishers, Westport, Conn.

### Chapter 5

1. Ideas reprinted from *Convenience Clothing and Closures* with the permission of Donahue Sales, Talon Division of Textron.
2. *Aids and Adaptations*, The Arthritis Society, Toronto. Reprinted with permission.
3. Idea courtesy *Handy, Helpful Hints for the Handicapped* by Julius D. Lombardi, distributed by the National Easter Seal Society, Chicago, Ill. Reprinted by permission.
4. *Aids and Adaptations.*
5. Suggestions reprinted courtesy the National Easter Seal Society from *Self-Help Clothing for Children Who Have Disabilities.*
6. All three ideas courtesy Julius D. Lombardi, Northeast Association Post Stroke Clubs, Inc.
7. Excerpted from *You Can Do It from a Wheelchair* by Arlene E. Gilbert. Copyright © 1973. Reprinted with the permission of Arlington House Publishers, Westport, Conn.
8. Ideas ("put on slacks while lying down"; "take off slacks while sitting up or lying down") courtesy the National Easter Seal Society.
9. Lombardi, Northeast Association Post Stroke Clubs, Inc.
10. The National Easter Seal Society.
11. From *Aids to Independent Living: Self-Help for the Handicapped* by Lowman and Klinger, copyright © 1969, Blakiston Division, McGraw-Hill Book Company. Reprinted with permission.
12. The National Easter Seal Society.
13. Lombardi, Northeast Association Post Stroke Clubs, Inc.
14. The National Easter Seal Society.
15. Idea by James Wirtel, reprinted with permission from *Accent on Living* magazine, summer 1980, copyright © 1980.

### Chapter 6

1. All safety information reproduced by permission from *Transfers for a*

*Patient with Acute and Chronic Conditions,* 1970, Sister Kenny Institute, 2727 Chicago Ave., Minneapolis, Minn. 55407.

2. *Ibid.*

## Chapter 8

1. Crib adaptation information reprinted from *Independent Living for the Handicapped and the Elderly* by Elizabeth Eckhardt May, Neva R. Waggoner, and Eleanor Boettke Hotte. Copyright © 1974 by Houghton Mifflin Company. Used by permission.

## Chapter 11

1. A *Stroke in the Family* by Valerie Eaton Griffith. New York: Delacorte Press, 1970. Reprinted with permission.

## Chapter 16

1. From *Aids to Independent Living: Self-Help for the Handicapped* by Lowman and Klinger, copyright © 1969, Blakiston Division, McGraw-Hill Book Company. Reprinted with permission.

2. *Ibid.*

## Chapter 18

1. Courtesy *Handy, Helpful Hints for the Handicapped* by Julius D. Lombardi, distributed by the National Easter Seal Society, Chicago. Reprinted by permission.

2. *Ibid.*

3. *Ibid.*

## Chapter 19

1. Courtesy *Handy, Helpful Hints for the Handicapped* by Julius D. Lombardi, distributed by the National Easter Seal Society, Chicago. Reprinted by permission.

2. Wheelchair-loading ideas courtesy of Sue Owen.

## Chapter 24

1. Material reproduced with permission from *Transfers for a Patient with Acute and Chronic Conditions,* 1970, Sister Kenny Institute, 2727 Chicago Ave., Minneapolis, Minn. 55407.

## Chapter 26

1. Reprinted with permission from *Accent on Living* magazine, summer 1980, copyright © 1980.

2. Both ideas contributed by Chantelle Ubelhor and reprinted with permission from *Accent on Living* magazine, summer 1980, copyright © 1980.

## Chapter 29

1. *Jobs for Handicapped Persons: A New Era in Civil Rights,* Public Affairs Pamphlet No. 557. New York: Public Affairs Committee, Inc. Reprinted with permission.

## Chapter 30

1. "Portable Planting Station Eases Garden Chores," *The Family Food Garden,* June/July, 1980. Reprinted with permission of The Family Food Garden, copyright © 1980, The Webb Co. Adapted from *The Redwood Book of Wood/Book of Could,* copyright © 1979, Simpson Timber Co., Seattle, Wash. 98164. Reprinted by permission.

# *Bibliography*

## GENERAL

*Access: The Guide to a Better Life for Disabled Americans* by L. Bruck. New York: Random House, 1978. Detailed consumer advocacy and economic information.

*Activities of Daily Living for Physical Rehabilitation* by E. Lawton. New York: McGraw-Hill, 1963.

*Aids to Independent Living: Self-Help for the Handicapped* by E. Lowman and J. L. Klinger. New York: McGraw-Hill, 1969.

*Handy, Helpful Hints for the Handicapped* by Julius D. Lombardi. Chicago: The National Easter Seal Society.

*Independent Living for the Handicapped and the Elderly* by E. E. May, N. R. Waggoner, and E. B. Hotte. Boston: Houghton Mifflin, 1974.

*Physically Handicapped.* Raleigh, N.C.: Extension Service, U.S. Department of Agriculture, North Carolina State University at Raleigh. Information on homemaking, grooming, and clothing.

*Self-Help Devices for Persons with Disabilities: Selected References* (Bibliography series L-6). Compiled by the Information Center. Chicago: The National Easter Seal Society, 1978. Books, periodicals published by the handicapped, addresses of sources, and a selection of catalogs (free).

*Sources of Information on Self-Help Devices for the Handicapped.* Chicago: The National Easter Seal Society (free).

## CARS

Conversion of Cars for Disabled Drivers. 219 East 44th St., New York, N.Y. 10017: Rehabilitation International. (Available in English or Spanish.)

Driver's Manual from your local Motor Vehicle Bureau. Gives driver's test requirements and sample questions.

Hand Controls and Assistive Devices for the Physically Disabled Driver. I.U. Willetts Rd., Albertson, N.Y. 11507: Human Resources Centre, 1977 (illustrations).

Hand Driving Controls and Special Devices. 107 S. Broadway, Room 7118, Los Angeles, Cal. 90012: California State Department of Rehabilitation, 1970 (free).

Teaching Driver Education to the Physically Disabled. I.U. Willetts Rd., Albertson, N.Y. 11507: Human Resources Center, 1978 (paperback, illustrations).

## COMMUNICATION/READING

(Compiled by the Reference Section of the National Library Service for the Blind and Physically Handicapped, the Library of Congress, Washington, D.C.)

"Communication and Vocational Aids" by Judith L. Klinger. In *Self-Help Manual for Arthritis Patients*. Atlanta: Arthritis Foundation, 1980. Pp. 89–98. $1.00. Sources of reading, writing, and telephone aids for individuals with arthritis.

International Guide to Aids and Appliances for Blind and Visually Impaired Persons. 2nd ed. New York: American Foundation for the Blind, 1977. 255 pp. $3.00. A full description, price, and address of source are given for each aid listed.

Library Service to Handicapped Persons. Washington, D.C.: Reference Section, National Library Service for the Blind and Physically Handicapped, the Library of Congress, 1978 (free).

Non-Vocal Communication Resource Book edited by Gregg Vanderheiden. Baltimore: University Park Press, 1978. lv. (loose-leaf). $12.95. Information about communication boards and other devices for persons with verbal and physical handicaps. Includes descriptions and illustrations of various devices in experimental stages and custom-made devices.

Reading Aids for the Partially Sighted: A Systematic Classification and Procedure for Prescribing by Louise Sloan. Baltimore: Williams and Wilkins, 1977. 150 pp. $12.95. Criteria for selecting and evaluating optical and non-optical reading aids. Illustrations accompany many of the descriptions.

## CLOTHING

Adapt Your Own: A Clothing Brochure for People with Special Needs by M. C. Beasley, D. B. Burns, and J. M. Weiss. University, Ala.: University of Alabama Press, 1977.

*Apparel Manufacturing for the Elderly and Physically Handicapped* by PTL Designs, Inc. P.O. Box 364, Stillwater, Okla. 74074: PTL Designs, Inc. A catalog describing garments that may be custom-ordered.

*Clothing Designs for the Handicapped* by A. Kernaleguen. Alberta, Canada: University of Alberta Press. Directions for altering clothing and patterns for men, women, and children.

*Clothing for the Handicapped: An Annotated Bibliography* by N. Reich. Tucson, Ariz. 85721: University of Arizona, School of Home Economics, 1979.

*Clothing for the Handicapped: Fashion Adaptations for Adults and Children.* Chicago Ave. at 27th St., Minneapolis, Minn. 55407: Sister Kenny Institute, 1977.

*Convenience Clothing and Closures.* 41 East 51st St., New York, N.Y. 10022: Talon/Velcro Consumer Education, 1975.

*Easy Fashions for You* by A. Burton and V. Trotter. Lincoln, Neb.: Independent Living Rehabilitation Unit, Dept. of Human Development and the Family, University of Nebraska.

*Fashion-Able*, a catalog of self-help items and clothing. Rocky Hill, N.J.: Fashion-Able.

*Fingertip Patterns.* 155 N. Belaire Ave., Louisville, Ky. 40206: Fingertip Patterns. Braille patterns catalog (free).

*Handee for You.* 7674 Park Ave., Lowville, N.Y. 13367: C. O. Smith. Catalog of fashions.

*Measurements, Guidelines and Solutions* by K. Caddel. P.O. Box 4150, Lubbock, Tex. 79409: K. Caddel, Textile Research Center, Texas Tech. University, 1977. Shows how to take body measurements of bedridden or wheelchair-bound person, how to adapt patterns.

*The Natural Creations* by K. Caddel. Lubbock, Tex.: K. Caddel, Textile Research Center, Texas Tech. University. Free brochure illustrating available patterns for men, women, and children.

*Sewing Techniques for the Blind Girl* by S. Jones. 1839 Frankfort Ave., P.O. Box 6085, Louisville, Ky. 40206: American Printing House for the Blind, 1970. Pamphlet on supplies, patterns, fitting; available in Braille and large print.

*Using Everything You've Got* by H. H. Wilke. Chicago: National Easter Seal Society, 1977 (publication E-58).

*Wings of VGRS.* 2239 E. 55th St., Cleveland, Ohio 44103: Vocational Guidance and Rehabilitation Services. A catalog featuring clothing and accessories that can be custom-altered according to your needs.

*Your Wheelchair Fashions.* P.O. Box 99, South Windham, Me. 04082: Wheelchair Fashions, Inc.

# COOKING

## General

*Mealtime Manual for People with Disabilities and the Aging* by Judith Lannefeld Klinger, written in conjunction with The Institute of Rehabilitation Medicine. Box (MM) 56, Camden, N.J. 08101: Campbell Soup Company, 1978. Much more than a cookbook. Offers cooking, serving, and other kitchen techniques.

## Cookbooks

*The American Heart Association Cookbook* by R. Eshleman and M. Winston. 7320 Greenville Ave., Dallas, Tex. 75231: American Heart Association, 1973.

*Cooking with Betty Crocker Mixes.* 9200 Wayzata Blvd., P.O. Box 1113, Minneapolis, Minn. 55440: General Mills, Inc. Betty Crocker, 1979. (large print, free).

*Cooking without Looking* by E. K. Tipps. 1839 Frankfurt Ave., P.O. Box 6085, Louisville, Ky. 40206: American Printing House for the Blind, 1965. (large print).

*Easy Ways to Delicious Meals—A Campbell Cookbook.* 919 Walnut St., Philadelphia, Pa. 19107: Volunteer Services for the Blind, 1974. (large print or Braille).

*Helping Hands Cookbook* by D. L. Amo and M. K. Doolittle. 133 Highview Parkway, Rhinelander, Wis. 54501: Helping Hands Books. (large print).

*If You Can't Stand to Cook* by L. Gifford. 1415 Lake Dr. S.E., Grand Rapids, Mich. 49506: Zondervan Publishing House, 1973.

*It Isn't Always Easy—But It's Possible.* 800 Sylvan Ave., Englewood Cliffs, N.J. 07632: Thomas J. Lipton, Inc. Booklet on teaching food preparation skills to blind people.

*New York Times Large Type Cookbook* by J. Hewitt. New York: Quadrangle Books, 1971. Available through the American Foundation for the Blind, Consumer Products Div., 15 West 16th St., New York, N.Y. 10011.

## Cookbooks for one

*Cooking for One* by E. Parker. New York: Harper & Row, 1976.

*Cooking for One Is Fun* by H. L. Creel. New York: Quadrangle Books, 1977.

*Cooking on Your Own* by H. L. Creel. New York: Times Books, 1980. Many recipes here are adapted from Craig Claiborne and Pierre Franey.

*Fearless Cooking for One* by M. Evans. New York: Simon and Schuster, 1980.

# DIABETES

## General

*Blindness and Diabetes.* Free from American Foundation for the Blind, Inc., 15 West 16th St., New York, N.Y. 10011 (1979).

(See also Booklets, Pamphlets, and Diabetes Forecast Reprint Series on page 264.)

*The Diabetes Fact Book* by Theodore G. Duncan. New York: Charles Scribner's Sons, 1982.

*Cookbooks*

*The American Diabetes Association/The American Dietetic Association Family Cookbook.* New York: American Diabetes Association, 1980.

*The Art of Cooking for the Diabetic.* Chicago: Contemporary Books, Inc., 1978. Basic dietary principles and recipes.

*Cookbook for Diabetics* by G. Maddox. Rocky Hill, N.J.: Fashion-Able. Over 200 recipes.

*The Diabetic Gourmet* by Angela Bowen, M.D. New York: Harper and Row, 1980.

*Enjoying Food on a Diabetic Diet* by Edith Meyer. New York: Doubleday, A Dolphin Book, 1974.

*Recipes for Diabetics* by Billie Little and Penny L. Thorpe. New York: Bantam, 1975.

## From the American Diabetes Association (2 Park Avenue, New York, N.Y. 10016)

BOOKLETS:   Price 50¢ each—$35.00 per 100 copies.

*What You Need to Know about Diabetes:* The Association's "fact book." Twenty-eight pages of basic information on diabetes in an easy-to-read question-and-answer format. The booklet contains detailed explanations of the disease, its early symptoms, and its control and treatment.

*Exchange Lists for Meal Planning:* New revised lists reflecting the most current thinking in nutrition for everyone concerned with good health. In large print with colorful illustrations, this 24-page booklet explains how to use food exchanges to vary the diet.

PAMPHLETS:   Price 15¢ each—$12.00 per 100 copies.

201 Career Choices for Diabetics
202 Travel Tips for Diabetics
203 Helping Your Child Live with Diabetes
204 What Is the American Diabetes Association?
205 Diabetics Are Desirable Workers
206 School Children with Diabetes
207 A Word to Fire and Police Personnel
208 Employment Opportunities and Protections for Diabetics
209 The Camper with Diabetes
210 Anger

DIABETES FORECAST REPRINT SERIES:   Price 25¢ each—$12.00 per 100 copies.

300 Back to School
301 Impotence: What It Is and What Can Be Done
302 Get Wise—Exercise
303 From Hamburgers to Haute Cuisine (eating out)
304 Think Thin (diet tips)
305 Diabetic Retinopathy
306 Vitrectomy Update
307 The Diabetic and Peripheral Vascular Disease

308 Feeling Funny Is No Joke (neuropathy)
309 Sick Day Management
310 On the Fast Food Trail (exchanges for fast food)
311 Fabulous Fruits (canning without sugar)
312 Save Your Teeth (dental care)
313 On Your Feet (foot care)
314 Solving the Food Label Mystery (how to calculate exchanges from labels)
315 Diagnosis: Diabetes (blood glucose tests)
316 Frank Talk about Oral Drugs
317 Living with Kidney Disease
Identification Card for the Wallet, 15¢ each, 2 for 25¢
PERIODICAL:   *Diabetes Forecast.* A bimonthly magazine for diabetics and their families: Price $6.00 for one year.

## DISABLED PARENTS

*Early Years* by M. Cornwell. Disabled Living Foundation, 346 Kensington High Street, London W14 8NS, England. A practical handbook for parents with various disabilities.

*Motherhood: How to Cope* by M. Cornwell. Disabled Living Foundation (address given above). A book for blind, deaf, or otherwise physically disabled mothers.

*Work Simplification in Child Care,* 28 pages, fully illustrated, available free from The School of Home Economics, University of Connecticut, Storrs, Conn. The result of a five-year study, this booklet includes a number of excellent, practical suggestions for dealing with the problems of raising children when the parent is disabled.

## HOUSING DESIGN AND HOUSEKEEPING

*Accessibility: Designing Buildings for the Needs of Handicapped Persons.* Washington, D.C.: National Library Service for the Blind and Physically Handicapped, Library of Congress, 1979 (free).

*Adaptations and Techniques for the Disabled Homemaker* by M. Strebel. Chicago Avenue at 27th Street, Minneapolis, Minn. 55407: Sister Kenny Institute Publications—A/V Dept., 1978. Gives directions for simplifying specific tasks.

*Barrier-Free Site Design,* American Society of Landscape Architects Foundation, Washington, D.C.: U.S. Department of Housing and Urban Development, U.S. Government Printing Office.

*The Bathroom* by A. Kira. New York: Viking, 1976.

*Bathroom Facilities Accommodating the Physically Disabled and the Aged.* Toledo, Ohio: Owens-Corning, c/o Fiberglas Tower.

*Current Materials on Barrier-Free Design Available from the National Easter Seal Society* (and Other Sources). National Easter Seal Society for Crippled Children and Adults, 2023 W. Ogden Ave., Chicago, Ill. 60612. Single copy free.

*Design for the Disabled.* Blacksburg, Va.: College of Architecture and Urban Studies, Virginia Polytechnic Institute and State University. Experimental designs for bathtubs, washbasins, and commodes for people in wheelchairs.

*Handbook for Design: Specially Adapted Housing,* VA pamphlet 26–13. 810 Vermont Avenue, Washington, D.C.: Veterans Administration, Dept. of Veterans Benefits (262), 1978.

*Home in a Wheelchair: House Design Ideas for Easier Wheelchair Living* by J. Chasin. Suite 300, 4330 East-West Highway, Washington, D.C. 20014: Paralyzed Veterans of America, Inc., 1977.

*Home Safety Roundup,* #A–210. 2023 West Ogden Avenue, Chicago, Ill. 60612: National Easter Seal Society. A free checklist for spotting potential hazards in the home.

*Homemaking Unlimited Series* by A. Burton and V. Trotter. Independent Living Rehabilitation Unit, Dept. of Human Development and the Family, Univ. of Nebraska, Lincoln, Neb. 68583. Includes:
"Easy-to-Use Kitchen" (EC 2200)
"No Stoop, No Stretch Kitchen Storage" (EC 2201)
"Easy-to-Use Sink Center" (EC 2202)
"Easy-to-Use Cooking and Serving Center" (EC 2203)
"Easy-to-Use Mixing Center" (EC 2204)
"Streamlining Household Tasks" (EC 2205)
"The Bathroom Made Safe and Usable" (EC 2206)
"Cleaning Supplies—Keep Them Handy" (EC 2207)

*Housing and Home Services for the Disabled* by G. Laurie. 2350 Virginia Avenue, Hagerstown, Md.: Harper & Row, Medical Dept., 1977.

*Housing for the Handicapped and Disabled* by M. M. Thompson. Washington, D.C.: National Association of Superintendents of Public Residential Facilities for the Mentally Retarded, 1977.

*How to Create Interiors for the Disabled: A Guidebook for Family and Friends* by J. Cary. New York: Random House, 1978.

*Ideas for Making Your Home Accessible.* P.O. Box 700, Bloomington, Ill. 61701: Accent Special Publications.

*Mary Ellen's Best of Helpful Hints* by Pearl Higginbotham and Mary Ellen Pinkham. New York: Warner Books, Inc., 1979.

*Self-Help Brochure.* Lumex, Inc. (See Appendix: Sources of Equipment and Information for address.) Gives an excellent picture of the self-help bathroom aids available and how they should be positioned in the bathroom.

*Streamlining Household Tasks* by A. M. Burton and V. Trotter. Homemaking Unlimited Series, vol. 6 (EC 2205). Lincoln, Neb.: Independent Living Rehabilitation Unit, Dept. of Human Development and the Family, University of Nebraska.

## MAKE-IT-YOURSELF

*Aids and Adaptations.* 920 Yonge St., Suite 420, Toronto M4W 3J7, Canada: The Arthritis Society. Instructions for aids to make yourself.

*Make It Cheap Manual,* Vols. I and II. P.O. Box 597, Middletown, Ohio 45042: The Independence Factory. Instructions on making aids yourself.

## FOR PEOPLE WITH THE USE OF ONE ARM OR LEG

### Books

*Handbook for One-Handers* by A. L. Danzig. 211 West 14th St., New York, N.Y. 10011: Federation of the Handicapped, 1966.

*Help Yourself: A Handbook for Hemiplegics and Their Families.* 3700 Pearl St., Washington, D.C. 20014: Butterworth, Inc., 1972.

*The One-Handers Book* by V. Washam. 1333 Moursand Ave., Houston, Tex. 77030: Independent Living Research Utilization Project, The Institute for Rehabilitation and Research. A basic guide to activities of daily living.

### Film

*The Homemaker with Use of One Hand.* Station K, Atlanta, Ga. 30324: National Medical Audio-Visual Center (Annex). M–2243–X, 28 minutes, 16mm, color, sound. Free on short-term loans to groups. Describes equipment, kitchen planning, and techniques of one-handed cooking and kitchen work.

## SPORTS

*Sports and Games for the Handicapped,* Reference Circular No. 79–1. Washington, D.C.: National Library Service for the Blind and Physically Handicapped, The Library of Congress, 1979.

## STROKES

Write to the National Easter Seal Society for their pamphlet *Selected References on Home Care of the Stroke Patient.* This offers a complete reading list of books, pamphlets, and other material on aphasia and hemiplegia.

*From the American Heart Association* (7320 Greenville Ave., Dallas, Tex. 75231)

"Aphasia and the Family" (50–002–A)

"Strokes, A Guide for the Family" (950–025–A)

"Up and Around" (50–026–A)

"Stroke: Why Do They Behave That Way?" (50–035–A)

"Do It Yourself Again—Self-Help Devices for the Stroke Patient"

All of the above are practical guides for day-to-day coping with stroke and its effects.

### Other books on strokes

*A Stroke in the Family* by V. E. Griffith. New York: Dell, 1970.

*Care and Rehabilitation of the Stroke Patient* by B. G. Cox. 301–327 East Lawrence, Springfield, Ill. 62703: Charles C. Thomas, Publisher, 1973.

*Communicative Aids for the Adult Aphasic* by Blanche R. Martin. Springfield, Ill.: Charles C. Thomas, Publisher, 1962.

*How to Recover from a Stroke and Make a Successful Comeback* by Clarence Longenecker. 2758 Milburn Ave., Baldwin, N.Y. 11510: Clarence Longenecker, 1977.

*Recovery from Aphasia* by Joseph M. Wepman. New York: Ronald Press, 1951.

*Speech after Stroke: A Manual for the Speech Pathologist and the Family Members* by S. Stryker. Springfield, Ill.: Charles C. Thomas, Publisher, 1978.

*Stroke Clubs: How to Organize a Group Program for Stroke Patients and Their Families.* Chicago: National Easter Seal Society, 1972.

## TRAVEL

### Travel guides

*Access to the World* by Louise Weiss. New York: Chatham Square Press, 1977, 178 pp. $7.95. Describes accessible hotels, health facilities, travel agencies, and organizations; includes a list of access guides.

*Access Travel: Airports; A Guide to the Accessibility of Airport Terminals.* Washington, D.C.: Federal Aviation Administration, 1976. 20 pp. Free. (Available from Consumer Information Center, Dept. 619–F, Pueblo, Colo. 81009.) A survey of 220 air terminals in 27 countries for 71 accessibility features. Updated quarterly in *Travel Planner and Hotel/Motel Guide,* a publication available in many travel agencies.

*Canada by Wheelchair.* Canadian Paraplegia Association. *Caliper,* journal of the Canadian Paraplegia Association, Spring 1974: 12–42. A list of Canadian motels, hotels, and resorts with accessible dining facilities and sleeping quarters. Article available free from the Canadian Paraplegia Association, 520 Sutherland Drive, Toronto M4G 3V9 Ontario, Canada.

*Dialysis Worldwide for the Traveling Patient.* New York: National Association of Patients on Hemodialysis and Transplantation, Inc., 1975. 61 pp. Free. (505 Northern Blvd., Great Neck, N.Y. 11021) A guide to dialysis facilities in the United States, Canada, South America, and Europe. Describes types of medical assistance available at each unit. Glossary includes dialysis vocabulary in French, German, and Italian.

*Highway Rest Areas for Handicapped Travelers.* 1111 20th St., N.W., Washington, D.C. 20210: U.S. President's Committee on Employment of the Handicapped, 1975. Free.

*List of Guidebooks for Handicapped Travelers,* 4th ed. Washington, D.C.: U.S. President's Committee on Employment of the Handicapped, 1975. 21 pp.

Free. A list of cities for which access guides have been published; covers the United States, Canada, and some European countries.

*Motel Guide for the Disabled for European Highways.* 2195 44th St., New York, N.Y. 10017: International Society for the Rehabilitation of the Disabled, 1975. Free.

*1978–1979 International Directory of Access Guides.* Rehabilitation International USA. New York: 1978. 16 pp. Free. (20 West 40th Street, New York, N.Y. 10018) Guides from 15 countries in North America and Europe covering air and rail travel, wheelchair accessibility to hotels, restaurants, and leisure facilities.

*Rollin' On: A Wheelchair Guide to U.S. Cities* by Maxine Atwater. New York: Dodd, Mead, 1978. 290 pp. $9.95. A travel planner and guidebook to 8 American cities: Chicago, Honolulu, New York, Philadelphia, San Antonio, San Diego, San Francisco, and Washington, D.C.

*Travelability: A Guide for Physically Disabled Travelers in the United States* by Lois Reamy. New York: Macmillan, 1979. 278 pp. $9.95. Includes information about travel by car, train, plane, bus, and ship. Gives a state-by-state listing of guides to barrier-free travel and answers medically related questions.

*Wheelchair Air Travel* by Clare Millar. 1975. 128 pp. $2.50. Box 7, Blair, Cambridge, Ontario, Canada.

*The Wheelchair Traveler* by Douglas R. Annand. 1978. 228 pp. $4.95. Write to the author: Ball Hill Rd., Milford, N.H. 03055. A listing of 3,200 accessible hotels, motels, restaurants, and tourist attractions across the United States, Canada, Mexico, and Puerto Rico.

*Wheelchair Vagabond* by John G. Nelson. Project Press, 1976. 132 pp. $4.95. 710 Wilshire Blvd., Santa Monica, Cal. 90401. Directions on how to plan a trip and how to fit out a vehicle for wheelchair traveling.

## VISION AIDS

*The New York Times Large-Type Weekly,* 229 West 43rd St., New York, N.Y. 10036. Offers discounts to American Association of Retired Persons members, as well as regular subscription to visually impaired people.

### Recording and tape information

*Choice Magazine Listing,* 14 Maple St., Port Washington, N.Y. 10050. Offers subscription to a series of 8 records, each of which includes 8 hours of articles, fiction, and poetry culled from such magazines as *The New Yorker, Harper's Fortune, Esquire,* and *Sports Illustrated,* among others.

*Recording for the Blind,* 215 East 58th St., New York, N.Y. 10022. Will tape educational material for blind people free of charge.

*Talking Books.* Inquire at your local library (see page 113 for qualification requirements) or write Talking Books, National Library Service for the

Blind and Physically Handicapped, Library of Congress, Washington, D.C. 20542, or obtain from American Foundation for the Blind or from American Printing House for the Blind (addresses on page 248).

*"Where Do I Go from Here?"* 3100 Oak Park Ave., Berwyn, Ill. 60402: *Dialogue Magazine.* A "talking book" for newly blinded people.

*From the National Library Service for the Blind and Physically Handicapped* (Washington, D.C.: Library of Congress). All available free.

Braille Instruction and Writing Equipment, 1978

Closed-Circuit Television Reading Devices for the Visually Handicapped, 1979

Magazines in Special Media, 1978

National Organizations Concerned with Visually and Physically Handicapped Persons, 1979

Reading Machines for the Blind, 1978

Reading Materials in Large Type, 1979

Reading, Writing, and Other Communication Aids for Visually and Physically Handicapped Persons, 1978

Subject Guide to Spoken Word Recordings, 1978

## WHEELCHAIRS

*Kitchens for Workers in Wheelchairs* by A. Alexander. Columbia, Mo.: Univ. of Missouri, Cooperative Extension Service, 1973.

*What You Can Do for Yourself* by P. Galbreaith. 381 Park Ave. S., New York: Drake, 1974.

*Wheelchair Bathrooms* by H. Schweikert, Jr. Paralyzed Veterans of America, Inc., Suite 300, 4330 East-West Highway, Washington, D.C. 20014, 1971. Hints on and equipment for constructing or altering a bathroom.

*The Wheelchair Book* by H. Kamenetz, 1969. Springfield, Ill.: Charles C. Thomas. How to choose a chair, mobility aids, lifts, transfers, care of chair, wheelchair sports, etc.

*The Wheelchair in the Kitchen: A Guide to Easier Living for the Handicapped* by J. Chasin and J. Saltman. Washington, D.C.: Paralyzed Veterans of America, Inc., 1973.

*Wheelchair Interiors* by S. Olson and D. Meredith. #E–52. National Easter Seal Society, 2023 W. Ogden Ave., Chicago, Ill. 60612, 1973.

*Wheelchair Prescription,* by M. Lee, D. Pezenik, and M. Dasco. PHS Rehabilitation Guide Series #1. Public Health Service Publication #1666, from U.S. Government Printing Office, Washington, D.C. 20402.

*Wheelchair Selection: More Than Choosing a Chair with Wheels* by B. Fahland with B. Grendahl. Rehabilitation Publication #713, Sister Kenny Institute, Chicago Ave. at 27th St., Minneapolis, Minn. 55407, 1976.

*You Can Do It from a Wheelchair* by Arlene E. Gilbert. Westport, Conn.: Arlington House Publishers. How to keep house, cook, and raise children while in a wheelchair.

# Index